✕RASPUTIN✕
The Man Behind the Myth

RASPUTIN

The Man Behind the Myth

A Personal Memoir by
Maria Rasputin
and **Patte Barham**

Prentice-Hall, Inc., Englewood Cliffs, New Jersey

Art Director: Hal Siegel
Designer: Joan Ann Jacobus

Rasputin: The Man Behind the Myth, A Personal Memoir
by Maria Rasputin and Patte Barham
Copyright © 1977 by Maria Rasputin and Patte Barham

Printed in the United States of America
Prentice-Hall International, Inc., London
Prentice-Hall of Australia, Pty. Ltd., Sydney
Prentice-Hall of Canada, Ltd., Toronto
Prentice-Hall of India Private Ltd., New Delhi
Prentice-Hall of Japan, Inc., Tokyo
Prentice-Hall of Southeast Asia Pte. Ltd., Singapore
Whitehall Books Limited, Wellington, New Zealand
10 9 8 7 6 5 4 3 2 1

Library of Congress Cataloging in Publication Data
Rasputina, Mariia Grigor'evna.
   Rasputin, the man behind the myth, a personal memoir.

   Includes index.
   1. Rasputin, Grigoriĭ Efimovich, 1871-1916.
2. Russia—Court and courtiers—Biography. I. Barham,
Patte, joint author. II. Title.
DK254.R3R35 1977   947.08'092'4 [B]   76-54231
ISBN 0-13-753129-X

All the incidents in this book, and all the people who reside in its pages, are actual events and persons. Much of the material presented is the result of Maria Rasputin's own observation. And all the rest was told to her by her father, her mother, the maid Dunia, the Tsarina Aleksandra Feodorovna, and the Tsarina's Lady in Waiting, Anna Aleksandrovna Virubova. The account of Rasputin's murder has been reconstructed from two sources: the partly fictitious narrative of his principal murderer, Prince Feliks Feliksovich Yussupov, and the story told by one of the Prince's servants to his sister-in-law, and by her related to me.

The names of all the characters in this book have been left unchanged.

Patte Barham

✠ONE✠

Although nearly three score years have passed since that fateful night, it remains fresh in my memory, untouched by the intervention of time. It is not that I cling to a recital of the events that occurred during that dark and dreadful period, as do those who clutch their griefs to their bosoms, but that an unreasoned fear —although it was to prove justified—and the trauma that followed, burned the impressions into my brain, like a scar made by a branding iron.

I remember that a blanket of snow lay over the silent city, cloaking the seething unrest of the populace, driven indoors by the polar chill. Overhead, the sky was a black velvet mantle, star-sprinkled like a handful of diamonds strewn across the bowl of the firmament, and the brightest of the jewels was mighty Jupiter, which my father had so often pointed out to me, gleaming down upon St. Petersburg, now rechristened Petrograd. But I could see that the stars were not to reign for long. Giving promise of more snow to come, new clouds had begun to form on the horizon.

On this night of December 16, 1916,* the citizens had some reason for their unrest. The year was ending on a note of despair, in contrast to the optimism that had flowed at its beginning, when the Tsar's armies had won victories at Lutsk, Czernowitz, and Ternopol in the great offensive launched by General A. A. Brusilov, which had advanced the Russian lines by as much as 125 *versts*.† But the arrival of fifteen fresh German divisions at the front had turned the tide against the Russians, some one million of whom had lost their lives, and all of the territory so arduously conquered had to be surrendered.

Dissatisfaction ran rampant throughout the population. At court, one faction was in all but open rebellion against the Tsar, and even more so against the Tsarina, whom they were calling, at least surreptitiously, *inostranka*,‡ overlooking the simple fact that she held nothing but distaste for the Kaiser and, as a granddaughter of Queen Victoria, was far more sympathetic to the British than to the Germans.

In their homes and in the streets the people were muttering their discontent, although the repressions instituted by Aleksandr Trepov, the new president of the Council of Ministers, made it unwise to speak aloud of such matters. Mother Russia was a powder keg, and all the people, both *aristokrats*** and *muzhik*,†† both pro- and anti-Nikolas, were sitting on top of it.

Yet, as I looked out of my bedroom window, I could find no sign of impending disaster. The empty streets were silent, and equally silent was the interior of our flat at 64 Gorokhovaya Ulitsa,‡‡ the home of my father, Grigori Efimovich Rasputin. But now the silence was broken by the rumble of a large black limousine as it braked to a halt in the street below. A lone figure emerged from the rear seat, the collar of his fur

*According to the Julian calendar. The Gregorian, or modern, calendar, which sets this date as December 29, 1916, was not adopted by the Russians until 1923.
†A versta is 3,500 feet; about two thirds of a mile.
‡foreigner (fem.)
**aristocrat
††peasant
‡‡Gorokhovaya Street

greatcoat turned up to cover most of his face, and the earflaps of his fur cap pulled down. The man, whoever he was, slammed the car door and passed from my view toward the back of the house, his footsteps crunching in the snow.

But there was nothing unusual about late visitors in my father's flat, and since it was so cold in the bedroom, I took off my robe and slippers and got into bed beside my sister Varya, who had slept through greater disturbances than this. I had even managed to fall into a light sleep after my father answered the ring of the rear door bell and escorted his unknown guest past the bedroom and into his study, from where the sound of their muted voices only served to lull me into a deeper slumber.

But I was soon awakened by another sound, one quite familiar to my ears. My father had gone to his bedroom and was calling to the maid, Katya, to help him find his boots, the ones with the patent-leather tops, and this was a certain sign that he was going to keep the appointment he had mentioned earlier in the evening.

I reached over and shook Varya, who was deep in seraphic slumber, and when she did not respond, I shook her again with greater vigor.

"Varya! Varya! Wake up! Father has a visitor and I think he is going out."

But Varya merely opened one unseeing eye and said, "Shhh, be quiet. Go away and let me sleep." She turned over, dragging half of the bedclothes with her, and was soon lost to the world of reality.

I sighed, and with some reluctance, stepped out onto the icy floor, my teeth beginning to chatter. I quickly found my slippers and wriggled my feet into them, at the same time shrugging back into my warm, red velvet robe. Somewhat less uncomfortable, I listened as my father's footsteps turned back to the study and heard the muffled voices renew their discussion. Taking a comb from the top of my dressing table, I looked into the mirror while running it through my hair. Again I noticed how much I was growing to resemble my father, particularly around the eyes, which, like his, were a deep blue, although his radiated a suggestion of some profound mystery. I was glad, however, that I had been formed after my mother, who, al-

3

though strong, was at the same time petite and feminine.

Silently opening the door, although there was little fear of awakening Varya, I slipped into the hall and moved down the hallway toward my father's study, almost colliding with him in the semidarkness, relieved only by a dim lamp casting its feeble rays out through the door of Katya's room.

"Oh, Maria, did we awaken you?" he asked.

"Yes, Papa, but no matter. Are you going out?"

"I must go, Marochka."

"You should not. You know what Ministr Protopopov* said?"

"Yes, I know. But this is an important matter."

"Oh, Papa, it's so late, and you need your rest. Can it not wait until morning?"

"Do not worry, Maria; I will soon return."

As he opened the door to the plain little study, a faint ray from the table lamp fell across my face. Papa noticed that lines of worry creased my brow, and he placed the flat of his hand across my forehead, as though to dispel my troubled thoughts. He always knew when any of his children were disturbed.

He repeated, "Do not worry; God will protect me. Go to bed now."

But my worries were not so easily diminished, for by that same light I had caught a brief glimpse of the visitor, a man with whom I had always felt ill at ease, and for whom, on this night as always, I experienced an unaccountable sense of dread, as though some icy demon were about to enfold me in its arms. My father reentered the study and closed the door partway behind him, so that I could not see them, but could still hear their conversation, and I eavesdropped shamelessly, for I had been seized by a sudden fear for Papa's safety. The other man in that study I had recognized as Prince Feliks Feliksovich Yussupov, tall and willowy, rather prettier than handsome, and exquisitely appareled in evening clothes beneath his open greatcoat. Although indoors, he still wore his fur cap, perhaps as a symbol of superior rank; a prince need not uncover in the

---

*Minister of Interior Aleksandr Dmitrievich Protopopov

house of a muzhik. In that brief glimpse, I saw Yussupov lolling languidly against the large table that served as Papa's desk, littered with books, papers, and a few of the many presents of fruit and other items brought by those seeking spiritual guidance or the exercise of my father's healing powers. There were gifts, also, from people who pursued him for his ability, real or fancied, to procure them favors at court.

And then Papa spoke: "Feliks, as you can see, I am very tired, and, also, I have been quite ill. Must it be tonight? Can it not wait?"

"No, Otyets Grigori,* it cannot wait. Princess Irina Aleksandrovna is suffering from one of her miserable headaches, and she can hardly bear the pain. You would not deny your healing gifts to my poor wife. As you love me, let me take you to her."

Papa sighed, "Very well, *moy malenki,*† give me but a moment to change into a fresh *bluza.*"‡

As he moved to the door, I stepped back into an alcove. I did not want to be discovered spying upon matters that were not supposed to concern me. But I could see through the open door, and it was evident by his expression that the prince was making no attempt to conceal his annoyance at this delay. I could see that Papa was bone-tired, and I knew that he would have given a great deal for a few hours of uninterrupted sleep. But I also knew that it was utterly impossible for him to spare himself when anyone needed his assistance. How many times had he told me of his vision of the Holy Virgin and of how she had fastened God's yoke upon him? And one thing I knew, God's servant, Grigori Efimovich, was not one to shirk his duty. If the lovely Irina Aleksandrovna needed him, he would go to her. He was weary, but, as he always said, God already knew that; and if He saw fit to send His servant out on this bitterly cold night, *tak i bit.***

I heard his narrow cot creak as he sat on it, and moved down to where I could see into his room, feeling that

*Father Gregory
†*my little one; a term of endearment*
‡*shirt; blouse*
**so be it

somehow I might be able to stop him, for the Holy Virgin had not appeared to me and I was under no such heavenly yoke as Papa bore. But when I came to the door, I found he had risen again, and was standing with his back toward me, before the *ikona* of the Virgin of Kazan, the form in which the Mother of God had come to him. Apparently renewed by this moment of prayer, he turned to the tall bureau by the window and opened the second drawer; and after rummaging through its contents, pulled out his finest bluza, the one the Tsarina had made for him with her own hands, its blue satin background embroidered with spun-gold cornflowers.

Papa had told me several times of his wanderings on the steppes of western Siberia, and how he had spent a whole year during his search for God without once changing his robes. But now he had become fastidious in the extreme. After his daily steam bath, he never failed to don fresh garments, and so active had he been on this day that he was changing into his third costume. Over the bluza he tied a golden sash, and I smiled to see him splash a little of his favorite cologne about his ears and neck, and comb a few drops through his usually unruly beard.

And then, to my surprise, as he looked into his mirror, he addressed himself, as though his reflection might have been another person.

"Well, Grigori Efimovich, you are a sorry-looking spectacle. But you have only yourself to blame. Your health is gone; your powers are gone; you are but a mockery of your former self. I'm afraid, my friend, that you are paying the price of your carousing."

But the blame was not entirely his. I knew that he was in almost constant pain from the knife wound he had sustained during an attempt on his life, and I knew that at times the pain was more than he could bear. At such times he would run out of the house and stay away until dawn, when he would return home. It was not until later that I learned he had spent the hours drinking and dancing with the Gypsies at the Villa Rodye as the only surcease from the ache in his abdomen. It was ironic that in order to relieve his agony he was ruining his health.

It was at this point in my chain of thought that Katya came to his door with the missing boots in her hand. She saw me and was about to speak, but I held a cautionary finger to my lips, which silenced her, and she continued on into the room to help him with his dressing. He drew on his finest pair of *pantaloni,** the blue velvet ones he wore only on special occasions, but I supposed that he considered his first visit to the Yussupov Palace on the Moika Kanal a special occasion indeed. Pulling on his boots, he struck a pose for Katya's approval, and when she reassured him with a smile, he visibly brightened. He got into his beaver greatcoat, the one given him in gratitude by the wealthy banker Ignati Porfiryevich Manus, whose niece he had healed after the finest physicians in St. Petersburg had despaired of saving her life.

Thus prepared for the cold ride to the Moika Palace, he came out of his room together with the prince, but instead of retreating so that he would not see me standing there, I flew to his side, clutching him by the arm.

"Papa," I began, "Papa. . ." But the words would not come, the unutterable words that would have told him of my chilling premonition. How can one give expression to abstract fears? How can one speak with certainty, when that certainty is based on something as ephemeral as my foreboding?

I know that Papa understood what was in my heart, for he answered my unspoken plea, saying, "If it is God's will, no harm can come to me."

He placed his arm about me and led me back to my bedroom. Before I could climb back into bed, he held me to his breast, and the warmth of his paternal kiss told me once again of the great love that he possessed. His affection nearly overwhelmed me, and I realized that I loved him even more than I had ever known. The moment was so poignant, so filled with a composite of devotion and fear for his safety, that the tears began to run down my cheeks. But he stopped my weeping with another kiss and wiped away the tears with his fingers.

And once more he repeated, "Do not fear, Marochka. Nothing can happen to me unless it is God's will."

I said, "Yes, Papa," and got into bed.

He went around to the other side of the bed and

*trousers

7

kissed Varya lightly on the cheek. Then standing for a moment at the foot of the bed, he made the sign of the cross over us, right to left, in the Eastern Orthodox fashion. And then he was gone, his shoulders slightly stooped, as though bowed down by some great weariness, and my tears began to flow anew. The premonition of danger returned, and no attempt to overcome it could rid me of the feeling that I would never see him again. I heard the back door close, and heedless of the cold floor, I rushed to the window. It was frosted over, and at first I could not see out. But I rubbed the pane with my fingers until I had made a clear, round area, and there I stood, waiting for my father and the prince to appear.

At last, I heard the crunching footsteps coming from the rear of the house. They came into view, Yussupov holding my father by the arm, as though fearing he would slip away at the last minute. I did not know why that was the impression I received, but I suppose it was a part of my dark foreboding. And suddenly the premonition was too strong to resist. I tried to open the window, thinking to call down to him that he must not go with Yussupov, but the window was frozen fast and I could not budge it.

Feeling helpless and hopeless, I cleared my little patch of clear glass once more and watched as the prince half helped, half pushed my father into the limousine. As he entered the car, Yussupov reached out one elegant hand and closed the door. The automobile left the curb with spinning wheels and sped recklessly down the street. I watched it for a few moments, but it was soon gone from my sight.

"Oh, Papa," I prayed aloud, "come back to me." And still weeping, I climbed back into bed, for I had become quite chilled standing at the window, and continued to shiver even after I had pulled the covers over me.

For what seemed a very long time, I tried to believe that he would come back, but it was no use. My mind was a whirlwind of turbulence and I ceased to think in a lucid manner. I remember that I cried aloud at one point: "Proshchaitye,* Papa." And I fell into a troubled sleep.

*farewell

8

⚴TWO⚴

The year of 1871 was, to say the least, fateful, filled as it was with developments that may have held only passing interest at the time, but which, taken together, were to eventuate in the complete disruption of the world social order. In France, Paris fell to the armies of Bismarck, spelling the end of Le Deuxième Empire; in Italy, a king of the entire nation was finally enthroned; and in Germany, the former petty kingdoms and principalities were welded into an empire. And all of these events contributed, unintentionally to be sure, to the vicious tyranny that was to come, a tyranny of an oppression beyond the wildest imaginings of the principal actors, Napoleon III, Victor Emmanuel II, and Wilhelm I; the tyranny known as communism.

And on the distant steppes of Siberia, another actor made his entrance onto the stage of world history, one who, even more than the others, was opposed to the Red purpose and who, if his words had been heeded, might well have pre-

9

vented its advent. He, too, however, was an inadvertent contributor to that very tidal wave of oppression to which he had been so strenuously opposed.

On the night of January 23, 1871, a great meteor burned its flaming path across the sable skies of western Siberia. A "shooting star" of such magnitude had always been taken by the God-fearing muzhiks as an omen of some momentous event. And, although they were not aware of it, a momentous event had indeed occurred. The arcing path of the meteor turned downward over the little village of Pokrovskoye, but before it could come to earth, the last of its substance was burned away, and at that very moment, a seven-pound boy was delivered by Anna Egorovna, the wife of Efim Akovlevich Rasputin. He was their second son and my father.

As soon as she could be up and about, my grandmother, being a most devout daughter of the Church, bundled up her newborn son, and handing him over to my grandfather, as I so often heard her tell it, admonished him: "Carry your son gently, Efim Akovlevich, but not so gently that you will drop him. No, no, not that way. You are as clumsy as your plow horse. Here, hold your arms like this."

She rearranged his grasp of the baby into a reasonable facsimile of the proper way, a way that all women seem to know intuitively by the time they receive their first dolls. "There, now, that is the way to hold him."

Having determined, according to her version of the incident, that there was a reasonable chance my father could survive the journey, she led the way toward the house of the *svyashchennik,** muttering in barely audible tones, although sufficiently loud for her discomfited husband to hear, as, of course, was her intention: "Men! All they are good for is to work in the fields. With things that really matter, they are utterly worthless." She punctuated her brief homily with a sniff of righteous indignation, and feeling much better, she arrived at her goal. Finding him at home, she took Otyets Pavel in tow and marshaled her little procession into the church next door, where, with all due ceremony, my father was anointed with

*priest

10

holy oil and immersed in the baptismal font, and the time-honored phrase was pronounced over him: "The servant of God, Grigori Efimovich, is baptized *vo imya Otsa, amin, e Sina, amin, e Svyatago Dukha, amin.*"*

My grandmother was also fond of recounting how her Grischa proved to be an exceptional child. Almost from the start, he displayed an intelligent awareness of objects, in contrast to the dim, unfocused consciousness of the usual baby. He fought against the restraint of his swaddling clothes, refusing to submit to them as his elder brother, Mikhail (Mischa), had done. He was able to draw himself up to a standing position by the time he reached his sixth month, and began toddling about the *isba*† in another two months. Although he responded to words that were spoken to him, he did not begin to talk until he was almost two and a half years old, which was much later than Mischa. But once he had begun, Grandmother said that he displayed a most active imagination. At the time when he was undergoing a brief illness, he told her that a beautiful lady had come to sit by his bed, soothing him until his fever had been dispelled. It was obvious that she did not believe in the "beautiful lady," but she did find it curious that he had been instantly cured. Listening to her tale, for what turned out to be its last telling, after I had learned something of my father's spiritual history, I was not so sure that the "beautiful lady" was not something more than merely an imaginary pretty woman.

Grandfather used to relate how Grischa enjoyed a singular sort of communication with the farm animals. Standing beside a restive horse, he could lay a hand on its neck, say a few quiet words, and the beast would at once become calm. And when he was present at the milking, a cow would give down without resistance. One of Grandfather's favorite stories concerned the time, during the noon meal, he mentioned that one of the horses was lame and might have suffered a pulled hamstring. Hearing this, Grischa quietly rose from the table and went out to the barn, and his father, following to see what would happen, saw his son stand by the horse for a moment,

*"in the name of the Father, amen, and the Son, amen, and the Holy Ghost, amen"
†peasant's house

11

as if in deep thought, and then go to the animal's rear leg and place his hand directly on the hamstring, although he had never even heard the word before, and certainly did not know what it meant. Again he stood in silence, his eyes closed, his head slightly thrown back, until, as though determining the healing had taken place, he stepped back, patted the horse, and said, "You're all better."

My grandfather said that he could hardly believe the little drama he had just witnessed, and as soon as Grischa returned to the house, he led the horse out of the stable and walked it about for a bit, amazed that it did not limp or give any other sign of discomfort. From that time on, Grischa was a sort of spiritual veterinarian to all the farm animals, and soon his "practice" extended to all the beasts of Pokrovskoye. And, of course, it was not long before he was also serving the human population as well.

When he went out to play, he did not indulge in childish games, as did the other children of the village, but would stare at, or rather into, the sky, for it seemed as though he could see deeply within the vastness of that great blue bowl. Or he might become absorbed for hours in contemplating a simple blade of grass with such rapt attention that his mother would sometimes fear he was "not quite right" in his mind. But his strangest and most misunderstood faculties were those of precognition and clairvoyance. Sitting in the warm kitchen while his mother baked her bread or prepared the family dinner in that huge brick stove, he would suddenly announce, without prior warning: "A stranger is coming."

And in time, perhaps an hour later, a stranger would come, knocking at their door in search of work or something to eat. And such people were never turned away with empty stomachs. My father told me that he could hardly recall an evening meal at which there was not someone at the table besides the members of the family.

But there was one such power without which he would have been much happier, the ability to predict a death in the village. As a rule, he suppressed these ominous presages, yet there were times when the words tumbled out before he was aware of what he was saying, and his father would wonder

12

what sort of a son the Good Lord had seen fit to bestow upon him. Was it a blessing or a curse? Only Khristos knew, and here my grandfather would cross himself.

It was futile to tell a lie in Grischa's presence, for he knew what was in the speaker's mind and heart. A horse trader, attempting to enhance the selling price of an animal, might expand upon its fine bloodlines and superb stamina, but Grischa, drawing his father aside, would say, "What he is saying is just not true; I can see that he lies."

At which my grandfather, like any uneducated man, faced with some incomprehensible phenomenon, would only become angry and shout, "What do you know about horses, you stupid boy? Dmitri Sergeyevich is an honest man; he would not cheat me. Go off and play, and leave such matters to your elders."

Grandfather felt that such things were the work of the *dyavol*,* and although not a notably religious man, he would cross himself again. It certainly could do no harm. And sometime later, when the horse failed to live up to the trader's glowing promises, Grandfather would blame its condition on some ailment contracted after the deal had been consummated, rather than to admit, even to himself, that there might have been some truth in Grischa's warning.

During those years, my father's sole companion was his brother, Mischa, who was ten, two years older than Grischa. Although my father kept to himself for the most part, when he was in the mood, he liked to go off with his brother for hikes in the woods, or to fish and swim in the Tura River, which flowed past Pokrovskoye. It was on a warm summer's day that tragedy entered the Rasputin household, a tragedy that was to have a profound effect on Papa. The boys had gone down to the river for a swim, and because their favorite place was already taken by a noisy group picnicking along the bank, they went a little farther downstream. Mischa, having been the first to undress, plunged into the water, and when he attempted to stand up, found himself sinking into a hole. As he vanished from sight, Grischa, who had now finished removing his own clothing, ran

*devil

13

to the edge of the stream. Crying, "Mischa, Mischa," he thrust his arm into the swiftly running river at the point where he had last seen his brother, but the panicking Mischa seized the arm, and in trying to pull himself out of the hole, managed only to drag Grischa in after him. The two boys clung to each other, struggling to regain their footing, but were being carried away by the rapid current. Fortunately, they were seen by a passing farmer, who rushed to the bank, and reaching out as far as he could, grasped one slippery arm. Clinging together, as they were, he was able to haul both of them ashore.

By the time they were pulled up onto the bank, both boys were thoroughly soaked, and each of them developed a severe case of "inflammation of the chest," the only name the villagers had for pneumonia. Since the nearest doctor was at Tyumen, about 120 versts away, the only medical help available was that offered by the local *akushyerka*,* whose ignorance of *materia medica* was profound. The good woman did what she could, but Mischa's illness was beyond her poor powers, and at the tender age of ten, he slipped away from his grieving family.

My father, whose constitution was stronger than that of his brother, pulled through, and after a long period of recuperation, made longer by the sorrow he felt at Mischa's death, he returned to his former state of health. But his cure was only physical; in his soul there lurked a deep depression, and he became moodily quiet and hyperactive by turns. His unpredictable behavior was a trial for my grandmother, and as she told me, she never knew what to expect next. One day, he would be off wandering in the forest of giant larches and birches, trudging over the grass now tinged with brown in anticipation of the coming winter, avoiding all companionship and brooding over his sorrow; and on the next, he would make a pest of himself about the house, getting in his mother's way and shouting loudly, until she felt that she would lose her mind.

His long illness, and the shock he had suffered upon learning of Mischa's death, produced an additional effect on his

*midwife

14

life. His psychic powers vanished for a time, and when they did return, their force was somewhat diminished and they were never restored to their former intensity. But he had never placed a high value on them or considered them as anything out of the ordinary, and he was hardly aware that he no longer was able to predict coming events or to read the contents of others' minds.

Entering his fourteenth year, my father passed into a new phase, his interest, which soon blossomed into a pre-occupation, with religion. Although he had not learned to read or write, skills he did not acquire until his later years in St. Petersburg, he possessed a remarkable memory and could quote whole passages of the Bible from having heard them read but once. Whenever the svyashchennik read from the Scriptures, Grischa would pay close attention, and thus it was that on a certain Sunday, he was, perhaps, the only member of the congregation who took note of a teaching of the Khristos, delivered without emphasis by Otyets Pavel, which, in the English of King James's translators states, "The kingdom of God cometh not with observation: Neither shall they say, Lo here! or, Lo there! for, behold, the kingdom of God is within you."

Grischa left the church that day in a pensive mood. What did this teaching mean? Was it literally true that God's kingdom—and, therefore, God Himself—was within each human being, and perhaps, each animal as well? If it were true —and who could doubt the words of the Khristos?—why did the Church not dwell on such an important teaching? Why did Otyets Pavel speak of heaven as though it were somewhere far off in the sky?

As his mother and father hurried home for the Sunday dinner that had been kept warm on the back of the great stove, Grischa mumbled some excuse and set off toward the woods. This was a matter requiring some thought. It was not to be heard in the course of an otherwise dull sermon and then quickly and conveniently forgotten. Why, those words meant—they could only mean—that God was within him, Grigori Efimovich, and to find Him, one need only direct his search inward. God was not to be sought in a church; one did

15

not address Him in some distant heaven. He was here, inside, this moment—and forever.

He found a spot where the grass was still green and the ground beneath it soft, under the shade of a tall larch, and there he took his seat. He began attempting to direct his mind inward, experiencing some difficulty at first, but as he continued his efforts, it became easier to enter that inner temple where God and man come face to face. A great sense of peace settled over him like a downy blanket, and with a feeling of joy, he lost himself in meditation. As he did so, a glimmer of light arose in his mind's eye, that "third eye" of which the mystics speak; a scintilla, a faint gleam that began to expand even as he watched it. And as it grew, it approached, nearer and nearer, brightening as it came, until what had been a soft golden glow suddenly erupted in a blinding white flash. It is hardly to be wondered that he was momentarily taken aback, recoiling in some apprehension, a frail tentacle of fear clutching his heart. He recovered at once, but that brief instant of misgiving had been sufficient to disperse the warm benison of his meditation, and he was wrenched back into a consciousness of the outer world, a world that was, for the moment, quite alien to him. He remained seated, hoping once more to dive deeply into the abyss of the spirit in which his little self would become lost, merged with that Great Self, but to no avail, and at last he realized that, by drawing back from the brink, as it were, of the abyss, he had deprived himself of a profound spiritual experience.

"O Heavenly Father," he prayed, with all the fervor that overflowed his heart, "I repent my fear. But, Father, it was only a little fear." The tears were streaming down his cheeks as he concluded, "Hear my prayer, and let me see Your light once more."

But there was no answer; the gates to the kingdom had slammed shut, leaving the supplicant outside, and after a time, he arose and slowly made his way home.

I can still remember, although I was only ten at the time, how Papa, on one of his visits from St. Petersburg, took the three of us children for a walk in the woods, and pointed out the very tree under which he had sat. He took his seat, as he had done so many years before, and asked us to join him in

16

a semicircle at his feet, and told us of that strange event. I know now that he was a truly outstanding religious teacher, for he had a way of making everything quite clear, even to us. I hung on his every word, and I am sure that Mitya and Varya did too. He explained the way we should meditate and had us try to do it, and I closed my eyes and sat there feeling nothing, for I was not a born mystic, although I believe Varya did gain something, for she was a little slower than either Mitya or I in responding when Papa said, "That will be enough for the first time."

On the way back to the house, he told us of the state he was in at that far-off time, of his melancholy, of his lack of appetite, of the way he refused the dinner that Grandmother had saved for him. And as soon as Grandfather left to see to the livestock, she drew Papa aside, cradling his face in her hands, forcing him to look at her, and asked, "Grischa, what is it? What has happened to make you so sad?"

"I cannot tell you, Mama; you would not understand."

"A mother always understands her child. Whatever it is, you can tell me."

"No, Mama, it is not something that can be told. There are no words to describe it. It was—different."

"Try, Grischa, please try. Perhaps I can help you."

"Well, I will try. But I don't think you will understand. I can only say—how can I put it?—that I almost saw God."

"Grischa!" She was horrified. "That is almost blasphemy. Only great saints can see God. Whatever you do, don't tell your father; he would most certainly punish you. Don't tell anyone. Come now, let us forget all that you have just said. Eat your dinner and I am sure you will feel better."

In my memory, I can almost hear her saying those words, for she always felt that a hearty meal would cure almost any condition, physical or mental, with the possible exception of a broken limb, and even then it would help. To please her, he ate the food she placed before him without actually tasting it. She could not comprehend what he had revealed to her, but as the days wore on with little change in his attitude, she was wise enough to know that his indrawn state involved more than a mere desire to avoid his fair share of the farm work, although

17

his father was not so sure. In fact, everything about Grischa began to offend his sense of what a good son should be. Grandfather attended church regularly and considered himself a reasonably religious man, but he also felt that religion could not be permitted to interfere with farming, and a boy who went about his chores, mooning and uttering vague observations about the relationship of God to man, could not be performing his required duties in an acceptable manner. I think it fair to say that Efim Akovlevich was never to understand his strange son, although when, in later years, he saw him receiving the attention, and even adulation, of the aristocracy of St. Petersburg, he began to realize that there might be more to the boy than he had thought. But all that was still in the future; as for now, all he wanted was for Grischa to bend his back a little more and help with greater alacrity in the never-ending work. And as time passed, the boy did begin to apply himself with some degree of industry, although there were times when he would stop in the middle of a furrow, lean on his hoe, and become lost in meditation.

When Grandfather found him idling, he would roar, "Get to work, you lazy good-for-nothing. How are we to eat if we don't dig?"

At best there was an uneasy armistice between father and son. Occasionally, Efim Akovlevich found it necessary to goad his son on to greater effort, but the work did get done, and the farm prospered. Grischa was strange, he felt, there was no doubting that. Why, he never wanted to make friends with the other boys of the village, good boys who did what their fathers asked without having to be constantly prodded. But Grandfather was unable to peer into his son's mind, and even if he had been able to have done so, he would have been thoroughly confused, for that mind was filled with but one thought, the desire to renew and expand upon that first experience, the near approach of illumination. But, as he often told me, illumination is like a skittish horse; once rebuffed, however slightly, it can only be enticed back with great patience. His sole interest lay in achieving God's grace, and, preoccupied in this fashion, he did not feel lonesome, and resisted being forced into companionship with other boys.

18

Having been urged by her husband, Grandmother finally spoke to Grischa about his desire for isolation.

"Your father and I are worried about you. You have no friends and you never play with anyone."

"But, Mama, I have a friend; I have God."

"Grischa, Grischa, I know God is your friend; He is a friend to all who pray to Him. But you have no companions, no one to play with."

"God is also my companion."

"Now that is just what I mean. Don't talk like that." She was becoming angry with her recalcitrant son. "You moon about the farm, or go off into the woods, all by yourself. It is not healthy to be so alone."

"All right, Mama." Grischa knew when he was beaten. "I will go and play with the boys."

He had no feeling of loneliness, but if it would make her happy, and keep her from nagging him, he would do as she asked. His heart was not in it, however, and he went to play without any idea that he would enjoy what lay ahead. As young people will, the village boys sensed that there was something different about him, and differences usually lead to animosity. He had had a few previous encounters with the youngsters, who had, on occasion, gathered around to bait him. He did not like to fight, so, although there had been sufficient provocation, he had always tried to turn their belligerency aside. As one might have expected, they did not understand his pacifism, and were under the false impression that he was a coward, thereby doubly deserving of their taunts, with an additional shove thrown in for good measure.

As it fell out, he had no sooner arrived at a field that all the boys used for a playground, when he was cornered by three of them. They were obviously irate that he would dare set foot on their sacred territory.

The largest of the three strode up to Papa, his face red with anger, and shouted, "*Malodushni,** we don't want you here. Go away!"

Grischa tried the soft answer that Otyets Pavel had

*coward

said would turn away wrath. "I am doing you no harm, and I would like to play here."

But the boys were not to be so easily put off, and raising his fists, the leader bellowed, "If you want to stay, you will have to fight."

When Grischa made no move, the boy, now overflowing with confidence, struck out with his fist, a blow Papa turned aside with a quick upthrust of his arm. Frustrated by the failure of his first attack, the boy lashed out wildly, and as Papa told me, he did not think this was the time to turn the other cheek. He saw an opening between his opponent's madly flailing arms, and with one well-placed blow, felled his assailant like a stricken ox. As the boy sprawled on his back, his only movement a slight twitching of his eyelids, his companions encouraged each other to avenge their fallen leader.

"It was just a lucky punch," cried one.

And the other replied, "He's no fighter. Boris will feel better if we finish the malodushni off."

They bore in upon Papa from both sides, but remaining cool in the face of their blind rage, he made short work of them. With all three of his attackers rendered *hors de combat*, he left the field to the vanquished, troubled by his unwonted pugnacity, for he had actually enjoyed the brief battle. But now that peace had been restored on the playground, there was no peace in his soul. He felt that he had fallen further from God's grace, and sought a secluded spot where he could pray for forgiveness unobserved. He made his way to the river, walking along the bank until he found a place hidden from the landward side by some heavy brush, and there, with the Tura running clear and blue at his feet, he offered up a long and heartfelt prayer. Yet, although he was filled with earnest repentance, it was to be some time before he regained his earlier sense of the nearness of God.

However, he gained one benefit from the fight; the village boys stopped badgering him and began treating him with greater respect. None of them had any stomach for a trial by combat with the conqueror of Pokrovskoye's leading bully and his two cohorts. But these things were of little concern to Grischa, whose mind was fixed on his spiritual quest. Of even less concern to him was his greater popularity with the village girls, who rather approved of his somewhat shy and non-aggressive attitude toward them, although a few of them secretly wished that he would not be quite so nonaggressive as he was. It had come to be a private little joke among them that he was not yet aware of the difference between the sexes, and several of them, impressed by his truly outstanding sign of masculinity, conceived a certain willingness—if not eagerness—to be the first to demonstrate the exact nature and purpose of that difference, although they could see that such an undertaking might present a real challenge. In regard to his supposed unawareness, however, they were mistaken, for by the same means that had led to their knowledge of his physical attributes, he had learned about theirs.

In fact, as I well knew, all of the villagers came early to this knowledge, since it was the custom for all the people to go bathing during the warm summer months in one of the quiet pools that dotted the shores of the Tura, entering the clear blue water in a state of natural innocence. Later, they would lie about on the soft grassy bank, drying themselves under the hot sun. While it was considered an act of serious misconduct for a man to stare at a woman, the younger people of both sexes were able to satisfy their curiosity by covert glances that told them all they wanted to know about certain anatomical facts. It may seem strange to those who have not grown up under this custom, but I can attest to the fact that there was nothing of embarrassment in it, nor did it lead to any unseemly behavior. At all other times, the people went about in sufficient clothing to satisfy the most puritanical of souls.

But Grischa could not have cared less about such matters; he had other, more compelling, interests, his mind a veritable torrent of spiritual questions, the answers to which seemed ever on the verge of being discovered, only to elude him just as they appeared to be within his grasp. His chief question, as always, concerned the light. Would it ever return? It had been revealed to him, he knew not whence or how it had come, that the light had become manifest to take him for Itself, that It was God, and that once It had taken possession of him, he would belong, body and soul, mind and heart, to God. And he wanted to be God's own, whatever that might mean. It seemed to him a treasure of greater value than the combined wealth of Mother Russia and the Holy Church.

Such was the state of his mind, and it constituted a formidable competitor for whatever desires the maidens of Pokrovskoye might have entertained. And so the girls were constrained to seek other companions for their dances and covert strolls through the woods on the long, balmy summer evenings, with the blazing stars hanging low over the Siberian steppes, to match the blazing desires of their youth—and Grigori Efimovich Rasputin, aged fourteen, was left to search for his God, alone and in peace.

❆THREE❆

However, Sudbina* was to rule otherwise. Whatever that lady had in store for Grigori Efimovich Rasputin, it was not to be the life of a celibate monk. As is so often the case, her decree was carried out in a most devious manner. Seldom does she approach her target directly, lest her hapless victim discover her plan and frustrate her will before it is too late. And thus it happened in Grischa's life, for he was lured into each catastrophic step along the seemingly innocent path, never becoming aware of what lay at its end.

The manner in which the will, or perhaps whim might be a more exact term, of Sudbina was executed was related to me during those last grim days in Petrograd by one of the actors —although a minor one—in the drama which was, in large measure, to dictate the course of my father's life. My grandfather had operated his farm with such efficiency that there was a large surplus of grain remaining after the local mill had bought

*Fate (fem.); personalized here as the goddess of fate.

all of his crop it could use. And it did not take exceptional wisdom to conclude that he needed to trade in some larger city, the closest one being Tyumen, a veritable metropolis in his view, harboring some fifty to sixty thousand souls at the time. The city was an important center of commerce, on the best route to China. And thus it was to Tyumen that he decided to ship his grain.

The one member of his family he could most easily spare for the eighty-mile journey was my father, and so it was to him that the monthly task was delegated. Grischa, now sixteen, was delighted at the prospect of spending a few days on the road, during which he could apply himself to almost constant meditation, while Ivan, his favorite horse, hauled the wagon with little need for direction from his beloved master.

Papa loved the vast sweep of the western Siberian steppes, the forests of stately larches and tall birches, the prim little farms, where whole families worked in the fields, waving to him as he passed; this was the Russia he loved, and would always love. These were the real people. And years later, when he was living in St. Petersburg, he made frequent invidious comparisons between the city folk, aristocrats and commoners alike, and these hardworking, and for the most part pious, muzhiks. He was also to contrast the beautiful natural fields and trees of Siberia with the gilded and gaudy onion-shaped domes and spires of the city buildings, and once remarked, "The very air of St. Petersburg bears the stench of decay."

Although he was not much of a businessman, Grischa had been well instructed in the minimum price he could accept for his produce, and by bargaining for a somewhat higher figure, was usually able to exceed the minimum, thereby turning his monthly visits into profitable ones. And thus, what had begun as an experiment became a regular fixture of the family economy.

After several of these marketing trips, he was driving along the main street of Tyumen which led to the road home, when he hauled back on the reins, stopping Ivan dead in his tracks. Out of the door of a shop bearing a sign proclaiming it to be a *modistka,** there had just floated a vision of surpassing loveliness, her blond curls peeping out from beneath a jaunty

*modiste

24

white bonnet, her slender figure draped in a lilac silken gown, with lace at the neck and wrists and a tiny bustle. To the young and impressionable Grischa, she was the epitome of all that was most desirable in womankind. For the first time in his life he knew desire, although a dichotomous desire to be sure, half worship and half sensuality, wanting both to prostrate himself before her shrine and to possess her in some nebulously conceived fashion beyond the scope of his present knowledge or comprehension. But even as he longed to hold her, he sensed that it could never be. Such a goddess was not for him, a muzhik and the son of *muzhika*. *

The object of Grischa's adoration was Gospozha Kubasova,† one of the five daughters of an officer in the Tsar's Artillery. Polkovnik Danilov Danilovich Shchagov,‡ although born into a family of some position and wealth, had squandered his fortune in the gaming rooms of Moscow, and had been on the verge of a scandal over his failure to pay his gambling debts, when his commanding officer, General Kubasov, called on his junior with a warning that any further gambling was out of the question, and that he would have to pay up; the alternatives being a dishonorable discharge or an honorable retirement. The general appeared to strongly favor an honorable retirement, which was but another term for suicide, although Kubasov showed a marked lack of enthusiasm for this solution. It was at this point that the conversation was interrupted by the entrance of the polkovnik's daughter, eighteen and newly home from finishing school. The general, forty years her senior, had been a widower for some five years, and this fresh beauty succeeded in driving all thoughts of the grim mission upon which he had come completely from his mind.

"Polkovnik Shchagov," said the general, "will you not introduce me to this lovely little flower?"

Irina Danilova thought his courtly manner somewhat stuffy and old-fashioned.

"A thousand pardons, General," replied Shchagov, who had forgotten protocol, teetering as he was on the brink of disaster, "this is my eldest daughter, Irina."

*plural of muzhik
†Madame (Mrs.) Kubasova
‡Colonel Shchagov

The general took her hand, kissed it warmly, and held it, looking into her eyes with what he hoped was a gallant and impassioned gaze, for a longer time than was absolutely necessary. Irina Danilova blushed prettily, as well-bred young ladies were trained to do, making no effort to withdraw her hand. It was obvious that the old soldier was charmed, and knowing something of her father's predicament, she was not about to permit an opportunity of restoring the family honor to slip away, however tenuous.

When she was finally given leave to retire, General Kubasov turned to his host. "Shchagov," he said, "you have a little treasure there; in fact, I might even say a small fortune." He laughed at his own little joke, and Shchagov, thinking he could see which way the tide was running, joined in. The general continued, "Perhaps," for he was not one for subtlety, "a way out of your misfortune can be found."

In his desperate straits, the polkovnik was ready for any proposal that held promise of saving his honor, and his life. And so it was not long before the two men reached an agreement, one that included a marriage and the transfer of a substantial sum of money. In this manner did the fair maiden become Gospozha Irina Danilova Kubasova, and for a while, she was content with her life as the wife of a senior officer in Moscow. There were gay parties and grand balls enough to suit any giddy young girl, and there were always handsome young officers with whom one could flirt. And when she became bored with her elderly husband and his all too infrequent and feeble attempts at lovemaking, there seemed to be a plethora of courageous young blades willing to risk their commanding officer's wrath, and their military futures, for the stolen delights of a furtive love affair.

But then the general retired, and the parties and balls were less numerous, and the opportunities for extracurricular romance even more rare. Added to that, old Kubasov, who had large estates in Poland and the Crimea, insisted on taking her to the dullest of them all, the one at Tyumen, as soon as the snow thawed, leaving the roads passable. There they would spend the summer and early autumn, until the threat of the long winter finally drove them back to Moscow. Irina Danilova would

26

not have minded going to the Crimea, where there were a number of summer resorts with their attending gaiety, and always a cluster of eager young men, but the general cared little for eager young men, preferring the quiet, bucolic life at Tyumen, and pout as she would, Kubasov could not be swayed.

So, during each summer, her boredom was profound. Surrounded by six female servants, she had no work to do. There was a fine library, but Irina Danilova had not been taught to appreciate good literature at her finishing school, which had specialized in transforming the daughters of the better families into young ladies, and, thus, the books represented only another bore. Caring little for reading, she cared even less for hunting and fishing, which were the principal occupations of the landed gentry of Tobolsk Province, of which Tyumen was the largest city. Restless and apathetic by turns, she found only one way of breaking the tedium of the long summer afternoons. Ordering around her *kolyaska** and taking one of the maids along, she would drive the short distance into town to go shopping. For a spoiled young woman, used to the finest shops of Moscow, Tyumen held few charms, or little desirable merchandise for that matter, yet it was better than languishing about the big house with nothing to see but the dark wood-paneled walls and the even darker, heavily upholstered furniture.

It was while she was on one of these shopping tours that she was first seen by Grischa, and as he gawked at her, overcome by a refined type of beauty quite foreign to him, she also saw him. His ill-concealed admiration touched her for a moment, but masculine approval was nothing new to her, and the customary little thrill that she experienced when one of the handsome young officers undressed her with his eyes was not there. After all, he was, as anybody could see, a simple muzhik, hardly a human being, and certainly not the sort to be permitted any of the privileges, even the visual ones, she readily accorded to the men of her own class.

However, without realizing the cause, Irina Danilova felt a lightness of heart she rarely enjoyed during a stay at

*carriage

27

Tyumen. She even joked a bit with her favorite maid, the buxom and blithe Olga, on the way home. There had, after all, been a difference in the way the muzhik had looked at her and the openly sensual glances of her more sophisticated admirers, for his expression had held more of adoration than of lust. And so, on second thought, she was more pleased than offended, and her maids profited from her unusually happy disposition. There were times, and they were frequent, when, feeling like an exile, she would fly into sudden rages at the slightest infraction, berating them in parade-ground terms her father, the old soldier, would have envied.

The next day, when she went into town, secretly hoping to see the awkward youth, she was disappointed, for Grischa had left on the return trip to Pokrovskoye. The 120 versts between Tyumen and his home seemed endless; every clop-clop of Ivan's hooves was carrying him farther and farther from the Celestial Being, and he could only visualize her as a semiamorphous form flowing mistily about the central image of her shining eyes and smiling lips. Shutting out the view of the scenery he had so loved, he passed the hours in counting each hair of that golden head and caressing a cheek he imagined to be as soft as pink velvet. Once he was home, he could hardly contain himself during the month that followed, longing for the day when he could start back to Tyumen. And, although it seemed that the time dragged, it helped him to erase the dreary hours if he held his beloved before his mind's eye, wondering if she would be wearing the same lilac gown, or some other. And then a wayward thought, an unbearable thought, would force itself into his daydreams: Perhaps he would not see her at all. Forgotten was his search for God, his inward turning to find the truth of his own being; forgotten—and unregretted.

Even dreary days will pass, and at last, the time for his departure arrived. He hitched Ivan to the wagon, and could hardly bring himself to take valuable time to give his mother a farewell embrace and kiss his father on both cheeks, as was the custom. But how different were his emotions as he started down the rough dirt road. Now he was going toward his loved one, and would no longer be reduced to imagining her beauty.

If only she were there—she had to be there—his very life depended upon her being there.

And she was. Without even stopping to sell his produce, he drove directly to the main street of Tyumen, and there he spied her kolyaska, its horse tethered by a hitching strap to an iron weight resting on the cobbled pavement. Halting Ivan, he waited impatiently for Irina—although he did not then know her name—to emerge from the shop, and it was not long before she made her appearance, chatting animatedly with the maid Olga. To his delight, she stopped in midsentence when she caught sight of him, stared at him for an instant, the faintest ghost of a smile touching her seductively full red lips. But then, catching herself, she looked away, resuming her conversation with Olga in an even more animated manner, as though to demonstrate to anyone who might have observed her brief lapse that he meant nothing to her. But Grischa had already buried that little smile in the fastness of his heart, a treasure never to be relinquished. He watched her mount into the kolyaska, still chattering away, and drive off. After she had gone some distance down the street, he gave cautious pursuit, staying far enough behind so that, as he thought, he would not be detected. They passed a very long, rather low, stone wall marking the boundary of the Kubasov estate, and he followed until he saw her turn in through a pair of massive wrought-iron gates, the Kubasov crest emblazoned on each. He stopped, waited a moment, and then turned back toward town in order to proceed with the business that had brought him there.

That night, a grounds keeper reported to the general that he had chased a young man who had been sitting on the wall, but that the miscreant had jumped into a wagon and fled, as though the dyavol himself had been after him. Kubasov went about the house, double-locking all doors and windows as a precaution against thieves, but Irina Danilova knew who had driven that wagon and, to her surprise, found she was pleased. She and her coterie of servants were not concerned with possible lawbreakers, for, in spite of Grischa's prudence, Olga had seen him out of the corner of one big brown eye, and without turning toward him, had managed, under the guise of appearing to look at her mistress as they chatted, to give her a running account of the pursuit. And, once they had arrived home, they regaled the other maids with a narration, slightly embroidered, of the incident, including a rather unflattering description of the new admirer.

As for Grischa, he could think only of that smile. Perhaps she loved him; not, of course, as much as he loved her, but maybe just a little. She must love him; why else would she have smiled? The prospect that lay before him was as intoxicating as the strongest wine, and he dreamed of what might be in store, although he was as yet unaware of the specifics in question, but was galvanized by his abstract notions and desires. Although he had transacted his business, no human power could have started him on the road home. He had to see her again. And he found a spot outside of town, sheltered by heavy brush, where he planned to spend the night. When he had tethered Ivan near some tall grass where he could browse, he unrolled his blanket and mat on the floor of the now empty wagon and settled down to sleep. But sleep was a long time in coming, for his brain seemed to throb with thoughts of the goddess of loveliness.

He awoke late the next morning, and contrary to his usual practice, made no effort to arise until the sun had climbed high in the heavens. He had nothing to do until the afternoon, when she—he did not know what to call her—came into town. And when she came, he planned to be there. Well before her usual time for her shopping tour, he drove to the modistka shop, and pulled Ivan up across the street. His period of waiting was not long, for he soon spied the familiar kolyaska coming toward him. When Irina Danilova saw him, she gave a little laugh of triumph, and turned quickly toward Olga, giving her some brief instructions, to which the girl agreed with a broad smile. As they drew to a stop, the young women alighted, the mistress to dart into the shop, while Olga crossed the street toward Grischa with the obvious intention of speaking to him. Breathlessly, he got down as she approached, and hardly believing his ears, heard her say, "Gospozha Kubasova bids me give you this message: In one hour, you are to take a seat upon a certain wall; I think you know the place. Do not be late." With that, she turned on her heel and followed her mistress into the shop.

Although he had some trouble in breathing, and something seemed to be clutching his heart, as though an octopus had penetrated his chest and was attempting to stop its beating, there was virtually no power of earthly origin that could have prevented his mounting that wall before the appointed time. Except for a gardener working over a distant flower bed, there was no one in sight as he sat swinging his heels against the hard stone surface. As he waited, he let his eye rove over that part of the vast estate visible to him, and he noted that it could have contained the entire Rasputin farm within one of the enormous lawns surrounding the great house, standing far back behind a grove of tall birches. Everywhere he looked, the landscape was green and lush, except for a long and rather narrow pond lying at the foot of a gentle slope that dropped away below his swinging feet. Across the turquoise pond was a rustic footbridge, at the far end of which stood a somewhat ancient summer house, badly in need of a fresh coat of paint. Looking past the little house, his gaze was at once drawn back to it by the appearance of his beloved at the open door. Without her familiar bonnet, the cascade of her golden curls, falling halfway to her waist, almost stupefied him, and his dazed state was in no degree alleviated as he noticed her dress of some pale green material, tight in the bodice to show off her sensual breasts, and cut daringly low at the throat. He remained spellbound atop the wall, stunned by her beauty, as she moved forward to the little bridge, and hardly believing this could be happening to him, he watched her as she glided out to the center of the span, and standing there—he could only think of an angel—she beckoned to him, and pointed toward the summer house.

The angel retreated and vanished through the door. Fearing to lose her at this juncture, Grischa half leaped, half fell from the wall, and followed her with giant strides. Coming quickly to the door through which she had disappeared, he could count his heartbeats, and his head seemed on the point of bursting as he entered. There, in the center of the room, stood his adored one, smiling at him in a most encouraging manner. He was transfixed, every drop of his blood urging him forward, but every muscle immobilized by his awe of approaching so hallowed a being. Quickly perceiving the state he was in, she opened her arms with apparent abandon, unmistakably

31

inviting him to come to her. Being so solicited, he somehow forced his feet to carry him into her embrace. Once within her arms, he was enraptured; her delicate fragrance, the soft seduction of her body, unshielded from his touch by the soft frock, the mystique of her femininity, all seized his senses and he melted into her grasp, his hands caressing her slender waist.

But the method of procedure beyond that point was a lesson he had yet to learn, and so he merely stood, holding her tenderly, in ignorance of the part he was expected to play. However, the worldly-wise Irina, sensing that she had caught an inexperienced youth in her web, took the lead in the little drama, acting as she never would have done or found it necessary to do, with the young blades of Moscow. Reaching her hand down to the front of his trousers, she grasped him gently, releasing him for a moment, then touching him again; the result being, as that seasoned campaigner well knew, that he was tantalized almost beyond endurance. A rush of passion welled up in him like molten lava in a volcano, and realizing that she had achieved the desired result, she ceased her efforts, telling him to undress and come to her quickly. Turning from him, and leaving him with strong outward evidences of her own ecstatic stimulation, she made her exit through a door leading into the next room.

In a fever of excitement, Grischa tore off his clothing and, stripped to the skin, followed her through what he felt certain was to be the gate to his paradise. In the gloom of the darkened chamber, he could barely distinguish his love, lying on a sofa, although, to his disappointment, he saw that she was still fully clothed. Wondering if she was obeying some peculiar custom of the upper classes, he was suddenly made shy by his own nudity, but the fire within him had burned away any niche where reason might reside. He moved toward her, now certain that some heretofore unknown bliss was but moments away. And then Irina Danilova raised one shapely arm and spoke one single word: *"Teper!"* *

As one, the heavy draperies covering the room's four windows were thrown open by the four maidservants who had been stationed behind them. The shock of the sudden light and

*now

32

the sight of four additional clothed females, where he had expected but one naked girl, penetrated his fantasy-clouded consciousness, and it began to dawn upon him that he had been made the butt of a most cruel hoax. Frozen into inaction, while his mind tried to make some sense of what had befallen him, he was further shocked when a fifth girl stepped forward with a bucket of cold water and threw its contents over him. Recoiling from the sting of the icy liquid, he tripped and fell over a sixth girl who had dropped to her hands and knees behind him.

Almost as soon as he crashed to the floor, all of the girls, save the mistress, who was clapping and laughing and urging the others on, were upon him like a pack of she-wolves tearing at a stray lamb, teasing and tormenting him, touching his outthrust organ in those lascivious ways that only as a group would they have dared employ. It was a divertissement, a game played by bored young women the world over, no less, for example, in the Trobriand Islands, when a suitable victim is caught while crossing a field during harvesttime, than in the factories of the larger Russian cities, before the joylessness of communism put an end to such sport.

A more experienced male will even find some pleasure in the carefree sexual romp of a covey of nubile girls, but there was no pleasure in it for Grischa, who suffered, even as he was being ravished, from the shattering of his romantic dreams and his desire for the cruel Irina.

The youngest of the girls, just fourteen, and but newly employed by the Kubasovs, was Dunia Bekyeshova, who quickly left off her part in the game when she saw the grief-stricken countenance of their plaything. Standing apart as the others continued with their voluptuous sport, she could feel only pity for the poor youth. And something more than pity, for there was born in her breast an emotion to which she was quite unaccustomed, and one from which she was never to recover. Somehow she knew, without knowing how she knew, that she was to play a more significant role in his life.

As for poor Grischa, once they had finished with him, the girls carried him out and dumped his now unconscious form, unclad as it still was, onto the ground in front of the summer house. And there he lay, he knew not how long.

33

✕FOUR✕

Consciousness returned to Grischa on sluggish feet, almost as though he were resisting sentience and the unpalatable reality that would come with full awareness. But his comatose state could not last forever, much as he wished that it would, and at last he opened his eyes to a world lacking, insofar as he was concerned, in any virtue.

As he awakened, he began to find little centers of pain throughout his body, bruises and scratches that had resulted from the mistreatment he had received. And behind all of these was a greater pain, one of the soul rather than the body, and one that he struggled to repress, knowing somehow that it could not be borne at the moment. Without thinking, he brought his hand down to one of the more insistent hurts, and only then discovered that he was totally without clothing. He was seized by a sudden panic; here he was, out in the open, with nothing to cover him. But as he looked about wildly for something, anything, with which to drape himself, he spied his clothes piled neatly at his side, left there, he felt certain, by some kind soul. He did not know it, of course, but the sympathetic Dunia had returned to gather up his things from where he had dropped them in his frenzy to join the treacherous Irina Danilova.

Thankful that he would not be faced with having to appear publicly in a state of nature, he quickly dressed and ran limpingly across the rustic bridge, up the slope, and to the wall, over which he managed to scramble. The faithful Ivan was still waiting patiently for him, and climbing painfully into the wagon, he was grateful that at least this much mercy had been vouchsafed him. He took up the reins, told Ivan to head for home, and the horse began pacing off the versts to Pokrovskoye.

And now, Grischa had nothing with which to fill his mind but a review of the events of the last few hours. What follows is the story recounted to me by Dunia, to whom Papa had told it, since she had been present at the first part of the incident. As he drove toward home, he tried with all his strength to avoid a confrontation with his catastrophic fall from grace, but the memory was too fresh, and it broke through his every attempt to ward it off. It all rushed in upon him, like a great flood, and he was helpless to stem it. Central to his torment was the laughing face of Irina Danilova, obviously enjoying his discomfiture, clapping her hands in glee and urging her girls on to even greater efforts. He could see it in all its horrifying details, details he had little noticed when they occurred, but displayed now as though projected on a screen by a still-to-be-invented slow-motion camera. Here were the girls—he could see each of them quite clearly—clutching at him, grasping his organ for an agonizing moment, screaming with excitement as children do at their play, their flushed faces coming close and receding, their voices mocking him, and all the time driven forward by the insatiable Irina. He had, he recalled, begged them to leave off, shouted threats and pleaded for mercy by turns, but nothing he could do or say had any effect upon the inflamed harpies who had been aroused to a feverish state, their cheeks red, unable to refrain from any action that occurred to them. And always there was Irina Danilova; her face, too, was red, the tip of her tongue protruding between her white teeth, obviously aroused by what was being done to him. He could find it in his heart to forgive the servants; they had only done their mistress' bidding, but Irina, the beautiful, false Irina, how loathsome she was. How could she have done it? What made her want to do it? Why? Why? He sobbed aloud in the throes of his agony. What had caused her to hate him so? Had he offended her in some way? He could not recall any act of his that she might have considered offensive. Then why? The question kept ringing through his head. Oh, Irina, I loved you. Why? Why? Why?

Without realizing it, for his tear-blinded eyes were oblivious to the road taken by the wagon, Ivan had hauled him through Tyumen, and they were now on the road to Pokrovskoye. His whole being was one amorphous mass of unadulterated misery, and his mind played and replayed the scene in the summer house. And always he saw Irina; in his imagination he could see her, even when the body of one of the maids was interposed, as though they were transparent and only she had substance. And always there was her gleeful face, that hateful face, the tongue tip between those white teeth, panting in some dreadful passion as she watched his struggle to escape, growing ecstatic at his every failure. There was a deep and insistent ache in his groin, but he hardly noticed it, so rapt was he in mental anguish.

He was suddenly aware that the wagon had not moved for some time, and he noticed with a start that the night had fallen. Out of the depths of his despair, he realized that he had to do something about Ivan, who was looking back at him with what only Grischa would have recognized as reproach. The good fellow could not be made to stand between the shafts throughout the night, and so Grischa climbed stiffly down, every muscle a throbbing torment, and unhitched the horse, tethering him to one of the wagon wheels and removing the rest of his harness. Almost automatically, he unrolled the bit of padding in the wagon bed, and pulling his rough homespun blanket over himself, he lay down to sleep. But it was hours before sleep came. The visions that had haunted him on the road returned, and for the hundredth time he relived the terrible scene, the laughing girls, their exhorting mistress, the impudent handling of his anatomy; all this ran through his head until he thought he would go mad.

Finally, in exhaustion, he fell into a fitful sleep filled with fantasies, and he dreamed of Irina, always Irina; those barely parted lips, those white teeth, that pink tongue tip peeping between them. Then there were wolves, she-wolves worrying him with their muzzles, and the leader inciting them to greater efforts, her snarling lips parted and a slavering tongue lolling out between the cruel fangs. He cried out, and the sleeping Ivan, startled by his master's cry, whinnied and tried to pull free. But quiet again descended upon the travelers, and Grischa was back with the girls, who were at the same time wolves, and the leader of the pack, the bitch-wolf, who was also Irina, egging them on, and he awoke with a groan just as they were about to tear his flesh. Again he dozed off, and the whole horrendous charade was repeated, until the sun rose at last over the distant trees on an otherwise flat plain.

Thankful that the terrible night was ended, he arose, still sore in every bone and sinew, rolled up his blanket and pad, hitched Ivan to the wagon, and set off for the day's ride. He had not stopped to eat his meager breakfast of black bread and the tea he usually made with water boiled over a roadside fire, for food was the furthest thing from his mind. Whatever hunger he might have felt was buried deep beneath the mound of his other woes. And so he let Ivan find the way, while he sat brooding over his sorrow and humiliation. That was the word that had found its way to the front of his mind: *unizheniye.** It was a mental reaction that had been crowded out of his thoughts by his even stronger grief and dismay over the treatment that had been meted out to him. But now, having run those emotions through the wringer of his distraught mental processes for endless hours, thereby drawing some of their poison from his wounds, the full crush of his unizheniye at the hands of the maids and their mistress descended upon him. And under this new burden, he groaned once more. What a comical figure, what a *grubiyan,*† he must have seemed to them, and particularly to Irina Danilova. She would not have treated him so if she

* *humiliation*
† *clodhopper; yokel*

37

had not thought him a grubiyan. She, a fine lady, must have considered him little more than an animal. She had not even deigned to partake of their sport; she was above such things. His misery increased, even above the level of his previous anguish. It was bad enough to have been used in that way, but how much worse to realize that he had not even been worthy of her participation. That was it—and now he was in an agony of self-deprecation—he was too base a creature for her to enjoy except at a distance. She had thrown a sacrificial animal to the wolves and had remained merely a spectator of its immolation.

And now his misery was complete; a feeling of abject degradation pressed down upon him, until he thought life a curse beyond all bearing. Perhaps God, in His infinite mercy, would relieve him of this burden; how wonderful that would be. Surely, he could not be expected to continue as he was, plunged into an ocean of torment, an ocean that was engulfing him. And he went on for some miles, brooding in this vein, until the black night overtook the travelers, Grischa and Ivan, and the boy once again unhitched his faithful horse, tying him so that he could crop the brown, though still nourishing, grass beside the road.

His train of thought having been broken for the moment, he felt the pangs of hunger and stuffed some of the black bread and sosiska* he carried in his knapsack into his mouth. Having hardly slept during the previous night, he was more tired than he realized, and almost at once fell into a deep sleep. There were dreams, but they were hazy and ephemeral, scenes that dissolved into other scenes, meaningless phantasmagorias of little significance. But suddenly, he was lying on a floor, and try as he would, he could not rise. He struggled, but in vain, until a large bevy of ravishingly nude women floated down from a distant ceiling to surround him, led, as he had known they would be, by Irina Danilova. She looked down upon his unclad form, sneering and laughing, clapping her hands in delight, and reached out one delicately slippered foot to touch him. But, as the tip of her toe made contact, she withdrew it in disgust. Pulling her scarlet cloak closely about her, as

*sausage

though she could not bear to risk even its slightest brushing against him, she drew herself up in towering disdain.

"Take him out," she cried, "and throw him away. Of what use is a lowly muzhik to me?"

The women stooped as one, and picking him up as though he were a feather, carried him out through a pair of great carved doors. Although it was bitterly cold, the women took no notice of the temperature, but held him still, standing at a stiff attention as though they formed a military unit awaiting the next command. He could see that they were in the open, but could find no distinguishing mark on the vast flat area which seemed to extend into infinity. There was heavy snow on the ground, the glare of its whiteness nearly blinding him.

Suddenly, Irina Danilova issued her command: "Dispose of the grubiyan!"

The women, in unison, repeated the order: "Dispose of the grubiyan!"

They swung him, back and forward, and again, and on the third swing, they released him to soar outward. He sailed through empty space for some time, not knowing whether he was face up or down, nor whether he was rising or falling, there being no feature by which to judge. And then he was back in the wagon, half covered by snow and chilled to the marrow of his aching bones. The first snow of winter was falling, early to be sure, but falling nonetheless. Ivan was snorting, the steam rising from his distended nostrils, and Grischa quickly hitched him between the shafts. There was no way of knowing how long it would last, and it behooved them to get home before they became lost on the road.

He let Ivan trot at a faster than usual pace, the horse needing the exercise to keep warm and yearning for the comfort of his stable. Grischa, on the other hand, could only sit on his rough board seat, wrapped tightly in the blanket to keep out the cold. The rutted road forced him to brace himself so that he would not be thrown out by every bump they hit, and he was quite sure that they hit them all. But, in a way, it was a blessing, since it prevented him from thinking his black thoughts. And in this manner did he arrive back at the farm shortly after noon, to find his mother beside herself with anxiety as to his safety. Even Grandfather greeted him with some warmth, and as soon as he had rubbed Ivan dry and placed him in his stall, he sat down in the wonderfully warm kitchen for his first decent meal since his departure.

But once he had eaten and made his accounting to his father, there was little to occupy him, and he fell back into his dark ruminations, plunging deep into a black stream of consciousness from which he was unable to rise. Anna Egorovna clearly saw that her son had suffered some blow, apparently— she sighed in relief—not a physical one. She knew something must have occurred in Tyumen that was tearing at Grischa's very soul, and she determined to do what she could to help him. She waited for him to say something, anything that might give her an opening, but he would not speak of whatever was troubling him. And, finally, she could contain herself no longer.

"Grischa, *dorogoi*,* what is troubling you? What has happened to upset you so? Tell me; let me help you."

"It is nothing, Mama. I will be all right."

"How can you say 'It is nothing'? I can see it is something. All I ask is that you tell me what it is."

"Truly, it is nothing. Please believe me."

"I know you don't want to worry me, but I can't help worrying when I see you like this. Come, tell me."

Grischa could not answer; he could not tell her of his shame; and so, without a word, he grabbed his coat and cap and ran out into the snow, stumbling his way to the barn, where he sat by Ivan's side and spoke of his woe. Anna Egorovna was a stubborn woman, especially where her loved ones were concerned, as I would learn in my time, but Grischa—my father—was in every way her son, and could match her in obstinacy. She sensed that whatever was troubling him ran far deeper than any depth she could plumb, and she resigned herself to a role of silently watching and praying for his speedy recovery.

But her prayers were not to be answered for some months, not until the spring had burst once more upon the

*dear

40

fertile lands of Tobolsk Province. And then, they were answered in a way she could not have imagined in her wildest dreams, a way that would have shocked her if she could have foreseen it, and foreseeing it, could have recognized it as an answer.

There was a woman in Pokrovskoye who had been widowed at an early age, and it was rumored among some of the older boys that she was a willing accomplice in sexual frolics. Actually, none of the boys had any evidence for their rumors beyond the fact that when she went for a swim in the Tura, she moved rather sinuously as she sunned herself on the grassy banks. This is not to say that any such activity on her part would have been startling or unusual, for there was more than a little copulating going on between the young people of that part of Siberia. Yet, strangely enough, this activity was covered by a strict, though unwritten, code. Undue promiscuity would brand a girl as a harlot, and a boy who refused to marry a girl he had made pregnant was subject to dire punishment, which might include castration in some of the villages. It was an accepted fact that few, if any, of the girls arrived at the altar as virgins, although most of the premarital sex occurred between those who were planning to marry.

The young woman in question, Natalya Petrovna Stepanova, although far from being the scarlet woman of the village, had her natural desires, and when a *brodyaga** knocked at her door one night in search of a meal, she welcomed him not only to her board, but to her bed as well. It was her misfortune to be observed as she admitted the man to her humble dwelling by the local *splyenitza,†* who ran as fast as her old legs would carry her to the Rasputin farm, since Grandfather was the headman of Pokrovskoye, and to him she sputtered out the scandalous story. On his way to the Stepanova isba, he stopped to enlist the aid of one of his friends, feeling that it was important to have an additional witness to the grave offense.

Arriving at the widow's place, Grandfather, under his own version of the "no-knock" law, pushed the door open and found the lady entertaining her caller in the most intimate

*vagabond
†gossip; one who gossips

41

fashion. The two men, egged on by the waspish voice of the old splyenitza, dragged the unfortunate woman out of bed—the brodyaga taking to his heels and escaping in the process—and hauled her off to Otyets Pavel's house for safekeeping. The splyenitza, glorying in her new position of prominence, spread the word throughout Pokrovskoye, and soon most of the villagers had gathered before the church, hotly debating a suitable punishment even before they had been made aware of the charges or evidence against the woman.

The sinner was finally brought out, two men holding her by the arms, and paraded to the church, where she was made to stand confronted by her fellow townsmen. The elders, as befitted their rank, were in the forefront of the crowd, disputing the evidence, the depth of her sin, and the proper disposition of the matter; their loud voices—since it is a well-known principle that he who speaks the loudest speaks the truth—were raised in hot discussion, although they had been in substantial agreement from the start.

Igor Guryanovich Yegorov, the dean of the elders, stated the case succinctly: "She is no better than a *prostitutka*,* and should be dealt with like one."

Anton Sergeyevich Smilodov agreed: "You are right, Igor Guryanovich, but how are we to deal with her?"

Igor Guryanovich stroked his white beard for a moment, searching for an answer. The onlookers realized that he was deep in thought, and breathlessly awaited his decision. At last, his face brightened, and the crowd prepared to hear his words of wisdom. And his words overflowed with wisdom.

"Efim Akovlevich," he said, "you are the headman of Pokrovskoye; what is the punishment for a prostitutka?"

It was now Grandfather's turn to look thoughtful. And then he, too, came to a decision: "We have had no case of *prostituciya* in our village within my memory. But Otyets Pavel can tell us what the Holy Church says we should do."

Otyets Pavel looked out over the assemblage, which by that time included almost every one of the twelve hundred inhabitants of Pokrovskoye, waiting until absolute quiet had

*prostitute (prostituciya: prostitution)

42

fallen upon his audience. He had not long to wait, for he was a large man, made to seem even larger by his robes and high priestly hat. And he represented all the majesty of the Holy Church. When there was no sound but for the almost silent weeping of the prisoner, he handed down his decision, as though he were standing at the very peak of Mt. Sinai: "The Church has proclaimed the punishment for a woman taken in sin." The crowd grew even more quiet, if that were possible.

"Natalya Petrovna Stepanova," he intoned, making her very name sould like a synonym for harlotry, "you have been taken in the very act. Hear, then, your punishment. You shall be stripped bare, and you shall be whipped out of the village. You are herewith severed from the congregation of Pokrovskoye, and you are forever exiled from this village. Tak i bit!"

With the two men still holding the dangerous criminal by the arms, Efim Akovlevich stepped forward to carry out the decree of the svyashchennik. Grasping the front of her dress in one muscular hand, he gave it a sharp pull, tearing the simple garment from her body. Natalya Petrovna screamed at being so exposed before her fellow villagers, and pleaded with her guards for something with which to cover her nakedness, but the elders showed no sign of compassion in their suddenly keener eyes. She struggled to free at least one hand with which to partially cover herself, but the men held her firmly. Another of the elders produced a pair of shears that he had brought along for the occasion, and these he handed to Efim Akovlevich, who proceeded to crop the woman's hair close to her head. Thus shorn of even the small protection to be had from her own hair, she was a pitiable object indeed. But there was no mercy in the hearts of the elders of Pokrovskoye, and she was powerless to defend herself.

And the worst was yet to come. A saddled horse was brought up, the woman's hands were tied together by one end of a piece of rope, the other end of which was tied to the saddle. The people, men and women alike, formed a double row, and Efim Akovlevich whacked the horse on its haunch with the flat of his hand. At once, the beast started up at a slow trot between the lines of vengeful villagers, who had armed themselves with sticks and leather straps; whatever was at hand. My father, who was present during the entire spectacle, although he took no part in that deadly gauntlet, described the scene to me, and even after the passage of so many years, he was still horrified at the memory.

"Here were these people," he said, "good friends and neighbors, even my own father, although, thank God, not my mother, lined up to beat a poor woman whose only sin was that she was caught doing something that many of her judges had done. It was terrible," and here he closed his eyes, and covered them, as if to blot out the scene. "And the most terrible part of it," he continued after a moment, "was the looks on the faces of the ones who were there to beat her. The fools did not know that their sin was far greater. Their eyes were almost popping out of their heads; their lips were drawn back in fiendish grins; they were eager to inflict the utmost harm upon her."

As the horse started down the lines, the woman had to run to keep from being thrown off her feet, and the people began to lash and flail her with their weapons. She screamed in agony as the blood began to flow, but no heart was so soft as to leave her unscourged. Her screams, and the shouts of her tormenters, frightened the horse and it began to run faster, so that she stumbled and fell, and dragged along the ground, she offered a choice target for the vicious blows. Her only blessing was that she became unconscious and did not feel the last of the flogging administered to her bleeding back. Thus was Natalya Petrovna bidden Godspeed by her former friends and neighbors.

She had an additional piece of good fortune in that it had rained heavily earlier that day, and the ground had been turned into a soft liquid mud. Thus, although cold and soggy, it did far less damage to her flesh than if it had been dry and firm. As the horse dragged its unconscious burden away from the village, the gauntlet lines dissolved, and the elders assured each other that justice had been done indeed, and quite enjoyably at that.

Papa, glued to his place on the outskirts of the crowd, had wanted to cry out in protest, but he had been raised, as was the custom, to have respect for his elders, and this, alone, had prevented his making an outcry. But every instinct had demanded that he speak. Had they never heard that the Khristos had said, "He that is without sin among you, let him first cast a stone at her?"

Once the saturnalia of torture came to an end, he slipped away, unnoticed, and followed the clear trail left by Natalya Petrovna's dragged body until it turned off into a field, and hearing the horse's whinny, he moved toward the sound. Finding her senseless form still tied to the saddle, he undid the rope, and turning the horse's head back toward town, he spoke softly to it and watched it trot off down the road. Then he knelt by her side and began to examine the cuts and bruises on her back. She had been brutally wounded, her flesh a mass of contusions and abrasions, some of which were bleeding quite freely. She groaned and tried to rise, but Grischa placed his hand on her back and said, "Do not try to move. I will help you."

She recoiled from his touch, crying, "Please, haven't you done enough to me? I can bear no more. Oh, the pain is too terrible. Please go away."

But Grischa reassured her: "No. no, Natalya Petrovna, I have not come to hurt you. I want to help you."

The poor confused woman found it hard to believe that anyone from Pokrovskoye would show any sympathy toward her, and she asked, "Who are you, and why do you want to help me?"

"I am Grigori Efimovich. I believe I can heal your wounds."

Like everyone else in the village, she had heard of his healing powers. "But," she moaned, "you are the son of Efim Akovlevich. What would he say if he knew you were here with me?"

"I don't know—or care. I only know I can't let you lie here like this."

"Oh, Grigori Efimovich, if you can stop the pain, please do it. I can stand it no longer."

"I will try, but please lie quietly."

As gently as a mother with her babe, he touched each of the open wounds in turn, and as he did so, the bleeding stopped miraculously. The bruises, too, yielded to his touch, and little by little, her groans decreased as the pain abated. At last, she sighed in relief.

"Oh, Grigori Efimovich, I feel so much better. You are a saint, indeed. I don't know whether I could have endured much more. I think I would have died if you had not come."

Although he had never touched a naked woman before, he was no more aware of her unclad form than if she had been one of the farm animals, and thus he was surprised at her reaction to his request that she turn on her back so that he might heal whatever damage had been done to her frontal parts.

"Please don't ask me to turn; I—I just cannot. What they did—what happened back there—undressing me in front of all those people—no, no, I cannot do it."

"But it must be done. If you have open wounds, they are filled with mire. It might be serious; you could get blood poisoning if they are not cleansed."

He spoke in such gentle tones, his voice so soothing, yet insistent, that without further protest, she did turn over, and Grischa placed his healing hands upon each wound until it was healed.

Then he told her: "It is not far to the river. I will help you there so that you can bathe yourself. All this dirt must be removed. Do you think you can walk with my help?"

She said that she believed she could, and leaning heavily upon him as he placed an arm around her, they hobbled slowly toward the Tura. Once there, she tried the water's temperature with her toe, and immediately withdrew it. Shivering, she said, "It's too cold."

"I know it's cold, but you must bathe, anyway. Give me your hand so I can hold onto you while you get into the water."

Although nearly twice his age, she had gained such confidence in him that she took his hand and stepped into the river, the water coming to her waist. She gave a little shriek at the cold, and demanded to be pulled out at once. But he was firm.

"Kneel down until the water comes up to your chin, and wash off the mud—all of it."

She cried out, "Oh, I shall die; it's so cold."

Her teeth were chattering, but she obeyed her healer, and as she became acclimated to the frigid stream, she began scrubbing herself with her free hand. At last, when he saw that she was clean once more, he pulled on her hand and she came gratefully up onto the bank. He had removed his shirt, and using it as a towel, dried her shivering form as best he could. When she was reasonably dry, he took off his coat and helped her into it. There was a heavy thicket close by, and he led her there, searching until he found two small trees growing a few feet apart. With his bare hands as his only tools, he broke off pieces of the brush, and using the trees as his main beams, he built her a crude sort of lair.

"The sun will be up soon, and then you will be warm," he told her. "In the meantime, you can stay here in perfect safety."

He moved out of the thicket to the field, which was lush with tall grass, and gathered armloads of it to make her a bed. When it was piled deeply enough so that she could lie on it in some comfort, he said, "I'll come back this evening, as soon as it gets dark, and I'll bring you some food and clothing. Will you be all right until then?"

"Yes. I feel much better. I don't know how to thank you for your kindness."

"Please, I have done nothing. It is only what any Khristianin* would do."

"Yes, but what of those other Khristiane? They were anything but kind."

"It is not my place to judge them; only God can judge."

And with that, he left her. But he was back that evening as soon as it grew dark, bringing with him an old dress and a pair of shoes that had belonged to his grandmother, who had died a few years earlier. He had also managed to gather up some black bread and a container of his mother's good borscht, and sat with her while she supped it down greedily, it being her first meal in some twenty-four hours. When she had sopped up

---

*Christian (pl., Khristiane)

the last of the soup with the last piece of bread, Grischa, who had been waiting patiently, asked her how she felt.

"Thanks to you, I have very little pain."

"Can you walk with comfort?"

"No, my legs are still sore, but they do not hurt very much when I am sitting. Only, then something else hurts."

"Here, let me fix it for you. Lie on your face."

Grateful for his ministrations, she did as he asked, and felt the discomfort ebbing away at the touch of his healing hands. She felt something else, as well, for those hands stirred a sensation within her that she had thought her good neighbors had beaten out of her only a few brief hours earlier.

She sat up, and with her sweetest smile, made known her inclination to comply with whatever desires he might have. "Grischa, I have only one way of showing my gratitude for what you have done. If you like, you may make love to me."

He was troubled by her words. His still-unsatisfied urges, although dulled for a time by the cruelty of Irina Danilova, had begun to rise again, and her open invitation had an instantaneous effect upon him. But he also had scruples about taking advantage of what he believed to be no more than her sense of obligation. Beyond that, she was, in a manner of speaking, his patient, and he felt himself honor-bound not to avail himself of the easy opportunity she had presented. And so he merely shook his head, forcing his desire to the back of his mind.

It was difficult to refuse her, but he forced himself to say, "No, Natalya Petrovna, not now. Perhaps when you are well and strong once more, but you are still too weak."

Surprised at his rejection, for she was unused to a male reaction of that nature, she found herself in some confusion. Seldom had it been necessary for her to ask for that which most men she had known were eager to press upon her, and all she could do was to stammer out a response that did not come out quite the way she intended: "Very well, then; whenever you decide."

Grischa came, bringing food, every night for a week, and by its end, she was quite cured of her wounds. She told him of her plans: "I think I will take tomorrow's boat downriver to Tobolsk. Since nobody knows me there, I can start a whole new life."

He considered this for a moment and then, almost as an afterthought, handed her a *kosinka** he had "borrowed" from his mother to cover Natalya Petrovna's shorn head.

As she tied it on, she continued, "Late last night, I took a chance and sneaked back to my *khizhina*† and dug up a ruble I had buried in the floor. It will pay my way to Tobolsk, and I can live on what remains until I can find work."

A vague disappointment stole over him. He had hoped that when she was well, they might—she would let him—do whatever it was that men did with women. He started to reach toward her, but she stopped him, drawing back a little, a look of mild panic in her eyes.

"Not now, Grischa," she implored him. "It is still daylight and someone might see us. You know what they would do to me if they caught me again. Come tonight, after dark, and we shall see."

But he shook his head. "Tonight I must be with my family at the wedding of Ilya Antonovich Ivanov and Nadya Igorovna. I cannot come."

"Poor Grischa; I'm sorry, but I dare not."

He nodded his head in understanding, and arose. Taking her hand, he made his farewells, adding, *"Da khranit vas Bog."*‡ And left her without glancing back.

That night, after the wedding ceremony, the guests gathered in the square to feast and dance to the strident notes of Pyetr Dmitriyevich Ilyanov's *akkordeon,*** and standing on the sidelines to catch his breath, Grischa felt a tug at his sleeve. He turned to find two young men of about his own age beside him, and one of them whispered in his ear: "Hey, Grischa, come and have a drink with us."

Thinking the boy was offering him some tea or even light wine, he went with them to a secluded spot behind the

*kerchief
†hut; cottage
‡God preserve you
**accordion

church, where a third boy awaited them with a bottle of some white liquid.

"Here," the bottle bearer said, "try some of this. It's really good."

Grischa took a healthy swallow, thinking it would help to cool him after his long period of dancing, only to find himself nearly choking on the liquor. His throat burned as though it had been filled with hot coals, but he managed to smile, realizing that they had been trying to play a trick on him and had been waiting to see him gasp and strangle for their amusement. With a laugh, he said, "That was very good. What is it?"

"Vodka. Go ahead; have some more."

He had to go through with his pretense of enjoyment, and so he drank again, this time holding most of the fiery fluid in his mouth, and permitting only a little to trickle down in a series of small swallows. He passed the bottle to one of the others, and soon it came around to him again. In a very short while, he was quite drunk, although still able to keep his feet, but all reason had deserted him. One of the boys had left as soon as the bottle was drained, but two of them remained, and wanting, as boys will, to appear as men of experience, they began talking of their many conquests of women, each working his imagination to the utmost to create marvelous stories of their exploits. Casanova and Münchhausen would have at once surrendered their honors if they had been privileged to have listened to the improbable tales.

"I'd give anything to have a woman right now," said one of the young men.

"Do you think" his companion asked, "that we could get a couple of the girls away from the dancing?"

"Not with the way their mothers are watching them."

"Come, *tovarishchi*," * Grischa cut in. "If you want a woman, just follow me."

The boys fell into a straggling file behind him, and the three drunken youths made their faltering way out of the

friends; comrades

village. Staggering a little, and boasting a lot, the small band approached the place were Natalya Petrovna was sleeping in the shelter Grischa had made for her. The loud voices awakened her, and she sat up to find herself surrounded by three drunken young ruffians whose obvious intent was to possess her by whatever means might be necessary.

Frightened, she cried out, "What do you want? Why have you come here?" And then, seeing that Grischa was among them, she turned on him accusingly: "Why did you bring them here? I thought you were my friend."

The boys had but one purpose, and were not to be turned aside from that goal by words alone. But Grischa, whose head had cleared somewhat during the walk from the village, suddenly saw that he had been on the verge of committing an unpardonable offense against not only the woman, but God as well, and he stepped between her and them, facing them with outstretched arms.

"No," he cried, "we cannot do this thing. I was wrong to bring you here. Let us leave her in peace."

Standing there like some avenging angel barring the gate to their particular Eden, he gave them pause for thought. They were not eager to test their pugilistic abilities against Grischa, who, they remembered, had defeated the village champion and his two supporters. The fire went out of them, and grumbling about people who robbed other people of their fun, they stole away. Grischa, his head throbbing, the tears streaming down his cheeks, gave a great sob and ran off into the woods, not stopping to hear the woman's expressions of gratitude.

After running for some time, driven by some inner need to vent his energy, he at last came to a standstill, and falling to his knees, began to pray, begging God for forgiveness for the sin he had almost committed, the sin he had indeed committed in his heart. Gradually, the pounding in his head diminished and his tears dried. A peace of sorts came over him, as well as a new resolve. He had suffered two shattering experiences, both rising out of his having forgotten God in a vain effort to achieve sexual gratification. Others might pursue the pleasures of venery without sustaining repercussions, but for him such delights were not to be, at least not for the present. He seemed to know, without having been told, that he must forgo such sensual joys in order to achieve some higher goal. And on his knees, surrounded by the natural loveliness of the woodland, and the sun just rising over the distant horizon, Grigori Efimovich Rasputin knew the will of God and accepted it. And with his acceptance, a light began to glow before his inner eye, not so strongly as the one he had seen nearly three years before, but a light nonetheless. And it was to stay with him during most of his waking hours until it was replaced by an experience of even greater magnitude.

No longer did he stop in the middle of a furrow to become rapt in meditation; with the light to act as an inner guide, he found that he could do his work and still enjoy constant communion with God. As a consequence, Grandfather had no further cause for complaint, and there was peace in the family. And there were other blessings. As the crops ripened, Grischa began to fear that with the harvest would come renewed trips to Tyumen and the scene of his shame, and he prayed that he would not have to go. Much to his delight, then, when plans were already being made for his first trip, a *makler** drove up to the door with an offer to buy all of Efim Akovlevich's surplus. And while the price he mentioned was a little less than that which Grischa had received, the savings in time and effort more than made up the difference, so that a deal was struck on the spot. Thus, Papa's life was now serene and exactly what he desired. His erstwhile drinking companions were angry and refused to speak to him when he went out to walk about the village, but his mind was too full of his own concerns to care one way or the other.

And so passed the fall and winter, and with the coming of spring, a new round of plowing and hoeing and planting. And Grischa, now eighteen, and physically powerful, due to his hard work, was more a man than a boy. His labors, though strenuous, he took in stride, his light giving him wisdom and joy. And when he fell asleep after a hard day's toil, it was

*broker

52

with the name of God on his lips. He was contented, and felt that there was little more to be asked for himself, except the one boon he constantly sought, the immediate experience of God and the knowledge of his true self. Gradually, he became aware of a presence within, One with whom he was still unable to make contact, but whose existence gave him a warming sensation of well-being. And with this presence as his constant companion, he found he could perform his duties around the farm almost without thinking, and still practice the presence of God, as Brother Lawrence had so aptly put it.

When thinking of this phase of my father's life, I feel a sense of the near-miraculous, for he seems never to have had a spiritual teacher, or as the Hindus call him, a guru. I have never felt any leanings toward mysticism, but since that was Papa's way, I have read a little on the subject, and I find that while many men and women have experienced realization and illumination, very few have done so without the blessed guidance of someone who had previously trodden that path. The enlightened teacher knows of the pitfalls that lie in wait for the aspirant; he knows the stage of progress at which his disciple may have arrived; and he knows how to pilot him past the shoals and reefs into the safe harbor of that knowledge, "by knowing which," as the ancient sage had said, "all things are known."

Thus, totally untutored, except by his own mind and yearning for the truth, Grischa was plowing in the fields one day when the ever-present light began to expand. As he fell to his knees between the plow handles, the reins loosed by his unfeeling hands, the light seemed to burst into a thousand fragments, revealing an even whiter, more refulgent luster, and he heard celestial music, as though some vast angelic choir were heralding the coming of a most wondrous Being. And, as he opened his heart and his whole existence to this exaltation, there appeared in the midst of the glory a nebulous figure, moving toward him and growing more distinct, until it emerged as that of a woman in flowing robes. It came nearer, and to Grischa, who had ceased to breathe, there was given the knowledge that here was a vision of the Holy Mother, in the form of the Virgin of Kazan. And now she stood before him, a golden crown upon her head, surrounded by a pulsating nimbus of brilliant hues and gowned in a shimmering robe of white embroidered in gold and silver and precious stones, beneath a cloak of royal purple. Her right arm reached down toward him, palm outward, granting him the boon of illumination; her left hand was raised above his head, conferring her divine blessing. Tears coursed down his cheeks, as he offered a prayer of gratitude and devotion, asking only that she tell him how he might serve her. He gazed into her serene and shining countenance, enraptured, his heart so swollen with adoration that it seemed on the point of bursting. He was beyond all thought, realizing only that he was receiving a visitation from *Gospod Khristos** in the form of his Virgin Mother.

He remained on his knees, hardly breathing and without bodily sensation, until the vision began to fade. He was a little disappointed that she had not spoken to tell him of her design for his future. But even that was obscured by the over-powering worship that coursed through his whole being. And as the Virgin, radiating her divine love, faded from his sight, and the celestial choir from his hearing, he remained on his knees in wonder. What was her purpose for him? In what way did she want him to serve her?

At last, he arose, only then becoming aware, as the feeling returned to his physical body, that he had been kneeling on a sharp stone and that it had cut through the cloth of his trousers and bitten well into the flesh of his knee, which was bleeding. But it did not matter in the least; what was that slight discomfort when placed in the balance beside a visitation from the Virgin of Kazan? He was overflowing with the miraculous event, and felt he must tell his mother.

But a voice, firm and yet kind, spoke in his ear, and it was the same voice that had spoken to the healed leper after the Sermon on the Mount; and the voice said, "See thou tell no man. . . ."

And Grigori Efimovich wondered that such a miracle should be kept secret, and in his wondering there was woven

*The Lord Christ

another question: What did the Virgin Mother of the Khristos have in store for him? But even as he asked the question, he knew that he would be told in time and that the time would be chosen by God. And Grigori Efimovich left the plow in the middle of the furrow and led the plow horse back to the barn, and with hands still trembling from the overwhelming experience, he removed the harness, and curried the horse, and led him into his stall.

In describing this golden moment to me, he called it his "Awakening," or his "Spiritual Rebirth."

But in its aftermath, he could only stand in wonder.

FIVE

The spiritual experience that had overwhelmed my father, although profound, was by its very nature, tenuous. The Hindu rishis, or illumined sages, who systematized the whole of the mystic techniques in their writings, the Upanishads, Bhagavad Gita, and the Yoga Sutras of Patanjali, among others, tell us that samadhi, or illumination, has two levels: the lower, in which there is a vision of God in one of His manifestations; he who sees, and He who is seen remaining separate. And the higher, in which the seer and the Seen become one. They also tell us that, while the lower samadhi is a most intense experience, it will last only so long as the disciple continues to build upon it. There can be no standing still; one either advances or falls back. And my father was no one's disciple, having had no teacher to guide his footsteps on the spiritual path.

Few are those who hear of the path; even fewer are those who, having heard, attempt the upward climb; and fewer yet are they who persist to the end. But fewer than all of these are they who succeed without guidance. Those who fail are not to be blamed, for they have at least dared to assault the heights, and the appellation "fallen saints" that is assigned to them may or may not be merited, for even in their failure, they are far advanced above those who have never tried at all. However, the fallen saints do return to the everyday world and are apt to yield to the demands of the flesh, the demands, as Sri Rama- krishna put it, of "*Kama kanchini*," or lust and greed, the desire for sexual gratification and the so-called good things of life.

And so it was with my father. Floating, as it were, on a sea of bliss, he continued to enjoy his euphoria, indrawn and out of communication with the world of reality. He did not seem to hear anything that was said to him, took no notice of his mother, and pitied his father, who was always angry. For some time, they appeared to him to be creatures from another planet. He loved them; in fact, he loved all mankind, equally and without discrimination, and his loving attitude somewhat softened his parent's disposition toward him. But, of course, the feeling did not last, and as he gradually returned to earth, he again took up his labors, so that peace was restored.

But Grischa was restless; his inner light had vanished, and although he prayed constantly for some further sign, there was none. It became difficult for him to pray, and he entered a dry period, one in which he could not arouse in himself any interest in things spiritual, however hard he tried. It was as though his total supply of spiritual energy had been expended in that one explosion, leaving nothing behind. As his "dark night of the soul" continued, in spite of all his efforts, he became discouraged, and at last, unable to bear it any longer, he took to spending his evenings at the local *kabachok*,* where there was at least some gaiety and a sense of living; where there was plenty of *slivovits*† and vodka to rouse the spirits of a man, and plenty of girls with whom one might dance. He discovered that he loved to dance, and did so with such enthusiasm that he would exhaust more than one partner during an evening. He was even happier when an occasional band of Gypsies passed through the village and pitched camp for a few days on the out-

*inn; tavern
†plum brandy

57

skirts. These were people after his own heart. There was always a fiddler to play the wild, sometimes sad, sometimes gay, music, and this, in itself, was intoxicating. And, like himself, the Gypsies never tired of dancing, and could go on until the small hours of the morning.

There were also feast days, when the whole village would turn out, and old Pyotr Dmitriyevich would play on his ancient akkordeon, and everyone, young and old alike, would dance until they could stand no longer. It was at one such festival that my father met his match. The tall and shapely girl that he had chosen as his partner loved dancing as much as he, and the villagers watching them agreed that they made a handsome pair. Her blond hair was in sharp contrast to his brown, unruly thatch, but she was nearly as tall as he. During a pause, while Pyotr Dmitriyevich took a few moments to refresh himself with a long draft of *pivo*,* the young couple strolled off from the crowd.

Grischa introduced himself: "I am Grigori Efimovich Rasputin, at your service."

And she replied, "Yes, Grigori Efimovich. I am Praskovia Fedorovna Dubrovina."

"Praskovia Fedorovna; what a beautiful name; almost as beautiful as its owner."

She blushed and smiled: "You are too kind. I do not think I am beautiful."

"Ah, *milochka*,† you do yourself an injustice."

She blushed an even deeper shade of red; his use of the endearing term so early in their acquaintanceship was, she thought, a little forward.

Grischa was about to continue when Pyotr Dmitriyevich began to play again, and the girl, pleased that the ardent swain had been halted at just the right point, quickly said, "There is the music. Come, let us dance again."

And the young couple made their way back to the floor, to whirl and dip and leap in the prescribed manner for hours on end. When, at last, the dance was over and the citizens began returning to their humble cottages, Grischa asked

*beer
†my dear

his new friend if he could escort her home, to which she gladly assented. They were in no hurry, and strolled hand in hand along the dark path, until Grischa, overcome by a feeling warmer than friendship, stopped and took her in his arms to deposit a fervent kiss upon her willing lips. And that is all that Father and Mother ever told me of their first meeting, but I could tell from the way that each of them spoke of it that for them it was a magic night; never were the stars brighter, never were the scents from the fields and flowers sweeter, never was the breeze more balmy.

And it also seeped out at various times when the subject came up that this euphoric state of their ambience continued for another three months, at the end of which period Grischa announced, without apparently astonishing either of his parents: "I have something to tell you."

Anxious to impress them with what he was about to reveal, he struck a most solemn note: "I am going to be married."

Grandmother, knowing the answer well enough, still asked the question: "Who is she? What is her name? Is she a good girl?"

Grischa replied, "She is a girl whose family has recently come to Pokrovskoye. Her name is Praskovia Fedorovna Dubrovina. And she is a wonderful girl."

It was now my grandfather's turn. "What makes you think she is the right girl for you?"

"I just know she is the right one. She is so beautiful; her eyes are so big and black; her hair is like *shyelk** from an ear of *zyerno*.† She loves to dance as much as I do, and she is so graceful. Oh, she is the right girl; I know it. She . . ."

But his rhapsody was cut short by his mother: "Grischa, she may be *pryekrasnaya*,‡ but is she *poslushnaya?*** With her love of dancing, she seems a little giddy for my taste. After all, farming and managing a family is a pretty serious affair."

*silk
†corn
‡beautiful
**manageable

"Mama, we have talked about it, and I know she will make me a good wife, and a good mother for my children— that is," he finished lamely, "if we have any."

"Of course you will," Grandmother countered, thereby indicating a consent she had not been quite ready to give. It was always better to be absolutely certain in such matters. She grumbled a little, but was inwardly pleased; the boy had been staying out too late these last few months, and she had been worried about his health.

Grandfather quickly capitulated, he too feeling that it was high time his son got all those foolish notions out of his head and returned to the business of working the farm; there was always so much to do. And thus, the wedding was arranged, and like all weddings in pre-Soviet Russia, it was to be a festive occasion. Otyets Pavel tied the knot, literally, in the Orthodox tradition, and as the bride and groom came out of the church, the merrymaking began. The happy couple was quickly surrounded by the revelers, who serenaded them with Siberian nuptial songs, some of which were quite explicit concerning the duties of each of the newlyweds, many jests of an indelicate nature, and here and there a sly double entendre, all of which the happy pair bore with patience and a smiling fortitude.

Grandmother and Grandfather were no less content, feeling that Praskovia Fedorovna would prove to be a stabilizing influence for their son. She was not only a good, solid girl, but also three years older than he. And in this their judgment was proven correct. Grischa settled down to a happily married life, stayed home at night, and did even more than was required of him around the farm. He was delighted with his bride, who, as proof of her love, gave him four children in rapid succession, although, tragically, the first of these, a son, lived but a few months. Grischa felt the baby's death more deeply, if possible, than he would normally have done, for there came flooding back all the memories surrounding the death of his brother, Mischa, to whom he had been so attached. At the same time, he was overcome by the thought that he was, perhaps, being punished for having neglected his spiritual efforts for so long a time, choosing rather to enjoy the pleasures of the marriage bed. Almost as a form of penance, he began to pray again, not only during the long hours of the night, but as he went about his labors and, although he did not regain his former blessing of the light that had been his constant companion, he did receive a measure of comfort and solace from prayer.

Praskovia Fedorovna did what she could to alleviate their sense of loss by quickly giving birth to a second son, Dmitri, and at intervals of two years, daughters Matriona, or Maria, as I have always been known, and Varya. Father was further occupied in building a new home for his growing family, somewhat larger than his father's, and set apart from it, although still on the farm. This was a two-story house, the largest dwelling in Pokrovskoye. His work and his children's demands for attention did wonders in dispelling the heaviness in his heart over the death of his firstborn, and time, also a noted healer of wounds, did the rest.

But as peace settled upon the household, Papa began having strange dreams, consisting in the main of fleeting glimpses of the lady of his vision, the Virgin of Kazan. She seemed to be calling him, as though the Mother of the Khristos required his services. But the images drifted by, passing too quickly for him to comprehend their meaning or intent. All that resulted was an uneasy feeling in his bones, an unshakable feeling that he was disobeying a heavenly command, and he became moody and uncommunicative toward his loved ones. Praskovia Fedorovna began to wonder if she had in some way failed him in her wifely duties. Perhaps she was not all that he had hoped; perhaps there was something lacking in the way she responded to his lovemaking; although, search her memory as she would, she could recall no incident in which he had not seemed fulfilled. But she knew she was ignorant in these matters, knowing only what he had taught her, and it might be that he had not taught her everything a good wife should know. Could that be it? But there he was, out in the field, standing halfway down a furrow and leaning on his hoe, his eyes turned heavenward, as though seeking some answer there. Surely it was something other than a lack of sexual fulfillment; it might not have anything to do with her or her lack of proficiency.

And in this assumption she was correct, for at the moment he was pouring out his heart to the Virgin Mother, imploring her to tell him what he must do. More than anything in the world, he longed to do her bidding, and his frustration was that, while he knew she had some mission for him, he had been unable to learn what it was.

And then one day, driving the wagon home from the mill where he had gone to deliver a load of grain, he stopped to give a ride to a young man. As they talked, Grischa found that his passenger was a divinity student from the monastery at Verkhoture, and at once began to seek his advice, particularly on the subject of his vision and his recent dreams.

The student became very excited at what he was hearing and said, "It is clear that you have been called by God, and there is no question but that you must do His bidding. Not to do so would be a sin."

"But what must I do?"

"You should come to Verkhoture. The monks there will help you."

"But what about my family?" Grischa asked weakly. "I cannot just go off and leave them."

"How can a family be allowed to stand between you and your calling?"

"But I have no education. I cannot read or write."

"Schooling is not what counts, my friend. The question is: How strong is your faith?"

Having arrived home, Grischa stopped to permit his passenger to alight. "Don't forget," were his parting words, "the Lord will not wait forever."

Grischa waved a farewell and proceeded about his business with a heavy heart, his mind awhirl with unanswered questions. How could he leave Praskovia Fedorovna and his three little children? How would they live during his absence? Did he have a right to go? But this was followed by another, antithetical question: What of the account in St. Luke's Gospel?

> And another also said, Lord, I will follow thee; but first let me go bid them farewell, which are at home at my house.
>
> And Jesus said unto him, No man, having put his hand to the plow, and looking back, is fit for the kingdom of God.

All of those who came to know my father, all, that is, except his political enemies, were in agreement on at least one count: He was a kindly and humane man, with great love in his heart for people. And it was just this quality that made it so difficult for him to reach a decision over whether to go or stay. He felt an almost irresistible urge to begin his mission, but, at the same time, he could not bear to tear himself away from his family, with all the possible consequences of such an act. For days he pondered the problem, telling no one of the turmoil through which he was passing, but they could not help noticing something of his condition. And Praskovia Fedorovna could not rid herself of her sense of guilt, that somehow it might be her fault, even though their shared intimacies were most satisfying to her and, so far as she could determine, to him as well.

It was on such a night that, having fallen into a sleep of contentment, she awoke some hours later with the realization that her husband was not in bed with her. Turning over, she discovered him kneeling in prayer before the ikona of the Virgin of Kazan, and in the flickering light of the votive candle that always burned before it, she could see the damp sheen of his cheeks. Hearing her movement, he ended his prayers and returned to her side, and she could see the agony written in his face. She was stricken again with the thought that she had failed him, and there was an ache within her that forced the tears to well up in her eyes and spill over. He took her in his arms and tried to soothe her.

"Milochka, why are you crying? There is nothing for you to weep about."

And then it all poured out of her, all the pent-up emotions, the worries, the feelings of guilt, and she cried, "Oh, Grischa, I have seen how unhappy you have been for a long time. Am I to blame? Have I done something to displease you? Have I failed you in some way? Are you sorry that you married me? What is it?"

He looked at her in amazement. In his preoccupation with his own inner struggles he had not considered that she might be suffering too, that the outward signs of his mental turmoil might have appeared to her as a diminution of his love, and that she might blame herself for in some way having failed him.

"No, no, milochka, that has nothing to do with it." He took her hand and stroked it lovingly. "You have been a wonderful wife; I could not even dream of a better."

He kissed her tenderly, wiping away her tears with a gentle thumb, and climbing back into bed so that he could hold her in his arms and reassure her. They spoke softly, for fear of waking the children, and she listened in wonder as he told her of his spiritual experiences, beginning back when he was a lad sitting under a tree and seeing God's light for the first time. He hoped that she would be able to catch a glimmer of what he had undergone, while knowing that no one can fully understand the lofty reaches of the spirit who has not experienced them for himself.

And then he added, "I know that the Blessed Virgin wanted me to take up my cross, as the Khristos said, and follow Him. But I have not done it. I have spurned God."

"But you have not spurned God. You are a good husband and a good father; you lead a good life and go to church. What more can God want? What more can you do?"

"I am not certain. I know He has some work for me, and I think He wants me to know my own true nature also."

"But surely you know your own nature? You are a farmer, a husband, a father, a . . ."

"No, no, that is not what I mean. That is only how I appear to others. It is not what is on the outside, but . . . but what I am like on the inside," he finished lamely, desperately trying to express the inexpressible. "You see, the inner nature of every person is from God; in fact, it is God Himself. And it is that truth I must realize."

Mother was confused; she had only half understood the purport of his words; the words themselves were simple enough, but all that business about inner nature and outer nature—was distracting. But there was a more important question to ask, and dreading what the answer might be, she steeled herself to ask it.

"What is it in your heart to do?"

"I feel I must go where there are teachers, men of God, who can help me find the way."

Words suddenly began spewing out of her mouth, words she had not meant to speak, nor planned to speak, words to which she listened half in amazement and half in horror, for they meant a separation from a part of herself.

"You must do whatever is right, Grischa, and you must do it quickly. There is no time to waste. If God wants you to go, then you must go."

He looked at her in utter astonishment, having been certain that she would never agree to his leaving her. If he had loved her before, his love was redoubled, for she had made his task far easier.

"Thank you, milochka," were the only words he could find.

"When do you want to go?"

"I haven't made any plans. I suppose it should be as soon as possible." And he was suddenly overcome by a sense of guilt at leaving his family, and his responsibilities toward them, behind. "But what of you—and the children—and the farm work?"

"The crops are coming along very well; my father will come and help with the harvest, and the children are in good health. So there is no reason for you to worry."

"I love you. You have been a good wife."

"I love you too. Only, do not stay away too long."

They spoke tenderly for a while, and then my father, relaxed for the first time in weeks, fell into a deep sleep. But my mother could not sleep. She lay there, wondering what had ever possessed her to speak as she had. The last thing in this world she had wanted was for her husband to go off wandering in search of anything but their mutual happiness and contentment.

And thus it was that in the next few days, Grigori Efimovich set out to find his soul.

Ж

The monastery of Verkhoture was a great pile of brick and stone, surmounted by tall spires and domes and surrounded by a massive stone wall. As Grischa approached this huge conglomerate of masonry, he passed between green fields in which

65

he could see a number of monks working. Situated as it was at the foot of the Urals, the horizon was a panorama of hills and fertile valleys; altogether a picturesque, if somewhat awe-inspiring, vista.

One of the elder monks who seemed to be in charge of the students questioned Grischa, and upon being assured of his sincerity, readily accepted him into the community. And the old monk's judgment did not betray him, for the new devotee labored long and hard in the fields and in his studies. He did not mind the physical work, for it was similar to that which he had done at home, but it was the hours spent in prayer and meditation that he really enjoyed, and his genuine devotion aroused the notice of some of the senior monks. But what he lacked, a lack the good brothers could not fill, was the guidance of a truly holy man, one who could understand his visions and his struggle to recapture them.

And then one of his fellow students told him of a teacher, a *starets** named Makari, who lived in a hut in the forest surrounding the monastery, and he determined to visit the holy man at the first opportunity. There was one other factor beside the lack of mystical teaching at the monastery that brought him to this decision, and that was a division between the monks themselves. One faction consisted of those who followed a rigidly traditional view of the Orthodox tenets, made up for the most part of the older members of the community, sometimes disrespectfully called the Starovyerkya, or "Old Believers," after the separatist sect of some two hundred years earlier. At least they were called that behind their backs by their opponents who took a more modern and liberal stand, as they liked to think. The two factions were constantly at loggerheads over minor points of doctrine, and this dismayed Grischa, who could never have imagined that such nonessential matters might occupy the thoughts of men who were supposed to have a larger goal in view. Up to this time, it was the only facet of monastic life with which he could not find himself in accord.

He had not minded the cold and dank little cell that

*a lay holy man, sometimes a wanderer seeking the knowledge of God; one who has had some degree of illumination had been assigned to him; the narrow window in the thick stone wall, letting in more cold than sunlight; the narrow cot with its wooden frame and thin mat, supported by an interwoven rope base; its one rickety chair, and equally rickety table, and below all, its cold stone floor. These might well have discouraged a man raised in a world of comfort, but Grischa had slept on harder surfaces, including the great sheet of iron that had served the double function of a top for the huge brick stove in his parents' house and a bed, once a mattress had been thrown over it, and so he was quite happy with his environment, happy except for one little *mukha v mazhye,** and its name was Otyets Iosif.

It was not too long after he had entered Verkhoture that he was made all too aware of that mukha. One night, just after he had fallen asleep, he was shaken into full consciousness, and someone whispered in his ear: "Hello, Grigori Efimovich; I am Otyets Iosif."

Grischa sat up in bed and brought his eyes to a focus on a little roly-poly man with beady black eyes, soft, thick lips, and soft, pudgy hands, who was smiling at him in a more-than-friendly manner. The smile, which was more like a leer, made him feel uncomfortable, and although he was a physical match for ten like the little monk, there was a tension between his shoulder blades, as though he were in some danger.

"What do you want?" he asked.

"I want to be your friend. It gets lonely here, very lonely at times. I hoped we might be—friends."

As if to reinforce his point, he reached out one clammy hand, and with the spittle gathering at the sides of his mouth, he started to press Grischa's thigh. While never having experienced a direct approach by a homosexual, he had heard of the deviates and their practices, and though he was slow to judge the actions of others, he was quite certain of one thing: Such practices were not for him. He got to his feet, apparently intending to leave through the low door, and the monk threw his arms about Grischa's waist.

"No, no, stay awhile. Can't we talk together?"

*fly in the ointment

But Grischa wanted no conversation with him, and especially not the sort of conversation he was certain that Otyets Iosif had in mind.

"Some other time, Little Father; right now, I must go to the chapel."

He shook off the not-quite-encircling arms and made good his escape, but he was sure that this would not be the last of it. By using his meager furniture to block his cell door shut at night, he secured himself from any further surprise awakenings, but he could not always avoid the pursuit of Otyets Iosif, even though he became quite adept at ducking around corners or hiding behind obstacles whenever his pursuer approached.

But in contrast to this annoyance, there was the pleasure of his long talks with Otyets Feliks, who sat next to him at meals, and with whom he had lengthy discussions on all sorts of subjects, from the occult to reincarnation. Since Grischa believed in both of these, he was happy to find the elder monk concurred, and not only concurred but expounded upon them in such a way as to further deepen Grischa's belief. After listening to some of the other monks argue over trivial differences in scriptural interpretation, Grischa found that Otyets Feliks did much to improve his opinion of the monastery, and the time spent with him made the hours pass quickly.

It was not long after his midnight confrontation with Otyets Iosif that Grischa found time to visit the Starets Makari. With directions provided by one of the younger monks, he had little trouble in locating the hut. He had been told the story of this strange man who had been a profligate in his youth, spending his patrimony in drinking, gambling, and wenching, until he awoke one day with an aversion for pleasure.

Heeding the words of the Khristos: "If thou wilt be perfect, go and sell all thou hast, and give it to the poor, and thou shalt have treasure in heaven; and come and follow me," Makari did just that, and when the demands of the flesh grew too strong within him, he mortified his body with cruel, self-inflicted torment to drive out the monster of lust, until there was no carnal desire remaining. Having passed through the fire and storm of passion, and conquered himself, he now lived serenely in the forest, giving guidance to those who came to sit at his feet.

Prostrating himself before the starets, Grischa addressed him: "Holy Sir, how can I know the will of God?"

"You must pray to Him."

"But, Master, suppose I am on a high wall and I start to fall off. Should I try to save myself, or should I leave it in the hands of God, knowing that His will must prevail?"

"My son, your body is the temple of God; why should you let it be broken? Should you not preserve the temple?"

"I understand, Master. What of my visions? Are they real, or mere hallucinations?"

"What did you see in your visions?"

"One day, while I was working in the field, praying as I worked, I saw God in the blessed form of the Virgin of Kazan."

Without answering the question, the holy man said, "Come, we shall meditate together for a few moments."

Grischa closed his eyes, and, almost at once, he was absorbed in the inner self. How long he remained in that state he did not know, for he had no thought of the outer world until the starets laid a gentle hand on his knee.

He spoke with assurance: "My son, I have seen that your vision was real. The Holy Mother did come to you, and you must follow her."

"I want to follow her, Master, but how shall I do it? She has not spoken to me, and I have not seen her again. How can I know what God wants of me?"

"You must pray without ceasing for guidance and direction. Upon rising in the morning, you must dedicate that day to God. You must do every task as the servant of God. Take no credit for good deeds, but offer that credit as your sacrifice to God. Pray for forgiveness, repeating 'Kyrie eleison' at least five thousand times a day. When you can feel you have been forgiven, He will come to you."

"I will do as you say, Master. Should I stay at Vekhoture?"

"God does not dwell only in a monastery. The whole

world is His. He is always with you, watching over you. Know this, and act accordingly."

"Thank you, Master." He prostrated himself once more, and took his leave.

Back at the monastery, he was perplexed. The starets' answers had not entirely satisfied him, nor completely answered his questions, although he hoped they might serve as a pointer toward the course he should follow. Whereas he had previously been contented with his life at Verkhoture, he could not help recalling the starets' words—"God does not dwell only in a monastery"—and he pondered for a long time on whether he should stay or leave. But the debate was quickly resolved. Having neglected to secure his door properly one night, he was awakened by an awareness of peril. Looking up, he found that two hooded figures were bending over him, one of whom he quickly recognized as Otyets Iosif; the other, he soon learned, was Otyets Sergius. The latter held his face so close to Grischa's that he could feel the monk's coarse, red beard against his cheek.

Raising his voice, he roared, "What do you want?"

Otyets Iosif clapped a clammy palm over Grischa's mouth, at the same time saying, "Shhh, be quiet, my boy. We mean you no harm. We only want to visit with you."

The other monk chimed in: "Don't you know that the Bible tells us to love our fellowmen? Well, we are your fellowmen, and we want to love you."

Horrified at this frank statement of their intentions, Grischa leaped up, tearing himself loose from Iosif's hand, and yelled, "Get out of my cell. I will have no part in your perversions."

Yet the two monks were committed to achieving their goal, and they pressed forward to take him by force, if that became necessary. But Grischa seized Iosif by the throat, saying, "Leave this instant, or I will choke the life out of you."

Taken aback, Iosif stopped in his tracks and turned toward the door. Clearly, he had not expected such violent resistance, but he stopped at the threshold long enough to spit out a threat of his own: "No one speaks to me that way. You may play the barbarian with me, but there are many of us here. You will most surely not escape our wrath."

Grischa made a threatening gesture toward Otyets Sergius, who fell back and fled on the heels of his comrade. Grischa immediately slammed the door and secured it, and fearing that he had little enough time to take suitable action, he dressed, threw his few belongings together, tied them into a bundle, and prepared to make his departure. It was clear that the monastery was now merely a trap in which he could be destroyed if he remained. He opened the door, looked up and down the stone corridor, and seeing no one, quickly ran along it toward the outer door. Passing through the massive portals, he went down the front steps as though shod with the winged shoes of Hermes, and so came into the courtyard. Seeing no one guarding the gate, he slipped through it into the outside world, drawing a great lungful of fresh air.

⚒SIX⚒

The haggard, ragged wayfarer tramping the dusty roads of western Siberia would have been unrecognized by the wife he had left behind in far-off Pokrovskoye nearly a year before. Then, he had been well fed and neatly dressed, clean-shaven and shod in stout leather boots; but now he looked like what he was, a *strannik*,* so intent on his quest for enlightenment that his physical appearance was of no concern to him. And there was another change that would have confused my mother. He had grown a beard, brown with reddish tints, although this he kept trimmed, not so much for the sake of appearance as for convenience.

As he walked, he maintained his constant prayer: "Kyrie eleison; Kyrie eleison," hoping, through God's mercy, to recapture the vision of the Holy Mother that had once been vouchsafed him in the fields back home. But in this he had no

*pilgrim; wanderer

success; rather, an opposite effect had been intruding upon his meditations for some time, for instead of the image of the Virgin of Kazan, he had been seeing visions of nude women, beautiful and alluring women, women who fanned the flames of his passions kept in restraint for so many months. When such a phenomenon loomed up to interrupt his devotions, he was overcome with a sense of shame and guilt, and redoubled his efforts to raise his consciousness above such carnal thoughts. But it seemed that the harder he tried to banish them from his mind, the more persistent they became, until he was wracked by the internal struggle that was being waged. Defeated in skirmish after skirmish, he would throw himself to the ground in exhaustion, but even then he found no rest and could only roll about, tortured by the ever-present demands of the flesh. Bedeviled as he was, he could make no progress in his spiritual quest, and yet he would not concede defeat, but fought on, beginning the battle anew with the coming of the dawn, and grieving at his failure with the setting of each sun.

Never having had the benefit of a true spiritual teacher, my father was unaware of the nature and cause of his suffering, which had been explained fully a thousand years or more before he was born. The Hindu rishis, or sages, described a vital force they called the kundalini, said to reside in a nerve center, called a chakra, at the base of the spine. There are seven of such chakras, each corresponding to points at which bundles of nerves extend out from the spinal cord to activate various bodily functions: digestion and elimination, sex, heart activity, and others. The kundalini is said to rise through them during meditation. The normal, everyday man lives within the three lower chakras, which activate the digestive process and sexual drives. Only meditation will carry the kundalini to the higher centers, that of the heart giving rise to the love of God, that of the throat bringing continual communication with God, that between the eyes granting a vision of God, and the topmost chakra, at the crown of the head, bestowing the highest illumination.

However, a problem may—and frequently does—arise. In this elevating of the kundalini, it must pass through all the lower chakras, the third of which is the one that vitalizes the sex center, and if the aspirant is taken by a gust of passion, he may well be unable to continue with his meditation. It is at this point that the expert teacher becomes essential to continued spiritual progress. Many a man or woman of the purest intention has been trapped by passions too powerful to resist, especially when lacking proper guidance, and while their more self-righteous brothers and sisters may look upon them with condemnation, they are not to be blamed for a perfectly natural yielding to overwhelming forces.

When I first heard of his sexual excesses, or so they seemed to me, I was stunned at their revelation, and it was not until many years later that a chance meeting through mutual friends with a Hindu yogi brought me to an understanding of my father's mountainous problem, the demon that was activated by an innocent attempt to achieve illumination. In the eyes of the world, Papa was a sinner, and by the laws of the Church, there can be no question that he sinned, but I like to think that a just God can find it in His heart to make allowances for the sins of a man who was impelled by irresistible forces beyond his powers to withstand.

As the yogi said to me: "Ah, memsahib, your father had the misfortune of attempting to do what few men have been able to accomplish, the finding of samadhi without the aid of a guru. Do not think of him as a sinner, but as one who tried and failed. And who can condemn a man for trying? Is that not better than to have made no effort? Millions sit safely in the valley, while only a few have the courage to begin the mountain climb, and when these fail, the millions say, 'There, I told you. They did not have the necessary stamina for climbing.' The millions, you see, have the wisdom of ignorance, which is no wisdom at all. How can one know what is involved in climbing the mountain when he has not tried it? No, do not think of your father as a sinner, but as a failed saint. He did not accomplish the climb in this life, but be assured that he will reach the heights in his next life or the one after that."

I do not know if I believe all of the things that the yogi said, because, as I have already mentioned, I am not a mystic; I have some doubts, for instance, about reincarnation, which may be true, for all I know, but then again, it may not. I certainly agree with him in one thing, which, to paraphrase an old line, holds that "it is better to have tried and failed than never to have tried at all."

But my father did not know the nature of his adversary, the demon with whom he contended in vain. He thought it to be a weakness in himself, some lack of sincerity, and he forced himself to pray with even greater vigor; but the more he prayed, the more insistent became his urges. Things had come to such a pass that he was on the verge of giving up his quest and returning home in defeat.

It was in such a frame of mind that he approached an isba at the edge of a woods with the purpose of seeking a meal and a night's lodging. Wandering holy men, stranniki, were no rarity in Tsarist Russia, and few were the muzhiki who would risk God's displeasure by refusing to share their simple accommodations with such pilgrims as came to their doors. On the contrary, the people felt that their homes and lives were blessed by these visitors, and so Grischa felt certain that he would be welcome. The man who came to the door in response to his knock was a simple woodcutter, a big, bluff man with a kindly exterior, tired after a hard day's work. He invited the ragged strannik to share the evening meal and to spend the night, if he would be so good as to sleep on the floor. Grischa entered, giving his blessing to the man and his humble dwelling, as well as to the woodcutter's wife, when she emerged from behind a sheet that hung down from the low ceiling to set their bed apart from the rest of the one-room isba. At once, Grischa had a strong urge to flee, for the woman, although by no means a beauty, exuded an aura of sensuality, but he could think of no way of excusing himself without appearing ungracious and risking damage to the feelings of the kindly man. Every ounce of desire that he had been fighting back for weeks arose in him, and he had to do battle with himself merely to sit at the table and eat the plain supper the woman served to him. And this conflict was in no way eased by the woman, who kept jumping up to refill his plate, or to bring him another piece of bread, each time leaning over him so that he was made to feel the pressure of her breasts against his arms and neck.

Immediately after the meal, the husband arose, and

75

yawning mightily, said, "Holy Sir, please give me leave to retire. I have had a long and very hard day, so if you will permit me, I will go to bed. It is to be regretted, but we have no other bed for you, but if you will lie on that rug, my wife will give you a blanket. Good night, Holy Sir. Come wife, take care of our guest and come to bed."

Grischa assured him that the floor would make a fine bed, blessed the couple, and as the man disappeared behind the flimsy curtain, lay down on the floor. The woman, with a most provocative smile, brought a blanket and spent somewhat more time than was absolutely necessary in arranging it over him. Then she, too, disappeared behind the curtain. Grischa lay on his back for a while, trying to force his mind into the proper mood for his prayers and meditations, when he heard the deep and regular breathing of the sleeping man, and immediately afterward, the woman emerged from behind the curtain and made her way to the sink, upon which there sat a bucket of water. Pretending to take no notice of the guest, she withdrew her arms from the sleeves of her dress, permitting it to fall to her waist, and turning, in order to display her full, firm bust, she began to wash her body, lingering lovingly over each breast, dimly lit by the moonlight streaming in through the isba's lone window, and slyly glancing out of the corner of her eye at her intended prey to make certain that he was observing her. Assured that he was, she dropped her dress to the floor, and waited, nakedly, for him to make the next move. Aching as he was, he could not resist the invitation so openly extended, and sat up preparatory to rising and going to her. But, in sitting up, he found himself looking face to face at an ikona of the Holy Virgin hanging on the wall. At once, he threw himself back onto his rug, and rolling over, groaned with remorse at having entertained such lustful thoughts. The woman, seeing that she had been rejected, snorted in disgust and stepped past him to her own bed, from whence it became obvious to the ears of the suffering Grischa that she had awakened her husband to serve her needs. Even though Grischa understood that this was an act performed out of spite, aimed more at punishing him than of gratifying herself, for she made more of her erotic responses than would have been usual with a guest in the house, he suffered torments, and bit himself deeply on the wrist in an attempt to quell the flame she had aroused in him.

Even after all had become still once more, he could not sleep, but tossed and turned on the hard floor until the first rays of the dawn entered through the window. Unable to bear the thought of facing the woman in the morning, he gathered up his bundle, put on his boots, and quietly stole from the isba, staggering as though drunk through the woods, until he found a grassy slope leading down to a crystal-clear pond, and there, with the warming sun well up over the horizon, he lay down to sleep. But sleep was long in coming, for his brain was buzzing with a multitude of conflicting thoughts, following each other across the panorama of his mind like fitful pictures seen in a kaleidoscope. Even as he was fixing his inner eye upon the image of the Virgin, her holy form was replaced by the remembered view of the unclad woman who had been his temptress on the previous night.

In his misery, he cried aloud: "What good am I? How can I serve God, when I cannot even keep my mind from wandering?" And then the most terrible question of all: "Why does God not hear my prayers? Why does He not purify my mind? Since I am not worthy of His help, perhaps I should take my own life. Maybe that would be a suitable offering to Him."

Such intense and dire ruminations have a way of exhausting the mind, and when superimposed upon a sleepless night, are apt to cast the afflicted one into the blessing of sleep. And thus it was past the noon hour before he regained consciousness, feeling somewhat more at peace, the golden sunlight warming him, and a bird singing of its love to an as yet unseen mate. He looked up into the branches of the tree under which he lay, and found the songster, as well as another bird, hopping from branch to branch, as she slowly and indirectly approached her serenader. And as he watched them, a new idea impinged upon his despair, overlaying it with the comforting realization that here, indeed, was the key to God's world. Even the innocent little birds knew desire; how, then, could it be a sin? And with this new concept, much of his guilt began to fall away.

It was then that a different sound reached his ears,

the happy sound of girlish voices laughing and shouting, and he sat up to see three young women swimming in the little pond down the slope. As with all those who swam in the lakes and streams of western Siberia, these girls were quite nude, and the sight of their young bodies sent the fires roaring anew through him. But this time, unlike last night, he did not even contemplate withstanding the fierce gusts of his passion, but started running down the slope, casting off his garments as he ran, and had soon joined them in their sport. They greeted his entrance into their company with shrieks, not of fear, but of welcome, and having frolicked with him for a suitable period, so that he was no longer a stranger, they accepted his lovemaking, one by one, on the grassy bank. Clasped in their arms, he felt the months of frustration and torment drain away, and he became whole again.

Later that night, as he knelt under a sky filled with blazing stars, the last quarter moon having just risen, he prayed as he had not been able to pray in many months. And he realized that a giant barrier of unfulfilled sexual desire had been removed between himself and God. Now he could fix the image of the Holy Virgin in his inner eye, and what was more, she seemed to be smiling at him. Here was serenity, here was peace, here was the gate to the inner temple of God. He prayed and meditated for several hours, never once distracted by a feeling of restlessness of the sort that had afflicted him of late. And this was also important: He had no sensation of discomfort in his knees, but rather an almost total lack of sensation to interfere with his concentration. But the most blessed of all the blessings was the absence of any intrusion by lust-provoking images.

And thus it was on this brilliant night, when all the stars seemed to have joined in conferring God's benediction upon him, that his philosophy of spiritual awakening through sexual assuagement was born. Although only in the embryonic state, this philosophy was founded not upon base gratification—lust for the sake of lust—but on the certainty in his mind that God, having implanted desire in man's nature, would not then ask him to repress that desire. God was good and just, and would never stoop to injustice; He would not punish a man for easing his thirst with good cool water, nor would He punish him for quenching the flames of passion. There were those who, being of weaker sexuality, could deny their urges and not suffer unduly, but men like himself were made of stronger stuff; their needs were more demanding, more consuming, and the only way of defeating such desires was to yield quickly to them. What the moralists had overlooked was that man not only lusts, but is the product of lust. Without sex, God's universe would be barren and unpopulated.

And so the whim of Sudbina, the Lady Fate, was realized, and Grigori Efimovich Rasputin, through no design of his own, had been thrust into the path along which he would inexorably tread. Left to his own devices, working and meditating in the little village of Pokrovskoye, he might well have grown to manhood without more than the normal stirrings of passion; he might have achieved the spiritual heights of full illumination and the merging of his individuality with God, which crowds out any thought of lust; he might have become an outstanding ecclesiastical force, one of the great saints of history who move the world more surely than do any kings or dictators. But it was not to be. As I review the first thirty years of his life, I am amazed that he was able, in spite of the machinations of Sudbina, to advance spiritually as far as he did, armed as she was with three powerful weapons. These weapons were all clad in the forms of sexually attractive women: Irina Danilova Kubasova, whose thoughtless cruelty brought his awareness of sex to its most intense peak; Praskovia Fedorovna Dubrovina, my mother, whose tenderness and understanding had modified the harsh lessons of his first encounter, and taught him the place of love in human sexuality; and the three nameless girls in the pond, who had helped him learn that the expression of sex can be a liberating force against the demon of repression and frustration. It was in this greatly altered frame of mind that Grischa continued on his pilgrimage.

But, as though my father were merely a character in a novel, whose author, the Lady Sudbina, had organized the material of the plot so that one incident paved the way for the next, it was not long after his experience in and beside the little pond that he fell in with a most peculiar sect, the Khlisti, with a strange and unusual history. Founded in the seventeenth century by Danilo Filipov, a man with outstanding powers of

79

oratory, the sect gained adherents wherever he went, and his followers were fanatical and what may justifiably be classified as hysterical in their support of him. They practiced rigid disciplines, fasting and self-scourging, to drive out the devils of the flesh. And since their ways differed from those of the Church, they were hounded and persecuted by the government. The principal factor in saving the sect from utter extinction was the vow of absolute secrecy taken by all the members, and still some thousand of them were sent into exile in the cold fastnesses of Siberia. After the death of the founder and his successor, the leadership fell to a quite different sort of man, one Radaev, who, being a profligate by nature, changed the whole course of the Khlisti. He declared that he was totally under the control of God's will, and that he spoke with the voice of the Holy Ghost, and that his teachings, therefore, were true and not subject to criticism. And he led his followers into new practices, which were little short of orgies, with himself as the focal point of the most debauched sort of promiscuity. Authorities agree that he kept a sort of harem of thirteen women and satisfied himself with them en masse. His new rites gave the sect an even stronger public appeal than had those of the founder, and licentiousness reigned as a powerful competitor of the Orthodox Church.

Grischa had heard rumors of the Khlisti while he was still at Verkhoture, and it had even been said that some of the monks were practitioners of the erotic religion. But at that time, he had been intent on quelling the demands of the flesh, and had refused to have anything to do with them, or to listen to their strange and, to him, demonic creed.

The strannik came to an isba one evening, after a long day of walking and meditating, and went to the door to request food and shelter from the occupants, who responded to his knock with sorrowful faces. They made him welcome, but explained that their daughter was seriously ill, and they feared she might be dying.

Grischa said, "Please take me to her; perhaps I can be of some help."

Glad of even this faint glimmer of hope, they took him to the girl's bedside. She was unconscious, her only sign of life a shallow, almost inaudible breathing, and a feeble moan that occasionally escaped her lips.

Grischa turned to the parents, who were looking at him with a desperate, though silent, plea, and said, "Please leave me alone with her; I will pray by her side."

The husband and wife withdrew, and he fell to his knees beside her bed, placing one hand on her feverish forehead and closing his eyes in prayer. He was unaware of the passing of time, completely absorbed in his supplication to the Virgin Mother. The worried parents opened the door now and again and were amazed to see that he had not moved since they had first left him there. At last, the girl stirred, opened her eyes, and spoke to the healer: "What day is this? I know I have been ill for a long time. Did you cure me?"

"No, my child, I cannot cure anyone. It is the Lord God who has healed you. Now sleep, malyutka,* and you will be well when you awaken."

He left the bedroom and was immediately besieged by the anxious parents, overflowing with questions about the health of their child.

And he assured them: "She is sleeping now. She will be well in the morning."

They thanked him profusely and laid out for him the finest supper their poor home could afford. As he ate, the couple, elated over what he had done for their daughter, the miracle he had performed, questioned him about his powers, but he patiently explained that it was all in God's hands; that of himself he could do nothing.

The wife persisted, "I suppose you lead a very pure life, a life of chastity?"

"No, I do not believe chastity is important."

"Is that so?" she asked. "Are you, by any chance, one of the Khlisti? You speak as though you were."

He replied, "No, I am not. I have heard rumors, and I am interested, but I really don't know much about them." A thought flashed into his mind, and his next question was one to which he already knew the answer. "If you are members, please tell me of your beliefs."

* my child

81

The woman gasped and put her hand over her mouth, realizing that in her ebullience over her daughter's healing she had come perilously close to violating her oath of secrecy.

She could only stammer out, "I—I can't speak of such things. Perhaps our *vozhd** would be willing to explain it to you. I will ask him."

True to her word, she did what she had promised. Grischa had spent the night on the floor and had looked in on his patient in the morning to find her quite well again and demanding food. After seeing to her daughter's hunger, the mother left them for a while, but soon returned with a man of middle height and a rather stocky build, topped by a short blond beard and clear blue eyes. He was introduced merely as the vozhd, his desire for anonymity at this point being apparent, and after the customary handshake, he settled himself down for a talk with the newcomer who had healed a young girl of the village.

Opening the discussion, Grischa said, 'All I know of the Khlisti is what I have heard, and I suppose that most of that is just rumor."

"You are probably right, Grigori Efimovich," the vozhd replied. "Our secrets are very well kept. Let me begin by saying that the human body, as I am sure you know, is the temple of God."

Grischa nodded his assent.

"You also know that the strongest force within that temple is, after hunger and thirst, sexual desire."

Again Grischa nodded.

"What you may not know is that there are religious sects of all races and nations that give full recognition to this truth, and that instead of repressing this force, or, rather, trying to repress it, they encourage its fullest expression. For instance, in India there are certain followers of Krishna, who is their Khristos, and who was noted for his sexual prowess, whose devotees meditate while in the act of copulating. And there are the fertility rites in nearly all ancient lands, and many modern ones, in which people have intercourse in the fields in order to

*leader

82

set an example for their gods, who must be shown that it is time to fecundate the earth once more. Look at the Hindu temples, with their outer walls carved with figures of gods and goddesses performing every possible kind of sexual act. Consider the implications of the Shiva lingam, the representation of the sexual organ of the god Shiva, and the way it is worshiped. And there are many such symbols throughout the world. Why, the very cross itself was an ancient sexual symbol. It wasn't until the Church took control of Christian philosophy that puritanism came into power, and the agape, or 'love feast,' of the early Christians so scandalized the puritans that they finally banned it at the Council of Carthage, in A.D. 397."

"You certainly have studied the matter extensively," said Grischa, amazed at what he had been hearing.

"Oh, that is just a small part of it; there is much more. But there is no purpose in continuing with the list. I merely wanted to show you that ours is not a new concept."

"I can see that, but I had no idea such things existed."

"I hope what I have said has not shocked you."

"No, not at all. In fact, most of what you have revealed to me fits in with some conclusions I have reached. This much have I learned from experience: One cannot meditate with full concentration when the demon of lust is calling."

"That is why you will find the members of our sect happy and contented and, I believe, nearer to God than are the members of the Orthodox Church."

"I am sure you are right."

"Well, then, perhaps you would like to join with us in the rites we are to celebrate this very night."

"I thank you, yes."

"Very well. Your good host and hostess will bring you to the place. Until tonight, proshchaitye!"

"Until tonight."

Grischa and his two new friends left the isba after dark, and avoiding the dirt road, struck off through the woods until they came to a barn. Entering by a back door, they found a candle placed beside a set of stairs cut into the soil and leading down to a heavy door, upon which the man knocked in a certain way. In a moment, the door was opened from within and they were admitted to a rather dank dirt cellar, lit by several lanterns suspended from the supporting beams of the ceiling. The small room was innocent of any furniture, although the dirt floor was covered by some old carpets. There were six or seven people in the room, holding a general conversation with the vozhd, and these greeted the new arrivals warmly. The vozhd moved to the center of the floor, and the congregation quickly formed a circle around him. Grischa found a place between his hostess and another woman, at the same time noticing that women were in the majority; of the ten persons present, only three were men.

The vozhd began with a prayer that was part of the Orthodox litany, and for a time he followed the Church pattern. But, gradually, he veered away from this course and began to speak of what he called "the highest worship of God." This puzzled Grischa for a moment, until he caught the drift of what was being said, based on a concept that, since each of them was an incarnation of God, each should worship and love the others. Grischa understood the idea, for had he not prayed to, and meditated upon, the God within himself? And was not that same idea being taught here?

"Therefore, my children, love ye one another." It was more than an admonition; it was a command, and as one, the devotees immediately began to obey. As the vozhd let drop the plain black robe which had been his only covering, the circle of worshipers divested themselves of their clothing, and Grischa, not wanting to be conspicuous, did the same. He felt strange, somehow, standing next to his now naked hostess, who had seemed such a modest woman, such an average housewife, until now. The circle began to move, and the people were soon dancing about the still figure of the vozhd, at first slowly, and then faster and faster, until they were moving like dervishes in a ring. Except for the slap-slap of unshod feet, they made no sound, until at the height of the near-frenzy induced by their wild dance, one of the women broke from the circle with a wild cry and threw herself upon the vozhd, dragging him unresistingly to the floor, where they were quickly coupled in a passionate embrace. Even as he watched, Grischa was seized from the side, and was soon engaged in intercourse with a woman, before he realized that she was the mother of the child he had healed. The scene became a little hazy in his mind, but he was aware that as one of the outnumbered males, he had to serve double, and even triple, duty with the women who had been forced to await their turns.

Just as he was beginning to feel that he had no more to give, the vozhd, who had donned his robe, spoke from his position in the center of the room: "Ye children of God, the ceremony is ended. Go in peace."

The congregation quickly dressed, and, with their clothing, they had also donned an air of respectability, the respectability of honest and pious muzhiks. To see Grischa and his friends walking along the dark paths, one might have believed anything of them but that they had been so recently copulating on the rug-covered dirt floor of a dank cellar dug beneath a barn. The little party arrived home, the mother going directly into her daughter's room, and coming back quickly to report that she was sleeping peacefully. Tired as they were from their strenuous activities, they went to their beds, and the isba was soon filled with the stentorian breathing of those who sleep the sleep of the just.

And in the morning, an outside observer, seeing them at breakfast, would never have guessed that this was anything but a family group preparing for the day's labors. The man left for his work in the fields, and Grischa, turning to bid the wife farewell, and to thank her for her hospitality, found her standing politely, though rigidly, to receive his thanks. His impression was that if he had approached her with some sign of wanting to renew their lovemaking, she would have been as offended as any honest housewife at such temerity. Matching his attitude to hers, he gave his thanks and his blessing, and she in turn expressed her undying gratitude for her daughter's healing. These amenities fulfilled, he left the little isba, never to return.

As soon as he could find a secluded spot, he stopped and knelt in prayer, and to his great joy, found that it came easily. He had been half afraid that his activities of the previous night might have offended God, but it was obvious to him that the Lord was not offended with His son. After concluding his devotions, he resolved to become a member of the Khlisti, and perhaps even a vozhd in his own right. If meditation flowed so smoothly after a Khlisti ceremony, then it was obvious that they were on the right track.

And in this way did my father continue on his pilgrimage through Siberia, healing the sick and preaching his gospel of surrender to God's will. The simple and earthy wives of the muzhiks he encountered were whole-souled in their devotion to God, and they lacked the sophistication that would have enabled them to distinguish between the surrender of the mind and that of the body. Gathering them about him through the magnetism of his animal attraction, he preached his creed and his words had an aphrodisiac effect upon them. It was not his intention to seduce these good country women, and it was his belief that they were convinced by the pure reason of his tenets, but they were seduced, nonetheless, and he was soon celebrating his peculiar rites in any convenient place, the woods, a barn, or the isba of one of his converts. And always the women outnumbered the men; sometimes he was the only male in the group. Between his powers of healing and those of persuasion, his fame went before him, and the forming of new congregations became a simple matter of appearing at a place where several farms came together, or in a small village by the road.

Learned observers have long noted that the fervor of religious abandonment borders closely upon that of sex; the wholehearted worshiper is but a step removed from being seduced by her own religious ardor. The "hell-and-damnation" preachers of the American backwoods found, if they were so minded, that there would be little resistance to their desires after they had preached a fiery sermon. And in the case of Grischa, as in most of the others, the women had no regrets, nor did they hurl recriminations after their submission. I have met two women, who are still living, who attended my father's ceremonies, and they are in independent agreement in referring to him in terms one might employ in describing Christ.

Mention has been made of the Shiva lingam and other phallic symbols, and the way they were worshiped as the representations of the creative principle. When his female devotees danced their dervishlike dances around his nude figure, they, too, were drawn to the worship of his phallus, endowing it with mystical qualities as well as sexual ones, for it was an extraordinary member indeed, measuring a good thirteen inches when fully erect. Theirs was by no means a wholly lustful approach at the start of the rite, but a worship of God in His Priapean form; and whichever of the female disciples was the first to perform fellatio upon him did so in a sense of a religious practice. Of course, as their passions were aroused, there was a tendency to forget the ritualistic aspect of the ceremony, and the participants would fall into a general orgy, seeking whatever outlet for their lusts was available.

Invariably, after one of these rites, my father would spend long hours in meditation and prayer, and he would find that his concentration was undisturbed by any conflicting thought. His "dark night of the soul" was a thing of the past; no longer did doubts and dismal ideas creep into his mind, and he found himself truly happy in his work, the main part of which lay in healing the sick. And thus he spent a fruitful year on the steppes of Siberia, his fourth away from home. How long he would have remained cannot be estimated; it might have been many more years if it had not been for a fateful meeting with another Khlisti vozhd, who was also an ordained priest of the Orthodox Church. At first, the two men greeted each other as true fellow workers in the Lord's vineyard, and Grischa readily fell in with the other's proposal to hold a ceremony for not less than a hundred followers. Arrangements were made to use a large barn on the farm of a member of the sect, and since there were a number of adherents in the neighborhood, the congregation was easily assembled.

But, from the start, the ceremony was different from any in which Grischa had participated. The priest, as the senior of the two, and by right of his rank, celebrated the rite. In the first place, there was no preliminary prayer, nor the usual procedures of the normal church service, such as Grischa had learned and employed, but the celebrant launched directly into a type of black mass that he had devised for himself. All the participants were unclad from the start, and the prettiest of the women was chosen to serve as the altar itself, not to mention the chalice. The sacramental wine was poured into her navel, from which the priest drank; he recited the Lord's Prayer in reverse, and began performing acts of perversion with his female "altar" before Grischa's horrified eyes. Here was not a gradual building up of the fervor of the congregation, but a frontal attack upon their basest natures. And yet, the scene held a certain fascination for Grischa, once he had become entrapped by the lust that began stealing over him, and he found himself engaging in the general debauchery despite his initial revulsion.

For the first time in his experience, the aftermath of this dreadful orgy left him with a feeling of disgust, disgust at the whole proceeding, and disgust with himself. And to his dismay, he entered upon another dark night of the soul, although this time, it was of mercifully short duration. In medicine, one of the schools teaches a system known as homeopathy, in which a drug producing similar reactions to the disease itself is administered in small doses as a cure. And it may be said that Grischa was cured of his sickness of the soul by a sort of homeopathy. Stopping one night at an isba, he found his knock answered by a handsome, sturdy housewife. She welcomed him with more than the usual warmth shown by a prospective host or hostess, and as she set a plentiful meal before him, she informed him that her husband was away on a trip to some neighboring town, where he had gone to transact some business. It was quite evident what the woman had in mind, and Grischa was content to let matters take their own course. After a night spent in the bed of his eager and insatiable hostess, he took to the road the next morning with an entirely changed outlook on life, and his communion with God renewed in all its former plenitude. But one thought did intrude, a strong impulse to see his family and home once more. And when he arose from his devotions, he set his footsteps on the road to Pokrovskoye.

❊SEVEN❊

During the long years that her husband had been off on his pilgrimage, my mother had eagerly awaited some word from him, but none had come, for he had never learned to write. Although missing him sorely, she had otherwise managed very well; the farm under her efficient supervision had prospered, and her children were blossoming under the care of the servants she had brought in to run the household while she oversaw the farming. Altogether, the family fortunes had never been better.

Of the two servant girls, the first to arrive had been Katya Ivanova, a wiry, rawhide-faced woman, whose saving grace was an excellent sense of humor. And the second was the same Dunia Bekyeshova who had played such a peculiar role in the humiliation of my father at the hands of Irina Danilova Kubasova, by first joining in the sport, and later acting as the only one of the maids to have compassion for the victim. Of course, I did not know that part of her story until some years later, but I did take to Dunia at once. Although a local girl from

Tyumen, Dunia had traveled with the Kubasovs for several years, spending her winters in the midst of luxury in Moscow, and only returning to Tyumen during the warmer months. When she finally decided to leave that glamorous life for the simple Rasputin farm, no one thought to ask her what her reasons were for doing so, which was just as well, for she would have been hard put to explain her preference for Pokrovskoye to not only Moscow but Warsaw and even Paris, as Irina Danilova's personal maid. What no one, least of all my mother, suspected was that Dunia had fallen in love with my father, even as she pitied him for the plight into which her mistress had tricked him; and although she had no desire to deceive her new employer, she was driven to be near my father by a force over which she had no control. Even though her master was absent, it gave her some degree of pleasure just to be in his home, surrounded by his belongings and sweeping the very floors upon which he had walked. To her way of thinking, she had done well to exchange the easy life with Irina Danilova for the hard household work given her by my mother, and she was happy.

While Mother had received no direct word from Father, she had questioned every passing traveler, and had heard rumors of a holy man who healed the sick and preached the word of God, and she felt in her heart that the holy man could only be her Grischa. Then there were other rumors, of a strannik who practiced the sexual excesses of the Khlisti sect, but although the man answered the general description of her husband, she refused to believe that he would do such horrible things. Not her Grischa.

News spread slowly through Tsarist Russia at the end of the nineteenth century. The Trans-Siberian Railroad was not even begun until 1891, under the direction of Count Syergyei Yulyevich Witte, one of the ablest statesmen serving the Tsar. Witte later became a good friend of Father's, joining with him against the vast majority of influential men to oppose the war which, as Witte and my father foresaw, would end the Romanov dynasty and leave chaos in its wake. Witte was also the founder of the Russian gold standard, and a staunch supporter of

Russian industries, securing for them loans of foreign capital. But the railroad, which was to open Siberia up to large-scale increases in population, was not to be completed until 1905, and communications were difficult at best. Mother was forced to rely solely on rumor for whatever news she could glean of her husband.

Then one evening, just as we were all about to sit down for the evening meal, a stranger entered the kitchen without knocking. Surprised at this invasion, Mama looked up at the man with the tangled beard and long flowing reddish-brown hair, wondering what he wanted. He did not speak, but stood smiling down at her until something within her leaped in recognition, and she flew into his arms, crying, "Grischa!" The whole house was suddenly thrown into confusion, an extra place was set at the table, Dunia fetched up some wine from the cellar, and we children ran to throw ourselves upon him, while he knelt and grasped the three of us in his loving embrace, scratching our faces with his beard as he kissed us each in turn, again and again. I remember the joy of that night, the warm glow of security that pervaded the atmosphere, now that our family had been reunited. As we gathered around the table, we hardly gave him time to eat, what with a steady stream of questions, one being asked before the previous one had been answered. Finally, Mama called a halt to the chaos.

"Children," she said, "your father is hungry. Why not let him have his dinner, while we tell him what we have been doing, and then he can tell us of his experiences?"

We agreed, but this did little to stem the torrent of childish voices as each of us struggled to be the first to speak. Mama, however, soon restored some semblance of order to the proceedings, giving each of us a chance to speak in turn, starting with Dmitri (Mitia), then me, and then Varya. And after we had finished, she told him of the prosperity of the farm. By the time she had finished, he had eaten, and it was now his turn to tell us of all the things he had done and seen in his travels. This he did, after some careful editing, leaving out all those parts that would have shocked Mama, parts that I did not have filled in until some years later, after his murder. As he told his story, I happened to glance down at the end of the long table and saw Dunia, her eyes glistening with what I did not then recognize as love, as she followed every word.

And then some neighbors, hearing the festive sounds as they were passing by, came to the door and were welcomed and included in the celebration. And soon, others came, until the house was full, and we children were as excited by the presence of all those people as we were that our father had come home to us. More wine was brought up, and Dunia and Katya worked feverishly in the kitchen to keep the supply of *zakuski** abundant. It was a memorable night for me, one I will never forget. We children ran through the house, making as much noise as we wished, and no one tried to quiet us, because all the grown-ups were making even more noise. Someone brought out an akkordeon, and Mama and Papa began the dancing, which was soon joined by all the guests, until the house shook as in a high wind. And through the melee of twirling and leaping couples, I could catch an occasional glimpse of Mama's face, brimming with love and pride in her returned traveler, and Papa, beaming with the joy of his homecoming and his love for Mama.

Every once in a while the music would stop, and everyone would start talking, and there would form a small group around Papa to hear him tell of his wanderings once again. And we children would run up to him and he would take one of us in his strong hands and lift us up and hold us high, without missing a word of his narrative. And he would give the lucky one another scratchy kiss and a hug before putting him down. Mama forgot all about our bedtime, and we stayed up as long as our legs would hold us. My last memory is of finally dropping into a chair, completely exhausted, with the revel still going on about me. And I knew no more until the next morning. Dunia told me that she had carried me upstairs and put me to bed, but I was able to take pride in that I was the last to succumb, Mitia and Varya having given out before I did.

But not all of the residents of Pokrovskoye were elated at the return of the strannik. Not long before Papa had

*snacks; hors d' oeuvres

92

left home, Otyets Pavel had gone to his just reward, to be replaced by Otyets Pyotr, a more mercenary servant of the Lord. His calling came from monetary, rather than spiritual, sources, for, as employees of an established Church, priests were paid by the government, and Otyets Pyotr received not only his salary as a minister but also a stipend as head of the village school. In addition to this, there were fees for baptisms, funerals, weddings, and special prayers for the sick and the souls of the dead. All in all, it was a most lucrative position. And Otyets Pyotr saw Papa as a competitor for at least a part of his income, for now the sick were seeking not prayers, but healings, and those in search of spiritual guidance preferred the bread fed them by Papa, rather than the stones offered by the priest.

Already outraged at the rivalry presented by the up-start, Otyets Pyotr became infuriated when he learned that Papa intended to construct a subterranean chapel beneath one of the buildings on our farm. It was bad enough that Grigori Efimovich, a man about whom he had heard some scandalous rumors, seemed to the priest to be treating him with some contempt, although he had no real proof of this, and he certainly was polite enough when they happened to pass, but Pyotr felt in his bones that the contempt was there, lurking beneath the surface. So, when the chapel was completed, he decided the time for action had arrived.

The men who had helped in the digging of the little place of worship had done good work, and when it was finished, Papa brought out some ikons he had picked up in his travels and fitted them into niches in the earthen walls. From the very beginning, the people of Pokrovskoye flocked to the underground house of worship, and they continued to do so, even after Otyets Pyotr ordered them to have nothing to do with that "agent of the dyavol." The harder the priest inveighed against "that sinner," the smaller grew his congregation, until, at his wits' end, the svyashchennik betook himself to Tyumen to complain to the bishop. Fabricating a complaint out of the whole cloth, interlarded with some of the rumors he had heard, sifted together with what little he knew of the Khlisti sect, he spun a lurid yarn for the bishop, who was so horrified that such blasphemous goings-on should be taking place in a village of his see, he at once accompanied Otyets Pyotr back to Pokrovskoye to put an end to the debaucheries, taking with him a team of churchmen and police to root out the accursed offenders. The police, wearing peasant clothing, attended several of Papa's services, and stern-faced monks went about the village questioning those who had gone over to Papa's congregation. After a few days of thorough investigation, they all reported back to the bishop, who had been staying at Otyets Pyotr's house, adjoining the church, that they had seen nothing that could in any respect uphold the priest's allegations. On the other hand, the bishop, who knew a fraud when he saw one, came to realize that the priest was negligent in the performance of his duties and had given almost no spiritual guidance to his parishioners. In a final meeting at the parish house, the bishop rendered his verdict.

"Pyotr," he said, and his voice rumbled like not-too-distant thunder, "you are guilty of one or the other of two sins; either you have borne false witness against the muzhik Grigori Efimovich Rasputin, or you have come to me with a serious charge, without first having determined its truth or falsity. Which is it?"

The priest, having been certain that the hated Rasputin would be removed from his path, was taken aback. He had not thought that his complaint would rebound, with himself as the target. The accuser had suddenly become the accused, and all his pomposity dissolved in his abject terror over what might happen to him.

"Episkop,"* he whined, "I must confess to the latter of your charges. It is true; although I believed the tales that came to my ears, I did not investigate them."

"This is a grave error, and it brands you as a poor shepherd of your flock."

"I repent, Pryevoskhodityelstvo,† I am at fault."

"Very well. As for the accused, Grigori Efimovich Rasputin, I find him innocent of the charges you have brought; and not only innocent, but a true devotee of God, and a healer of the sick. I think, Pyotr, you not only owe him an apology,

*bishop
†Excellency

but you would do well to learn from him; he has much to teach you."

This fell as an additional blow upon the back of the defeated priest. His cheeks turned a deep, almost purplish red, and for a moment it seemed as though he might suffer a stroke. The hated muzhik had triumphed over him, him an ordained priest. It was not to be borne. But it had to be borne; that was the galling fact. That is, it had to be borne for now, but a time would come, of this he felt certain, when he would have his revenge.

But the Lord did not seem to be ready to deliver Grischa into the hands of the venal churchman, and his little chapel flourished, free from further ecclesiastical interference, and filled to overflowing at every service. He was, for one of the few times in his life, at complete peace with himself, his family, and his fellowman, all his fellowmen, that is, except Otyets Pyotr, who gave no outward sign of his hatred, but remained aloof in smoldering silence. Being at peace, he was also happy, and his happiness pervaded the whole family; Mama liked running the farm and was a contented woman, now that her husband was in her home and in her bed, a constant source of comfort and joy, and we children were made happy by his gaiety, playing with us even as he worked in the fields, telling us wonderful stories, some of which came from the Bible, and some of his own devising.

But if the Rasputin household was at peace, it was not so with Russia. Some of the theories of socialism had been preached even before the founding of Land and Liberty, a secret society of Marxist persuasion, which spearheaded the populist movement in 1876. Some three years later, a radical terrorist wing of Land and Liberty, Will of the People, was organized. But even with increased liberty, unrest, nurtured by those who sought power through a pretense of giving even greater freedom to the people, had begun to seethe throughout the nation, and by 1898, its socialist trend finally found leadership in the Social Democratic party, founded by Giorgi Valentinovich Plekhanov, who had introduced Marxism into Russia. He was joined in his efforts by Vladimir Ilyich Ulyanov, better known as Lenin, and the pair worked together, mostly in

Switzerland, toward a socialist take-over of their motherland. They found their big opportunity in 1904, with the outbreak of the disastrous Russo-Japanese War, during which they fomented strikes, culminating in the General Strike of 1905. The subsequent October Manifesto granted a constitution to the people, and a legislature, the Duma, and Count Syergyei Yulyevich Witte became the Prime Minister. By that time, the Social Democratic party had become divided into the Bolshyeviki* and Myenshyeviki† under Lenin and Plekhanov respectively, the former consisting of the extremists, and the latter, comparatively speaking, the moderates.

What details of these events seeped through to Pokrovskoye were inaccurate, to say the least; reports were either overblown or understated, depending upon the political sympathies of those who passed on the accounts orally in the long chain of communicators between St. Petersburg and Siberia. But they were sufficiently disturbing to encroach upon Papa's peaceful thoughts, and a vague feeling of having to accomplish some mission required of him by God began to permeate his meditations. Mama believed that he had received another visitation from the Virgin of Kazan, although he said nothing of it, in which she commanded him to go to St. Petersburg. In any event, the day came when we gathered at the door to bid a tearful farewell to Papa, waving to him until he had passed out of sight along the dusty road that would eventually bring him to the nation's capital.

Ж

St. Petersburg was then just over two centuries old. Begun on May 16, 1703, a beginning signaled by a salvo of massed artillery along the banks of the Neva River that ordered some twenty thousand laborers to start work, it was to be the monument of Pyotr Vyelikie‡ to God, Russia, and himself, although perhaps not in that order. The thirty-one islands, most of which were low and swampy, were to be connected by ornately designed bridges; there were to be magnificent palaces and

*members of the majority
†members of the minority
‡Peter the Great

96

government buildings with golden domes and spires, and parks and boulevards were created to please the eye in almost any direction one might look. From the first, it vied with Stockholm for the title of "the Venice of the North," and even before the city was fully built, it became the political and cultural center of Russia, and thus a magnet for members of the aristocracy and families of wealth, who added their own grandiose palaces to those constructed at the behest of Pyotr Vyelikie.

But the city in which my father arrived was not only a Venice of the North; many of the worthy churchmen thought a more appropriate appellation would have been "the New Sodom," for the principal product of St. Petersburg seemed to be pleasure in all its perverse and licentious forms. The chief occupation of the major portion of the populace was that of providing comfort and luxury for the aristocrats. And the aristocrats, fearful of the perilous future, acted in the manner that most people do when catastrophe threatens, turning to different forms of escape. Suddenly, the teachings of Helena Petrovna Blavatski, or Blavatsky, as she was known to the Western world, founder of theosophy, were widely studied throughout society. Many people were soon chatting of little else but the doctrines of karma and reincarnation, and the "Masters." Others took up spiritualism, until there was hardly a salon that did not have its "circle" for table-rapping. And those who were not completely taken with psychic phenomena were attending lectures by mystics and pseudo-mystics; anything, in short, that might give some meaning and purpose to their lives.

And while the ladies of the court were practicing yoga breathing and the ways of meditation, their husbands, or at least many of them, were seeking other means of escape from the harsh realities that threatened like a dark cloud on an otherwise sunny horizon. Never has greater sexual license prevailed in a social order. Numberless *filles de joie* roamed the Nyevski Prospekt at night, and numberless others inhabited the bordellos of the city. To staff them, girls were imported from Asia, South America, and Africa, including ten-year-olds, who were in great demand. One of the most certain signs of decadence is the desire for unusual forms of sex, the exotic foreigner who, purportedly, can offer some hitherto untried method of gratification. And to cater to these tastes came a variety of femininity, from slender English dancers, reputedly ready to accommodate their clients' strangest fancies; French cocottes, understood to possess a sophistication unknown to those of other lands; Hindu apsarases, wise in the ancient ways; and a liberal sprinkling of Chinese, Japanese, and Arab girls, brought to St. Petersburg on every ship that sailed into the Gulf of Finland. Exhibitions of every imaginable sort of depravity were to be seen, one of the favorites being a pantomime depicting a classroom in which a pretty teacher, enlisting the aid of her students, seduced, disrobed, and made love to one of her female charges. Staged in one of the brothels, this exhibition was performed within a few feet of the audience, and, even then, some of the bon vivants viewed the proceedings through their opera glasses. For the connoisseur, there were displays of bestiality and multiple fornications; and for the jaded, homosexual and transvestite houses. The only limits seemed to be those of the imagination.

Into this self-indulgent, though fearful society, there came a prince; not the heroic prince of the story books, but a prince of perverse fantasies, Feliks Feliksovich Yussupov. At the time of my father's arrival in the capital, the prince had just passed his eighteenth birthday, having been trained from the cradle for a life of degeneracy. This is a precise statement of fact, since his mother, who had wanted a girl, had provided a pink layette for him on his arrival.

Unfortunately for the young Feliks, his father left a void in his life, taking little interest in his training or his problems.

In his early youth, Feliks began showing definite signs of his homosexual tendencies, which he chronicled in his own autobiography, *Lost Splendor*.

And, along with his early presages of homosexuality, there was an as yet unawakened interest in sadism.

The Yussupov wealth was truly staggering, the result of two generations of well-planned marriages. Feliks' paternal grandfather, a commander of the Don Cossaks, was said to have been the son of Frederik William IV, King of Prussia, and Countess Tiesenhausen, maid of honor to the Empress Aleksandra, the King's sister. During a visit of the Tsarina to her brother, the King fell in love with the countess and wanted to marry her. There may or may not have been a morganatic marriage, although the maid of honor is thought to have refused, since she did not want to leave the Tsarina. In any event, the affair resulted in the birth of a son, Feliks Elston. He married Countess Elena Sergeyevna Sumarokova, and since she was the last of her line, there being no male heir, the Tsar granted him the right to take his wife's name and title. His son, Count Feliks Sumarokov-Elston, married Princess Zenaidye Nikolayevna Yussupova, and she, too, was the last of her line, and another Tsar granted him the right to take her name and title.

Thus, through a series of marriages and the generosity of two Tsars, the fortune of the illegitimate son of a King of Prussia and his descendants had increased until, beside a palace on the Moika Kanal in St. Petersburg, a gift from Catherine the Great to Feliks' great-grandmother, Princess Tatiana, there was also a vast estate at Arkhangyelskoye, near Moscow, with magnificent gardens, marble fountains, and rare and exotic birds. There was another house just outside Moscow, built in 1551 by Tsar Ivan the Terrible, and given to an earlier Prince Yussupov in 1729 by Tsar Pyotr II. Then there was a large estate at Rakitnoye, containing a sugar plantation, numerous sawmills, a wool-spinning mill, and several stock farms, where, among other animals, prize racehorses were bred. At Rakitnoye, in the district of Kursk, the family would stop for some hunting, while on the way to one of their estates in the Crimea, usually Koryeiz, on the Black Sea, between Yalta and Sevastopol, although they had another up in the mountains at Kokoz, and a house on the Bay of Balaklava. And these were but a few of the Yussupov land holdings, such as the one near Baku that stretched for some 125 miles along the shore of the Caspian Sea, and whose soil was rendered unfit for cultivation throughout a major part of its vast area by the oil that seeped to the surface. Having made this round, the family would return to the palace on the Moika for the winter. Wherever they traveled, their private car was attached to the rear of the train, its observation platform transformed into an aviary, the drawing room paneled in mahogany, the chairs upholstered in green leather, and the windows curtained in yellow silk. In the event that they wished to journey abroad, there was another equally luxurious car stationed permanently on the German side of the border, its wheels fitted to the different gauge of the western European tracks.

On only one occasion did Feliks' father make an attempt to assert his parental authority. Being a soldier, the elder Yussupov decided that his young son should receive a Spartan training and, to that end, had all the comfortable furniture removed from the boy's room, to be replaced by a cot and a plain stool, and a rather suspicious-looking cabinet, which he tried to open, but in vain. The next morning, his father's valet pulled him out of bed, pushed him into the cabinet, and drenched him in a shower of cold water. He screamed, but could do nothing to escape this indignity until the supply of water came to an end. He created such a furore—even to threatening suicide—that his frightened parents relented and thereafter left him pretty much to his own devices.

It is little wonder that the effeminate Feliks, knowing little or no discipline from this time and thereafter raised with complete permissiveness, felt that the world was his already-opened oyster. With a family fortune of over three hundred million dollars, particularly enormous by the standards of that time, and greater than that of the Tsar, he lived with the prospect of becoming the wealthiest man in all Russia, if not all Europe. In the meantime, his doting mother was more than generous in the matter of his spending money.

When he was twelve, he perpetrated what he considered a mere boyish prank, although there are not too many young males who would have thought it boyish. He and his cousin Vladimir, also twelve, decided to go out disguised as women. His mother's wardrobe provided them with the costumes, two of her finest gowns, complete with pieces of her most valuable jewelry. Donning fur-lined velvet pelisses, they awoke his mother's hairdresser, and saying that they were going to a fancy-dress ball, persuaded him to lend them wigs. Thus adorned, they went out to stroll the Nyevski Prospekt, mincing like a pair of courtesans. As this was the hunting ground for prostitutes, they were accosted by a number of men, much to their delight, and when they went on to the Medved,* a fashionable restaurant, they were a focus of attention, particularly on the part of some young officers, who invited them to supper in a private room. They had champagne, which quickly went to their heads, and Feliks removed a long string of pearls and began to use it as a lasso in an attempt to rope some people sitting at a neighboring table. The string broke, and having become the cynosure of all eyes, the boys decided that retreat was in order. Gathering up most of the pearls, they were forced to admit that they had brought no money with them and Feliks revealed his identity to the manager. They arrived home, believing that the escapade would not be discovered, only to find the next day that the manager had sent the bill to Feliks' father, who was not amused. Feliks was confined to his room for ten days, as was his cousin, a punishment he thought both cruel and unusual. But this was not to be his last experience of transvestism.

The young Yussupov received his first lesson in sex while staying with his mother at a hotel in the town of Contrexeville, where she had gone to "take the waters." He was then about twelve, and having little to do, had gone out for a walk in a park after dinner. He passed a summer house, and peering in through a window, discovered a young man and a girl making love.

He questioned his mother about what he had seen, but she could not bring herself to satisfy his curiosity, and he spent a sleepless night. The next day, he met the young man of the tableau, and asked, with a characteristic lack of regard for the niceties, if he was planning to see the young girl again. The young man was astonished, but when Feliks told him of having watched the proceedings on the previous evening, he said that he was to meet her at his hotel, and invited Feliks to join them.

Since his mother went to bed early, he had no difficulty in leaving their suite and making his way to his new friend's hotel nearby. The young man told Feliks that he was from Argentina, but before any more could be said, the girl arrived, and the next several hours were spent in their mutual sport. The nature of this sport, Feliks never elaborated on. He

*Bear

later was to say, "I was so amazed by what I had learned that, in my youthful ignorance, I failed to discriminate between the sexes."

While Feliks did not allow himself to be more specific, it does not require a trained psychologist to read between the lines and to extract the meaning of his phrase. Further support of this conclusion arose from an incident that occurred in Paris in 1960. A young homosexual with rouged cheeks and dyed hair happened by chance to be in the house of my daughter, who, of course, was Rasputin's granddaughter. When he discovered whose house it was, he laughed hysterically, and when he could gather himself together, he telephoned Feliks, shrieking his news: "Darling, you'll never believe where I'm calling from."

But it was his elder brother, Nikolas, who did more than anyone to advance Feliks' transvestite proclivities. Apparently amused by Feliks' undetectable female impersonations, he yielded to a whim of his mistress, a girl named Polia, to take Feliks with them to see some Gypsies perform at a cabaret. Feliks' "drag" was undetected.

Feliks accompanied Nikolas to Paris, where they decided to go to a ball, Nikolas acting as his younger brother's escort. Feliks was, of course, dressed as a woman. To while away the time before the ball was to begin, they went to the theater, where they were seen by King Edward VII, who was sitting in a stage box. After the intermission, during which Nikolas had gone to the foyer for a cigarette, he came back laughing, telling Feliks that he had been accosted by an equerry of the King of England who had sent to ask the name of the lovely young woman he was escorting.

Feliks was delighted and flattered.

Once back in St. Petersburg, Nikolas and Polia arranged for Felix to appear at the Aquarium, a fashionable café concert.

He borrowed his mother's jewels for the occasion and was enjoying tremendous success during the two-week engagement, until on the seventh night some friends of his mother's recognized him and the jewels he was wearing. There was quite a scene at home, but Nikolas took the blame, and the matter was soon forgotten. Feliks gave up his career as a girl cabaret singer, but continued with his feminine adventures, becoming more daring in his escapades, until finally his father sent for him one day. The elder Yussupov, brought up on a strict military regimen, was infuriated with his errant son, and related to him the stories that were going around about his activities. He likened his son to a guttersnipe and scoundrel, not fit to be in the company of decent human beings. He iterated and re-iterated a long list of grievances that had brought disgrace upon the family name.

When Yussupov was older and certainly more worldly, he often had reason to recall the confrontation with his father. However, he denied his father's accusation that he did not like women. On the contrary, he said, he adored them—except when they were not nice. He said he found, however, that there was more loyalty among men—something he felt most women lacked.

And so the stage was set for a heinous crime and, to me, a grievous tragedy. The villain—no less a villain because of his frailty—and his victim were waiting in the wings of history, and the curtain was about to be raised on a drama that even the Greeks would be hard put to match.

❌EIGHT❌

It was into this maelstrom of perfervid emotions that my father arrived, a city in ferment brewed of part revolution, part metaphysics, part debauchery, and part—and a very small part it was—of an effort to preserve national sanity. As a newcomer, he did not observe any of these activities during his first days in St. Petersburg, but he told me later that he could sense the discontent, the fear, and the reckless pursuit of some form—any form—of escape. He did not like the city, much preferring the natural beauty of his beloved steppes; the clean air, the open and frank people, the peaceful atmosphere. This was life as it should be lived, and not like the leprous-spirited dwellers in this hellhole. He almost doubted his mission, and if he had not felt certain of the directions he had received, he would have turned and retreated to his home and his family.

Once on the scene, he knew not what he was to do next, but he had long heard of a priest who held forth at the basilica on the Isle of Kronstadt, in the Bay of Finland, just off the coast of St. Petersburg, a man reputed to have great spiritual force, the far-famed Ivan of Kronstadt, and since it was Sunday, he determined to go and hear the holy man. He took a place well back in the congregation, and at once felt the basilica to be an oasis of peace in a turbulent city, although there was one unusual feature of the service, a public confession. Near the end of the service, just before the communion, and upon a given signal, nearly all of those present arose and began bawling out their sins for all to hear. Papa thought this one of the most curious sights he had ever witnessed; the good people telling each other, and God, of their transgressions, asking His forgiveness, and then marching down the aisle to receive the sacramental body and blood of the Khristos. But he also realized that the apparent comedy of the scene was not laughable, for here was the first display of true devotion that he had seen in many a month. Suddenly overcome by the realization that God was very close to him in this holy place, he knelt in prayer, giving himself, body and soul, to the Lord's will.

In the same way that one opium smoker knows another, so do men of high spiritual attainment; there is a sense that draws them together. And so it was with the Archimandrite Ivan, for he came down from the altar table and stood before Papa, taking him by the hand to raise him to his feet.

"My son," said Ivan, "I could feel your presence in God's house. The divine spark is within you."

"I ask your blessing, Father."

"Take God's blessing, my son," replied Ivan, and gave him communion standing, a singular mark of recognition, for few there are who have received the bread and wine thus.

"Stay awhile; I would speak with you after the mass," the priest requested, and Grischa bowed his head in assent.

When the congregation was dismissed, and were filing out of the church, Ivan beckoned to Papa, who came forward to be met by him at the rail, where he received an invitation to the adjacent monastery for the midday meal. He went gladly, and the two conversed long and earnestly of spiritual matters; Papa confided to his host the vision of the Virgin of Kazan, and the command he had received to come to St. Petersburg on some mission as yet undisclosed.

Ivan was impressed, calling his guest a true starets, and ended by inviting him to stay on at the monastery while he was in the city, an invitation he gladly accepted. The archimandrite told him that he wanted him to meet several other churchmen, and would have them to dinner that very night. These turned out to be Episkop Hermogen, of Saratov, who was one of the most popular men in Russia; the monk-priest Syergyei Trufanov, who had taken the monastic name of Iliodor, and was known for his ferocious sermons which drew enormous crowds; and the Archimandrite Theofan, inspector of the Theological Academy of St. Petersburg, and religious tutor to the tsarevich and tsarevnas, the royal children, and confessor to the imperial family. They were impressed by the words of the simple muzhik with all a muzhik's simplistic piety, yet with a profound grasp of mystical truth. In the discussion that ensued, they could see that his was not some heterodox theology, the sort that one might have expected of an unlettered wandering preacher, but an orthodoxy the equal of any man's. His prodigious memory of biblical passages was imposing when taken by itself, but his ability to give simple interpretations of the Gospels marked him as a true teacher of the Word. Arguments over dogma were of no interest to him; he felt that they were a waste of time that might better be spent in devotion to the Lord, for it had been the Khristos who had been sent by his Father to show the way, through both teaching and example.

And as he settled down to life in the Kronstadt Monastery, so different from that at Verkhoture, he began to forget, almost as though they had never been, his years with the Khlisti, and his sexual excesses while trudging across the steppes of Siberia. That was all in the past, having served his needs at the time, but no longer a part of his fabric, for now he was immersed in prayers that would lead him to the love of God and point out the way in which he could serve Him and thus discharge the mission that had been laid upon him.

After some days spent at the monastery, he was approached by Ivan, who, having had time in which to take the measure of his man, offered him membership in the Union of

True Russian Men, a group formed to oppose the revolutionaries and to give what support it could to the throne. The Union was composed of a number of leading churchmen, Hermogen, Theofan, and Iliodor among them, as well as several wealthy landowners and members of the aristocracy. They were all men of high religious principle, and Papa was happy to be made one of them, feeling that the Union might well be a tool for accomplishing at least a portion of his mission. He saw that prayer and politics would each have to serve their parts if Russia were to be saved from rebellion and chaos.

The hours spent in devotion, which now consumed nearly all of his waking hours, were giving him a growing awareness of inner strength and power. He sensed that the day would soon dawn when he must fulfill some role in the destiny of Mother Russia; it was clear that the future of his beloved land was in the balance, and that he must be prepared to play whatever part the Lord might see fit to assign him. He knew now that this was his mission, although the details would not be made known except in God's good time.

The bell had already begun to toll for Russia, and chaos was fast approaching. In little more than a decade, the empire of the Romanovs, with all its faults, would give way to something immeasurably worse. The viewer of that niche in history is somewhat like a member of the audience at one of the old motion picture melodramas; he may shout a warning to the ingenue as the clutching hand reaches out through a panel in the wall to seize her by the throat, but no shout will be of any use, for the scene has already been photographed and the event is beyond anyone's control. The innocent victim's role in this history is played by Tsar Nikolas II, whose only fault was his inability to take firm charge of events. While an autocracy may not be the ideal form of government, if there is to be a ruler, he must rule; otherwise, the ship of state cannot navigate the rough seas of world and national politics.

One of the principal weaknesses of the government was the corrupt bureaucracy, which had been partially reformed by Peter the Great, but like the civil service in all countries, at all times, had spread its quagmire of inertia throughout the empire. As the late Ludwig von Mises has pointed out, ". . . bureaucracy and bureaucratic methods are very old and they must be present in the administrative apparatus of every government the sovereignty of which stretches over a large area."[*] He also writes of bureaucracy: "It kills ambition, destroys initiative and the incentive to do more than the minimum required. It makes the bureaucrat look at instructions, not at material and real success."[†]

Thus, while bureaucracy is necessary to the operation of a large country, it is also stultifying, since no bureaucrat will do more than the task that has been set for him. And when to this lethargy the factor of corruption seeps in, the land will be administered badly indeed. This was one of the handicaps faced by the Tsar; the bureaucracy could not be moved to reform itself or its activities. The people of the world, who do not seem to profit from the mistakes of their ancestors, may yet be drowned in an ocean of bureaucracy.

Nikolas was a kindly man, and thereby hangs the tale of most of his woes. One thinks of the tyrant as the one most hated by the people, so that when a revolution against such a man occurs, it is only natural that he be executed. But the Tsar was not a tyrant, and had taken the first timid steps toward political liberalization, and yet he was hated by the revolutionaries, and when he was led before the firing squad on the fateful night of July 16, 1918, the world was stricken with dismay that the Bolshyeviki should have seen fit to murder this mild-mannered man. And not only the Tsar, but his Tsarina, the lovely Aleksandra Feodorovna, his four daughters, the Grand Duchesses Olga, Tatiana, Maria, and Anastasia, and the Tsarevich Aleksei. One would have thought that a fourteen-year-old boy could not have posed a real and present danger for Lenin, Trotski, Stalin, and Company.

The Tsarina had close blood ties to the British throne, having been the daughter of Louis of Hesse-Darmstadt and the Princess Alice, one of Queen Victoria's nine children. Nikolas also had links to the British royal family, his mother having been

---

[*]Bureaucracy (New Haven and London: Yale University Press, 1944).
[†]Ibid.

Dagmar, daughter of King Christian IX of Denmark, and sister of Alexandra, Edward VII's Queen. The name Dagmar does not appear in many of the history books, since, upon her marriage to Tsar Aleksandr III, her name was changed to Maria Feodorovna. But under any name, she was bitterly opposed to the union of her son, who was then tsarevich, to the strikingly beautiful Aleksandra Feodorovna, and it was only by the intervention of the strong-willed Victoria that the wedding was brought off. However, the Dowager Empress never accepted her daughter-in-law, even after she renounced the Church of England and was baptized in the Orthodox Church.

Nikolas and his bride embarked on a life of wedded bliss, flawed only by his mother's intransigence, but nothing Aleksandra Feodorovna could do seemed to mollify her. The Dowager Empress' antipathy spread through the court, and the sensitive girl felt herself surrounded by foes from the very beginning. And when Nikolas succeeded to the throne shortly after the wedding, his coronation was marred by a tragedy at Khodinski Field, when several thousand of the people stampeded during the distribution of the new Tsar's gifts to them and many were trampled to death. He wanted to cancel all of the receptions that had been planned, but his counselors prevailed upon him to attend a ball given that same evening at the French Embassy. Thus the seed was sown, as early as 1896, for the harvest of unrest among the *rabotniki*,* who felt that their new Tsar was indifferent to their sufferings and sorrows.

Nikolas was at once swept up into affairs of state, for which he had been given little training by his father, and these preempted most of his time, so that he had very few precious moments to spend with his bride. She began to feel abandoned and alone in a hostile court. From her point of view, she found little to admire about the nobility and aristocracy of her adopted country; they were venal and self-indulgent, and few were moved by any sentiment of patriotism. Self-interest ruled the land, from the lowliest civil service clerk, whose chief ambition was to stay out of trouble and thereby secure his position and achieve promotion, to all but a handful of the highest ministers of state, who clung to the status quo, while the whole nation

*workers; laborers

was in a ferment around them. Like a woolly mammoth that has been quick-frozen in a glacier, which, at first glance, appears to be quite normal, although actually immobile, so was the government of Russia, for no one wanted to be charged with showing the least spark of initiative, fearing that some higher official might disapprove and place a black mark on his record. Since all power resided in the throne, a strong Tsar might have saved the nation, a Tsar with outstanding administrative and organizational abilities, a Tsar who would have swept out the incompetents and time-servers. But Nikolas was none of these, and so the country moved but slowly, weighted down by the inertia of men who lacked imagination or ingenuity, outwardly prosperous, but inwardly decaying.

To make matters more difficult for the Tsarina, her first four children were girls, and the Dowager Empress at once set tongues wagging with her theory, spread by the gossips of her clique, that Aleksandra Feodorovna, by refusing to provide a male heir, was betraying Russia to the Germans, since she was of German extraction. Forgotten, of course, was her British heritage, far more influential in her character than the Hesse-Darmstadt strain. And, too, of course, the vicious detractors were ignorant of, or chose to ignore, the simple fact that the sex of the children had been determined by their father alone.

The sensitive Tsarina was unable to contend with the hostile atmosphere of the court, and she withdrew from the unequal contest, attempting as well as she could to shut out the external world, living within the smaller sphere of her family and a few intimate friends, among whom there was an ambience of harmony and love. Deeply religious, with a strong tendency toward mysticism, she encouraged Nikolas to adopt her interests, and there began to be seen a succession of holy men and pseudo-holy men, soothsayers and charlatans, mystics and mountebanks, in her court. All were welcome, but most particularly those who could, or were willing to, foresee a male heir. And, as a matter of course, word was passed through the ranks of the prophets and psychics of the Tsarina's desire. And many there were who availed themselves of the opportunity to make capital of her misfortune.

And, of course, the same word was passed in other

110

quarters as well. The Dowager Empress heard of these goings on, and rather than sympathizing with her daughter-in-law's desire to provide the heir that everyone, including that same Dowager Empress, wanted, she only increased the output of jokes about the Tsarina's supposed shortcomings. However, since all the seers were unanimous on predicting the early advent of a male heir, she began to believe that there must be some truth in their prophecies, and her belief was such that she began to experience all the usual signs of pregnancy. The court physician accepted these signs at face value and assured her that this time the child would be a male. When it became evident that the time for delivery had arrived, she retired to her chamber, attended by the entire staff of royal physicians, but after several days without any indication of labor, they made an examination and were forced to announce that her pregnancy had been of the hysterical type, similar to that of Queen Mary— "Bloody Mary"—of England. And this, of course, gave renewed life to the jesting of her enemies, who now said that the false pregnancy was a certain sign that she was quite mad.

All of these events were painfully embarrassing to the sensitive Tsarina, and now a new discomfiture was added, this one by the Holy Synod, the members of which had been most unhappy with the spate of seers and psychics that had been holding ascendancy over the royal family. Archimandrite Theophan was given the task, as confessor to the Tsarina, of declaring to her that her false pregnancy had been a punishment from God for giving ear to heretics, and that the Tsar must canonize a priest who had lived a century before, one Otyets Anhila, and that her penance was to consist of a pilgrimage to the tomb of the new saint, where she was to pray for forgiveness and cleanse herself in the waters of the adjacent well. And, to cap the climax, when she did go through the ritual of purification, she slipped and fell as she entered the water, exposing, so it was said, her derrière, and whether this was true or not, it added much to the gaiety of the capital and the Dowager Empress' circle.

My father never told me of the precise date upon which he first met the royal family, but it is likely that it occurred on October 31, 1905, for on the next day, November 1, the

Tsar wrote in his diary: "We have met a man of God—Grigori Efimovich, from Tobolsk Province." Papa was, at that time, still staying at the monastery, and Theofan, who had taken a particular liking to him, had been introducing him to many important people, among whom were the Grand Duchesses Anastasia and Militza, princesses of Montenegro, and the wives respectively of the Grand Duke Nikolai Nikolayevich and his brother, the Grand Duke Pyotr Nikolayevich, and it was at the home of the latter that Papa met the Tsar and Tsarina.

During the next three years, there were several additional meetings, and the royal couple enjoyed Papa's faculty of expounding the Gospels in simple terms, making the words of the Khristos come alive. But, other than their recognition of his spiritual qualities, he had no particular influence upon their lives, certainly not as much as did the dwarf Mitia Koliava, who was a protégé of Iliodor's, and who, when in one of his epileptic seizures, was believed to speak the word of God.

In the year prior to the first meeting, the Tsarina had finally given birth to a son, the Tsarevich Aleksei Nikolayevich. But with this happy news, there came sadness as well. The tsarevich was found to be afflicted with the disease that was the lot of all the male issue of Queen Victoria, the dread hemophilia, a disease passed on through the female line. The Tsarina, Victoria's granddaughter, had given birth to a hemophiliac, an ironic twist of fate, since only her son could inherit the malady, and the birth of a son had been her most ardent desire. Although, of course, the fault was not hers, she felt a sense of guilt that she should be the instrument of her son's suffering, and her life now revolved about his well-being. One of her first acts was to appoint a guardian of Aleksei's health; a sturdy sailor, one Dyerevyenko, was brought in to follow the child at all times, with the authority to prevent his engaging in any of the boyish activities that might result in his hurting himself, for the slightest cut or bruise might produce uncontrollable bleeding. Even the prick of a rose thorn could have proved fatal.

But it was well-nigh impossible to keep an otherwise healthy boy from doing something that might cause him to bleed a little; healthy youngsters shed many drops of blood, if only a few at a time, while growing up. And, of course, the inevitable happened. When he was four, he stumbled and fell while playing, but, unlike others of his age group, who are forever falling and getting up to continue their play, Aleksei was instantly disabled with pain and began to hemorrhage internally. He was carried to his bed, where he lay in excruciating agony, and Dr. Botkin, the royal physician, was hurriedly summoned. The good doctor did what he could, but was forced to admit that he was helpless, and that even his most powerful opiates were not equal to the task of easing the tsarevich's torment. Aleksandra Feodorovna stayed by his bedside night and day, not leaving him for even the hastiest meal, and Dr. Botkin remained in the sickroom as well, taking only the briefest periods for a much-needed rest. For three seemingly endless days, Aleksei continued to fail, his body twisted in pain, his face ashen and wet with perspiration. In the palace, and all through the city, special church services were held, and the nation prayed with one voice for the recovery of the heir apparent, but all to no avail, and it became increasingly clear that nothing short of a miracle could save his life. And there was no miracle in sight.

It was at this point that the Grand Duchess Anastasia went to the palace, and having access to the sickroom, managed to gain the Tsarina's ear.

"Vyelichyestvo,* have you thought of calling upon Grigori Efimovich?"

"No, dorogoi† Anastasia, it had not occurred to me. I know Otyets Grigori is a holy man, and I suppose his prayers would help."

"But, Vyelichyestvo, he is more than a holy man; he is also a healer, one of the greatest of all time."

"Oh, then hurry. Please bring him here at once."

The Tsarina was ready to clutch at any straw, and with the Grand Duchess' endorsement, the straw might not be too frail a one.

This and what is to follow was told me by the Grand Duchess herself a few years later; for a time, until things under-

*Majesty
†dear

went a change, it was one of her favorite stories. She rushed out of the palace, and waving her footman back into his place, for she had no time to wait upon formalities, ordered her coachman to drive with all speed to the Ducal Palace, where the horses, running as though they were pursued by a hungry wolf pack, brought her in record time. From there, she sent out several of her retainers to locate Papa, ensuring their enthusiastic participation in the search with the promise of a reward. And within the hour, she had her man, who agreed to go at once with her to the tsarevich's bedside. She had told her coachman to have the carriage at the door, and so no time was lost in making a swift return to the royal palace. Arriving at a side entrance, leading to the imperial apartments, they were quickly led by a butler up the back stairs, past no fewer than ten guards, standing stiffly at attention, and resplendent in their uniforms of the Royal Guards, and into the sickroom. As they entered, they were the cynosure of all eyes.

My father told me of the scene: Grouped around the bed were the grieving parents; the four young grand duchesses, sisters of the tsarevich; Gospozha Anna Aleksandrovna Virubova, lady in waiting to the Tsarina; Archimandrite Theofan; Dr. Botkin; and a nurse. Papa raised his hand, and making the sign of the cross, blessed the room and its occupants. He strode across the room toward the royal couple, greeting the Tsar with the familiar triple kiss and a hearty embrace, and then the Tsarina, more gently, but also with the triple kiss. She was not at all put out by this show of familiarity, as some of the courtiers were to be in the future, but took his hand reverently and kissed it.

Then he turned to the sick boy, and observing the pallid features wracked with pain, he knelt beside the bed and began to pray. As he did this, the others in the room were filled with his enveloping aura of peace, and irrespective of the degree of religious belief, each knelt as if overcome by a spiritual presence, and joined in the silent prayer. For a space of ten minutes, nothing was to be heard but the sound of breathing. And then he rose to his feet and stood looking down at his patient, a beatific smile on his glowing countenance.

"Open your eyes, my son!" It hardly seemed a

command, so loving was his voice. "Open your eyes and look at me."

As he spoke, the others arose, and to their amazement, saw Aleksei's eyelids flutter and open. The boy looked about him in some confusion at first, but his vision finally came to a focus on the starets' face, and ever so gradually, a smile began to form on his lips. The Tsarina's cry of joy shattered the stillness of the room, and the others joined in, but Papa signaled behind him with his hand for silence, and spoke again to the boy.

"Your pain is going away; you will soon be well. You must thank God for healing you. And now, go to sleep."

Aleksei closed his eyes and was soon sunk in the first restful sleep he had had for several days. Papa turned away from the tsarevich to address the royal parents, who were looking at him with an attitude of awe and reverence. They had seen a miracle performed before their very eyes, the miracle that alone could have saved their son.

"The tsarevich will live," he announced, speaking as one having authority.

And no one in that room doubted that he had spoken the truth. And thus, in a moment of high drama, the influence of Grigori Efimovich Rasputin was born, an influence enhanced by the dependency of the Tsar and Tsarina upon him for the well-being, even the survival, of the future Tsar of all the Russians.

NINE

From the very beginning of his stay in St. Petersburg, the way had been made clear for my father, almost, it seemed to him, as though someone—or Some One—were easing his path so that he would be free to pursue an as yet undisclosed purpose. He had no doubt that such was the case, and how could he have doubted, with the evidences of it all around him? There was that first day when Ivan of Kronstadt had invited him to stay at the monastery, and the friendships formed with the eminent churchmen. Theofan, in particular, had been of great assistance, introducing him into influential circles that finally led to the healing of the tsarevich. Theofan had also found him more permanent quarters, and a warm welcome from Grigori Pyotrovich Sasanov, a member of the Duma, and there he remained for several years.

The archimandrite had appointed himself to the post of Papa's counselor and guide, and as a muzhik fresh from the country, my father relied on his good judgment. It was Theofan who introduced Papa to the Grand Duchess Militza, and since both she and her sister, the Grand Duchess Anastasia, as well as their husbands, were deeply interested in mysticism and the occult, he made a profound impression upon them. Although devoted to spiritualism, and constantly attending séances, they transferred their devotion to Papa, and it was through their sponsorship, particularly that of Nikolai, that he was accepted into society, becoming famed as a spiritual teacher with remarkable gifts of healing and prophecy. And the degree of his acceptance was not diminished by the fact that he was a muzhik, with the crude, but civil, manners of a son of the soil. None took offense when he did not act in a servile manner, as befitted his station, but greeted one and all with an embrace and the three kisses of welcome, refusing to abide by the custom of the lower classes, which dictated that superiors were to be addressed as "Your Excellency."

The Grand Duchess Militza held social functions, attended by many of her friends, so that they might meet the starets and hear him expound his simple interpretations of the Gospels and God's will. And by the power of God residing in him he was able to heal many of their ailments. He was soon the principal topic of conversation, and even some of the higher churchmen expressed themselves as believing that he had a very special gift from God.

The royal family had an additional reason for holding Papa in high esteem. A Dr. Philippe, who had come from France to serve as their combined medical and spiritual adviser, had on his deathbed disclosed that he was but a forerunner of one who was to come, one who was greater than he. Although Dr. Philippe had begun life as a butcher's assistant, he had become a most competent practitioner, as well as having developed remarkable powers of clairvoyance. With his last breath he had whispered, "Another will come to advise you, and he will be exalted above me. He will speak with the voice of God. As you have loved me, love you also him. Please, hear him . . . listen . . . and follow. . . ."

It was as if John the Baptist were speaking of him who was to come after: "He it is, who coming after me is preferred before me, whose shoe's latchet I am not worthy to

117

unloose." And thus, one came to "make straight the way" for Grigori Efimovich Rasputin, one whom he had never seen.

Ж

Having spent more than two years away from home, Papa took advantage of the new Trans-Siberian Railroad to visit his family, and there was another all-night celebration to welcome him home. Mama had a genius for management, and he was pleased to see how well the farm had prospered. There was a brief period of happy reunion; Papa played with us children and worked on the farm, living the sort of life that he had always loved. And then, one night, shortly after we had all gone to bed, I heard Mama scream as if with pain. I ran to their bedroom and knocked on the door, but Mama said that it was nothing, and I should go back to bed. But before I finally fell asleep, I heard Mama and Papa speaking, although their voices were too low for me to distinguish the words being spoken. The next day, when I asked Mama what had made her scream, she put me off with some vague answer and refused to discuss the matter any further. And a few days later, Papa left once again for his return to St. Petersburg.

But then, Mama became really ill, and Dunia worked feverishly to help her, while I was sent to bring the akushyerka. And at last I found the truth, which could no longer be kept from me, that Mama was suffering from a hemorrhage which the two women stopped only after she had lost a good deal of blood. While Mama was recovering in bed, I was sitting with her one day, when a question occurred to me.

"Why didn't Papa heal you with his prayers?"

Mama replied, "I didn't want to worry him, so I kept it from him."

"But he must have known something was the matter when you screamed that night."

"No, I just told him that I had a cramp, but that it was all better in a little while."

At that point, Dunia entered the room and brought up a subject that apparently had been discussed before: "Praskovia Fedorovna, it is not safe for you to remain here. You should be in the hospital at Tyumen. Please, let me take you there."

But Mama had a fear of hospitals and said, "No, I will not be placed in a hospital to die. I want you to stop talking about hospitals. And while we are on the subject, I don't want you plotting behind my back. Promise me that you will not send word to Grischa about my illness. I'm afraid he would put me in a hospital, whether I wanted to go or not. Promise!"

"Please, Praskovia Fedorovna, don't ask that."

"Promise!" Her voice was very firm.

And Dunia gave the required promise, but I could see that she had misgivings about it.

In a few days, Mama felt well enough to go out into the fields; she always worried when she was not there to supervise the workers. But she had not been there very long when I heard Dunia give a cry, and run out of the house. I followed, and saw Mama lying in a crumpled heap where she had fallen. She was hemorrhaging again, only this time it was worse. Katya came out of the house, and between the three of us we got Mama back into bed, and then Dunia broke her promise. Running quickly to the post office, she sent a telegram to Papa, and the next thing Mama knew, she had been put into a comfortable carriage and was being driven into Tyumen. Too weak to resist, or even to complain, she was placed aboard the train, and in a few days arrived in St. Petersburg. The diagnosis was quickly made; she had a tumor, and a hysterectomy was indicated. One of the most distinguished surgeons in all Russia performed the operation, which was a complete success, and before she had been in the city two days, she was convalescing in the best private room in the hospital. Insisting that it was his privilege, the Grand Duke Pyotr paid all the expenses. And when she was released from the hospital, and it was time to return to Pokrovskoye, the Grand Duke provided her with a private nurse to accompany her and to care for her until she could be up and about. And, of course, Papa came back with her.

This time, Papa stayed with us for three months, and we children were delighted. He took us fishing down by the Tura, which we enjoyed, as can well be imagined, but he also made us observe all the rituals of the Church, including learning our catechisms, and our school studies, prayers before bedtime, and grace before meals. And, without fail, we attended church on Sundays and holy days. We were quite different in our natures; Mitia, the eldest, was going to be a typical farmer and was already showing a fondness for the horses and other animals, as Papa had, although he lacked Papa's gift of healing. Varya was still too young to exhibit any special characteristics, but played about the house, getting underfoot and making a nuisance of herself, as do all little children. But I was a natural-born rebel. In school, I could sense a certain enmity toward me on the part of Otyets Pyotr, and I knew that it could be attributed to his dislike of my father. So I repaid him in the only way that I knew how, by becoming an intractable pupil in his classroom. And for every punishment meted out by the priest-teacher, I would avenge myself. I particularly loathed having to learn my catechism, although not from Papa, but only from Pyotr, and when the correct answer was not forthcoming, he would give me a heavy thump on the ear. In retribution, I would wait patiently for an opportunity, and when he turned his back to write on the blackboard, I would flip spitballs at my classmates. When I had stirred them up to the point of retaliation, and the noise had mounted to an uproar, Otyets Pyotr would turn around to see who was causing the disturbance, by which time I would be sitting with my hands folded on my desk, and as beatific a smile as I could manage on my face. And although I am sure he had a fairly accurate suspicion as to the identity of the culprit in his moderately dull mind, he was never able to catch me *flagrante delicto*.

While most of my friends were boys, for I had early learned that they could be maneuvered into doing favors for me by the simple expedient of setting them to competing for nothing more than a smile for a reward, I did have a few of my own sex. My best friend was a girl named Lili, the daughter of a poor widow whose husband had been a farm worker. She and her mother lived in a little isba on the outskirts of the village, and because I felt sorry for her, I made it a practice to take her to my home after school, where she could warm herself beside the big stove and satisfy her constant hunger with a thick slice of fresh bread. We had been close friends for several years, until her mother remarried, when, suddenly, Lili, who had been gay and outgoing, became indrawn and uncommunicative. To my dismay, she began to avoid me; no longer did we enjoy the winter afternoons by the stove, and our secret exchanges of confidences about which boys were taking which girls for walks in the woods, and heaven knew what else. I was saddened by this sudden break and wracked my brains to find a possible cause, but I could think of none.

And then, while Mama was in the hospital, Lili unexpectedly took the first step toward renewing our friendship. Coming up to me on the way to school, she said, "Your mother was so kind to me, and now my mother wants to invite you to spend the night with us."

I was overjoyed at the invitation, having missed Lili's companionship, and my excitement was increased by the prospect of an adventure, for I had never slept away from home before.

So I quickly answered, "Oh, I would love to come. I'm sure Dunia will let me; I'll ask her right after school."

Seeing how badly I wanted to go, Dunia gave her consent and helped pack my nightgown and other necessities for the visit. I was walking on air as I arrived at the isba, but it was soon clear that this was not going to be quite the joyful occasion that I had imagined. The place itself was small and poorly furnished, even by the simple standards of Pokrovskoye, but that was not the principal reason for my misgivings. It was Lili's mother, pale and gaunt, with kindly, though sad, eyes and a disconcerting habit of constantly looking over her shoulder, as though in dread of some nameless horror. I also noticed, in passing, that the sleeping arrangements consisted of two bunks, built into recesses in the wall and covered by worn curtains.

And then the cause of the woman's nervousness became clear when her husband, Lili's stepfather, came home. With his arrival, the atmosphere became even more strained, and it was obvious that both mother and daughter were afraid of him. And some of this fear rubbed off on me, even though the man was pleasant enough toward me, pleasant in a way that a bear, which he somewhat resembled, might be. But,

121

along with the fear, I felt a strange sense of excitement, even if I could not determine its source. I was too young then to have a comprehension of the animal appeal certain brutish men radiate, and the sometimes overwhelming compulsion that can impel a woman to yield to their demands, as had been the case with Lili's mother. The man stood in the center of the little room, his feet spread apart, thumbs hooked into his belt, and smiled as the introductions were made, looking me over in a way that made me feel like a bird being appraised by a hungry snake. I had a feeling that some unknown danger was in that room, but I was also fascinated at the same time. He hardly took his eyes off me during the brief period between his homecoming and his wife's call to the evening meal. And it was at that moment that the strained peace fell apart.

Not seeing his familiar bottle on the table, he cried out, "*Radi Bog,** where did you hide my damned wine?"

"I haven't seen it," she answered, her voice tremulous and defensive.

He took her by the shoulders and shook her: "Don't tell me that. Where is it?"

"Please! I don't know."

He pushed her from him with such force that she fell to the floor, and he began to search, throwing anything that stood in his way to one side and cursing harshly under his breath. Lili and I shrank toward a corner in order to keep out of his way and watched as he finally found the bottle under his bunk. In the meantime, his wife had regained her feet and was attempting to recover a little of her composure and what remained of her dignity. Grasping the neck of the bottle in one hamlike fist, he applied pressure to the cork with his thumb, flipping it loose, and took a long pull at the wine. He thumped the bottle down on the table and took his seat, muttering so all could hear: "Damned woman, always hiding a man's wine. What good is she?"

I had never been so terrified and could hardly eat the meal, although there was little enough of it, for watching the man as he alternately drank and cursed, and the more he drank, the more he cursed, until he was thoroughly sodden and

*for God's sake

Portrait of Grigori Rasputin that now hangs over bed of his daughter, Maria, in her home in Los Angeles, California.

Rasputin and his children on the Rasputin farm in Siberia. Maria is on the left.

Rasputin family house in Siberia.

Rasputin surrounded by his followers in Siberia.

Anna Vyrubova, who arranged Rasputin's meeting with the Tsarina and her son, the Tsarevich.

Portrait of the Tsarina and the Tsarevich from a postcard sent to Maria Rasputin by Anna Vyrubova.

Friends in Rasputin's parlour in St. Petersburg. Maria Rasputin is seated in front of the standing man.

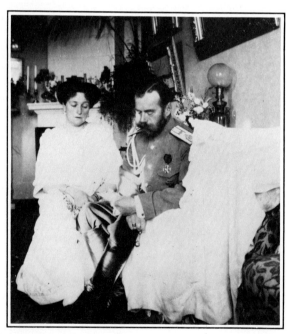

The Tsar Nikolas II and Tsarina Aleksandra during World War I.
The Bettmann Archive

Grand Duchesses Olga, Tatiana, and Maria, in mourning for Rasputin in 1917.
The Bettmann Archive

Prince Feliks Yussupov in Bovar costume.

Prince Feliks Yussupov as a young man.

Maria Rasputin, at the age of 30, when living in Paris.

Maria Rasputin as a wild animal trainer in an English circus, 1935.

Maria Rasputin and Patte Barham at Fremont Place, Los Angeles, Christmas 1975.

even more belligerent than before. Suddenly, starting up from the table, he opened his trousers, kicked the door open, and standing in plain view of the three of us, urinated on the ground. This was the most swinish thing I had ever seen, and I was disgusted, not because I was unfamiliar with the masculine anatomy, for I, too, had bathed communally in the Tura, and had played those games most children play when finding themselves free of adult supervision. But even the crudest muzhik had never done anything like that in my presence. The poor mother, no longer able to hide her embarrassment, hurried us from the table.

She warned us: "Stay away from him tonight. He is in a dangerous mood."

She shoved us toward the sink and urged us to hurry with our ablutions, but even as we were washing, I could see out of the corner of my eye that the man, who had stumbled back into the room, was leering at me with open mouth, the tip of his tongue at the corner of his wet lips. As Lili and I started toward our bunk, we had to pass the chair upon which he was sitting, and Lili, with obvious distaste, stopped to kiss her stepfather good night. I waited until the ritual was over, preparing to follow her, when the man lunged forward and caught me about the waist. Pulling me toward him, he held me close.

"Don't you want to kiss me good night?" he asked. "You kiss your own father, don't you?"

I decided that it would be best not to resist; the quicker I kissed him, the sooner would I be free of his grasp. But my dutiful kiss on the cheek was not enough. Still holding me in one arm, he took hold of my face by the chin, and turned it so that he could give me a wet and altogether disgusting kiss full on the lips. And as he was doing that, his hand began to rove over my body, touching me intimately as no one had ever done. I was thoroughly terrorized.

This proved too much for the distraught woman, and she pulled me away from him, screaming, "Take your hands off her, you filthy beast."

He laughed in his coarse way, and said, "What's the matter; can't a man have a little fun? That's what girls are for."

"Not these girls, you drunken pig." She pushed us

toward our bunk and turned back to face her husband, just in time to receive a glancing blow on her chin.

As she fell back against the wall, he yelled, "Then, ei Bogu,* I'll take you instead."

And with that, he seized the front of her flimsy dress, and giving it a downward pull, ripped it to the waist. As she stood helpless before him, he laughed at her, contemptuously, derisively, a laugh that repudiated a thousand centuries of human ascent from the jungle, and he tore off the rest of her clothing. She was weeping now, great sobs of shame and embarrassment, trying to cover her nakedness, trying somehow to avoid the spectacle that was being presented to her daughter and me. But her husband had no such inhibitions; if anything, he was further stimulated by the idea of displaying his prowess before us. He began to remove his own clothing, staggering as he tried drunkenly to remove his trousers, and cursing obscenely as he stumbled in the process.

Having clambered into the bunk ahead of Lili, I was facing toward the room as I lay on my side, holding the blubbering girl in my arms and trying to comfort her. Thus, I could not avoid witnessing the whole dreadful scene, much as those who find themselves present at a horrifying accident cannot force themselves to turn their eyes away, held by an overpowering fascination to observe every sanguine detail. Held as though in a vise, I watched as the man dragged his wife to the floor, forced her to admit him, and thrust viciously until he had accomplished his purpose. Suddenly, all was still in the little isba, save for Lili's sobbing and the heavy breathing of her stepfather, who now lay sprawled upon his wife, pinning her to the floor.

At last, Lili's tears stopped, and the poor child fell asleep in my arms. Both husband and wife were also sleeping, exhausted by their violent actions, and I saw an opportunity for easy escape. I got out of bed, very gently so as not to wake Lili, dressed, and crept on tiptoe around the couple. Opening the door quietly, I slipped out and then fled, blinded by tears of fear and horror, until I arrived safely home. Panting for breath, I found Dunia still up, and rushed into the protection of her

*by God

124

motherly arms. To say the least, she was surprised, having thought I would have been asleep with Lili.

"What is it, child," she asked, "what has happened?"

"Oh, Dunia, it was horrible."

"What was?"

"I can't tell you; it was too awful."

"Are you hurt?"

"No, no, nothing like that."

"Well, then, tell me. What made you run all the way home, like a frightened rabbit?"

I could not bring myself to tell her at first. But she persisted, and finally the whole lurid tale tumbled out. Of course she was shocked, but regaining her poise, she exerted every effort to calm me, and the combination of her words, and even to a greater extent, the soothing sound of her voice did restore some degree of peace in my mind and I was able to sleep at last.

One of the things that Dunia told me during those last chaotic days in St. Petersburg was of the debate that went on in her mind as to whether or not she should tell Papa, when he and Mama returned from the hospital. Should she preserve the peace by keeping the truth from him? On the other hand, was it not his right to know? She mulled this over for several days, finally telling him the whole sorry tale.

Papa's face turned white as he listened to the account, but he made Dunia promise not to say a word to anyone else, particularly Mama. And that night, after Mama had gone to sleep, he made his way to the isba where the outrage had occurred. Calling the man out, he said, in a voice uncharacteristically filled with anger: "How dared you to act as you did in front of my daughter? Maria is a young and innocent girl . . ."

But that was as far as he got, for the man, drunk as usual, raised his arm from behind his back, and in his hand there was an ax handle. Papa saw it as it descended, but too late to ward off the blow, and it crashed down upon his forehead. He fell to the ground, unconscious, and blood began to flow, staining the area around his head. The man's wife ran, screaming for help, and soon some men came and carried Papa home, where he was put to bed, suffering from a slight concussion. Dunia bathed the wound and bandaged it, stopping the bleeding, and he was up and about in a few days, although he bore the scar for the rest of his life, as can be seen in subsequent photographs of him.

When the story of the attack on their starets came to be known throughout the village, the people rose in anger, and a large number of men moved upon the isba with the determination to give the man a thorough beating and to drive him out of Pokrovskoye. But, although a drunk and a scoundrel, the man was no fool, and by the time the irate villagers arrived, he had gone, abandoning his wife and those of his possessions he could not carry.

One result of the incident was that Papa decided I should not stay in the village with the unhappy memories it might hold for me, and he had a long discussion with Mama in which he urged her to permit him to take me with him to St. Petersburg. He argued, and I agreed wholeheartedly, that I would enjoy many advantages not to be found in Pokrovskoye, good schools, association with people of culture, an introduction to the royal family, and a familiarity with good music and fine art. As soon as he could find a proper home, he proposed to send for Dunia to keep house for us. Mama was torn by the necessity for making a decision, realizing it would be better for me, but loath to be parted from her daughter. But when Papa promised to bring me back for occasional visits, she finally agreed, and it was not long before we set out for the nation's capital, he to continue with his mission, and I to begin an adventure.

✕TEN✕

A young girl of ten, no matter that her father may be an international figure, is no less impressed with the prospect of a long journey by express train from the far Siberian country to St. Petersburg, the most famous of all Russian cities. To my father it was home. To me it was a new world to be explored with all the enthusiasm and curiosity of my tender age.

With the modern convenience of air travel one has a tendency to forget the long, time-consuming rambles by rail. But it was fun—oh my, yes—such wonderful fun filled with all sorts of exciting events. For instance, we had no dining cars— not even on the express trains—and so the corridors of the railway cars were filled with the aroma of food prepared in as many kitchens as there were travelers. It was a wonderfully exciting array of scents that permeated even our private car where our own food baskets were laden with cakes, fruit, and food that would keep until we reached our destination.

Although we traveled in a special car, I was seldom in

it. My father ministered to his flock even in transit and hardly missed me as I wandered through the train, fascinated by all I saw and heard and found myself surrounded by people who were just as interested in me because I was the daughter of the mystical starets.

Of course, to me he was my father. I knew he had mystery about him that other men did not have. I knew he had healing powers that went far beyond anything the medical profession could account for—but he was still my father and I loved him. Consequently, I enjoyed talking about him to all those strangers who were so interested. I was always an outgoing person—still am—and it became a trip for me to remember.

America, of course, is my home now and I love my life in California, but there is even today no more beautiful place in the world to me than my recollection of that lovely Russian countryside I passed through en route to my new life in the big city.

I was in for a surprise on several levels in St. Petersburg. It was a center of social and political activity, being the winter quarters of the Tsar and his government.

In our small country village, where I had lived all my life until now, when my father had the opportunity to be home with us, it was fun and games and time spent by my father with his children. He played hide-and-seek and other games with us and read books to us, and I remember the joy in his eyes when he said or did something that made one of us happy.

In St. Petersburg it was totally different. I saw my father as a different person than I had known at home. He no longer belonged to us—he belonged to everybody. And they were all there, lining up day after day to exercise their claims to him. If I was jealous of the mob of adulators and admirers of my father (and I was), I was also intrigued by the almost holy tribute paid to him.

We did not have our own apartment at first. My father was friendly with a family named Sasanov. Mr. Sasanov was, like my father, a religious man—a member of the Synod— and because he was a busy man I saw very little of him. Their apartment was not large, but adequate. It was exquisite in furnishings and decor. The Sasanovs had two servants—a cook and a maid. It was a first-class home of the time and everything was immaculate.

In spite of the family informality, there was a lot of formal atmosphere about the home. The maid served all meals. It was a comfortable but strictly arranged life. Nothing was left to guesswork by the Sasanovs, whereas with my father, his life outside his work was quite loosely strung together and, in retrospect, even his work was disorganized. Had it not been for the stream of visitors who sought of him so many things, I believe he would have been appalled at the chaos in his daily routine.

I shared a room with the Sasanov's daughter, a girl four years my senior and hopelessly spoiled both by her parents and by an untold number of young swains who swarmed about her, much to her adolescent delight. My father was so busy at first he hardly had time to notice such affairs, but in due time it would come to his attention, or rather distract his attention. Marusa Sasanova was a strikingly attractive girl, and had she not been constantly chaperoned I am certain some young officer would have brought down a terrible scandal on her and her family.

Although the Sasanovs' apartment was adequate for them, or for house guests, it was never designed with my father's following in mind. Word spread that the starets was back and receiving guests. The Sasanov privacy was a thing of the past and their apartment filled with the lame, the halt, and the needy. These were always at my father's door looking for a kind word, a healing phrase, or often just a touch of my father's hand.

And now, with my father's influence at court, the politically ambitious came in droves. It was openly rumored that to solicit material favors the starets was the man to see. The stream through the Sasanov living quarters was constant: mothers with sons seeking positions in the civil service, businessmen looking for government contracts, people seeking introductions to cabinet ministers—they all flocked to see my father.

My father was a man who could never say no to anyone in need. He was a most dedicated and conscientious worker. For a time he tried to see them all. The sick he prayed for. Many of these were miraculously healed, and this created longer lines as the news of his healing abilities spread among the populace.

He had great insight into the character and nature of humanity. His was a clairvoyant power, although he would have been the last to call it that. Those who passed his rigid examinations (unaware that they were being psychologically tested) he tried to help in any way possible. He would drop a word to a minister or civil service commissioner, or whoever it was that might be able to help the petitioner before him. Many, however, were turned away when they could not pass the scrutiny of my father's keen awareness of purpose. These he dismissed with great tact and kindness, leaving them with the feeling that they had not been judged and found wanting. Papa never took it upon himself to judge the motives of others. "Only God," he would say, "has the right to judge."

None who sought my father's help and assistance ever went away disgruntled or bitter, even though they left without that for which they had come. My father's enemies were not among those who sought favors, solace, or comfort.

Yet a group of enemies was forming. They included fraudulent faith healers and seers, the leaders of bizarre mystical cults, purveyors of grotesque philosophies, and other quacks who had lost favor at court or in the aristocratic salons and drawing rooms. Soon these misfits were joined, however reluctantly, by Orthodox churchmen who were motivated by jealousy of the starets. They were strange bedfellows with a common purpose—to discredit and demean the man who had more influence than anyone in Russia outside the royal family itself.

Rasputin taught a loftier, more sublime sort of Christianity. It was a teaching understood by the common man, made all the more simple by my father's innate ability to explain in terms understood by even the most common plow-man. Because of this he was sought out more and more as the Orthodoxy was abandoned by the ordinary man in the street. Adding to the sting, the regular clergy saw their influence with the nobles and aristocrats being won away from them by this simple Siberian. Even the Tsar's ear was more available to

Rasputin than to the recognized Orthodox spiritual leaders.

It was inevitable that plots and subplots against my father were brewing in every jealous Orthodox mind in the realm. Yet the time was not right—the instrument of retaliation had not as yet come to light.

In the meantime the Sasanov home was over-crowded. My father became aware that he was imposing on the Sasanovs, although they never complained. He decided that he could no longer impose upon their generosity.

But it wasn't only his visitors that gave him cause to ponder his next move. He became aware that Marusa was not the best influence on me. True, I was fascinated by the way she handled her young men. But Papa was not fascinated and told me so.

"Maria," he said, perching me on his knee as he had so often done on visits to our home in Siberia, and which he almost never did now that we were in St. Petersburg, "you are too young to have your ears filled with the nonsense of a silly girl whose parents allow her to do anything she wants. You are far too young to be exposed to the attentions of these young men Marusa keeps company with. It is not right before God. Therefore we must move to our own quarters."

I, of course, denied that Marusa's escapades with the young blades influenced me in any way, but they did. Papa had some justification for his concern, and as I always did, I bowed to his decision with little argument.

"The sooner you are separated from that girl, the better."

When Papa said "sooner" it meant immediately.

But my father was a man, after all, and knew little about the mundane house-hunting, housekeeping chores that women in our day seemed preoccupied with—even if they were merely supervising their own help.

Realizing he would need assistance in finding a suitable home, he turned to a friend, Anna Aleksandrovna Virubova, the principal lady in waiting to the Tsarina. Father was rather a newcomer to the city and not as familiar with the proper places to live as those who had spent their lives there. Anna was the ideal person to help him.

I adored her because she always had time to tell me

things about the court and about the social events to which young ladies of my age were not invited.

Anna Aleksandrovna has sometimes been named as the person who introduced my father to the royal family. This is merely a myth, like so many others that surround the memory of a man who cannot answer for himself from the grave.

She told me herself she had been introduced to Papa by the Grand Duchess Militza, at her palace on the English Quay in St. Petersburg, recalling her excitement at meeting the holy man. "I must admit," she laughingly recalled, "I was quite shocked at his appearance. I saw an elderly muzhik, thin, pale of face, long hair, an unkempt beard, and the most extraordinary eyes, large and luminous. He was capable of looking into the very mind and soul of the person with whom he was conversing."

This was some two years after the Tsar had entered into his diary (1905): "We have met a man of God—Grigori Efimovich, from Tobolsk Province."

So the myth is just that—a myth.

Although she referred to my father as being "elderly," he was only thirty-six years old when they met. I suppose his sage appearance had something to do with that, and the beard merely added to his Moses-like appearance.

She recalled even more about that auspicious meeting. "Your father entered the room in a jaunty manner and embraced the grand duchess, shocking me beyond any belief that I might have had that I could be so astounded. He had the audacity to give her three hearty kisses on the cheek." She laughed as she remembered the event. "Of course, my dear, I was incensed with his ill manners and lack of propriety."

Offended or not, she did not hesitate to ask Papa the question she had come to ask him: "What of my forthcoming marriage?" She would not waste the opportunity because of Papa's lack of court graces. "I was engaged to a dashing naval lieutenant and had been assured your father would give me the right answers. However, when I was confronted with the close scrutiny of his piercing eyes I withdrew and asked the grand duchess to seek the advice on my behalf. He was so over-whelming—I'd never met anyone like him in my life."

Although her courage failed her, she still received a reply from Papa—albeit not the one she wanted to hear—because she ignored his message. Papa's ability to see into character and the future had given him a graphic picture of events to come, although their meeting had been quite brief. He later related the entire incident to me and I sat at his feet in a state of awe/love as I listened to the story he had previously unfolded to the grand duchess.

"I assured her the marriage would take place—and it will. But it will not be successful."

"How do you know that, Papa?" It was not that I doubted his words—merely that I was anxious to seek out the source of his wisdom. He only waved his hand through the air, and somehow that was supposed to satisfy my curiosity. Of course, it never did.

But despite his ominous prediction, she did marry the young officer. The ceremony was arranged by the Tsarina, who, in spite of her opposition to the marriage, made her a wedding present of a set of fine chairs.

Most young men of the upper classes were well trained in the ways of sexual pleasures either by mistresses or by courtesans. This was usually accomplished long before they took on the obligation of wedded bliss. Such was not the case with Anna's maladroit young lieutenant. His entire education of bedroom marriage had been gleaned from nonfactual salacious books and obscene jokes. Consequently he was as ignorant as any common lout in a lady's boudoir, made even more dis-astrous by the fact that Anna Aleksandrovna knew even less than he about such things. She had been puritanically raised and protected, as were all her compatriots, and although she had indulged in the fantasy of numerous flirtations and in-fatuations, there had never been any intimacies with the opposite sex other than polite pecks on the cheek. Young men of the day had other outlets for their more base desires and restrained themselves with their more chaste fiancées.

Thus, two unseasoned amateurs were left to their

own illiterate devices, once the wedding banquet had disappeared and the last guest departed.

"I'm not sure what happened," Anna told me in an intimate exchange of feminine feelings. "Either my husband was a latent homosexual or perhaps the excitement of the night rendered him impotent." She shrugged it off many years later as one might the remains of long-faded love letters from a once ardent admirer. "He was so drunk. The vodka merely gave him the courage to be crude. Without any consideration for my feelings or the sanctity of the moment, he practically raped me, although his mental capacities were far ahead of his physical ones. I was so overcome by shock and mortification I absolutely refused any further advances.

"He might have wanted to approach me differently, but it was too late. I would have none of him."

She explained that her resistance so enraged him that he pounced upon her as one would another man in a barroom brawl and proceeded to beat her as he shouted all sorts of obscenities, most of which she did not understand.

The memory suddenly became quite painful. She burst into tears as she remembered pleading with him to be merciful. "I only wanted him to go away and leave me alone," she sobbed. "I never wanted to see him again."

Realizing what he had done, he was at once sober and apologetic, but Anna wanted nothing to do with him.

"Oh, how I wish I had listened to the Tsarina and to your father. It was just as he had predicted. My marriage was in ruins from the first moment and there would be no reconciliation. I was a virgin when I married, and sex became to me what had been attempted by my husband on that horrible night. I hear of those who seem to enjoy it so much. I wish I could. To my dying day I shall remain virginal, and if I'm missing something great, so be it."

I felt sorry for her.

Ten years later, when, as a prisoner of the Communists, she was held in the Fortress of St. Peter and St. Paul, she was subjected to humiliation by drunken guards. She volunteered to be examined by doctors to prove that she was still a virgin—resulting in confirmation by medical authorities that she was indeed virtuous.

I hoped that fact might have ended the vicious gossip linking my father to Anna in a lewd and lascivious relationship —but it didn't. Even today there are those who whisper in polite company, and speak loudly when the traffic will bear it, of my father and Anna.

But such horrors were still in the future. Anna Aleksandrovna's problem of the moment was to find her friend a suitable apartment. A problem she solved with felicity.

Number 64 Gorokhovaya Ulitsa was ideal for Papa. It was somewhat off the beaten path, located in an unpretentious section of the city in a respectable neighborhood—and important to Papa, among the people. The house was recessed from the street, fronted by a small courtyard which was protected by a wall. The front court was entered through an archway.

Our apartment was on the third floor, which pleased Papa. He did not like being exposed to the disadvantages of first-floor living in a large city.

I was delighted that the apartment was so large—five rooms. For the first time in my life I did not have to share a room with anyone, and I quickly learned the value of personal privacy. But that was not what delighted Papa. Insofar as he was concerned the most appealing feature was the back stairway which emptied onto a side street, permitting Papa to leave and enter the house unobserved by the line of petitioners which often stretched down the three flights of stairs and out onto the front courtyard and street.

Papa was under constant surveillance by the secret police and the back stairs also permitted him the luxury of having important visitors come and go without being observed by the police, who seemed only to station themselves near the front, never the rear, entrance.

"Why do the police watch you?" I asked Papa one afternoon as two agents made themselves all too obvious across the street from our building.

"Oh," he shrugged, "for no good reason except something to keep them busy."

He was not concerned at all with their presence. "Everybody is suspect of something these days," he explained offhandedly. The Russians have always been overpopulated with bureaucrats and it is their need (nobody knows why exactly)—from the Tsars to Nikita Khrushchev and Leonid Brehznev—always to know everything about everybody.

If the surveillance by the Okhrana was intended to be covert, with no one seeming to know who ordered it, nor why, nor caring why (especially Papa), there was also uniformed protection, the source of which was obvious—the Tsarina. She ordered it for Papa's protection.

I once asked the Tsarina about the uniformed police officers. "My child," she counseled, "you are so young and there is so little you know of the intrigue at court—of political alliances. . . ." She paused as if to indulge a child's unwarranted curiosity. "There have been attempts on the lives of many who are friendly to the throne. I cannot afford the loss of your father. He is the savior of my Aleksei. You do not know, but until your father came with God into our home my son was given up as a hopeless case. The doctors with all their nostrums could do nothing for him. But the starets—a man of miracles from on high."

I knew that there were those out of favor with the Tsar who would like to see the elimination of the royal family. But I was an educated girl and I also knew that it had always been the same wherever there were rulers and those to be ruled. Some writers of books about the time have said that Papa was regarded as a villain who took careful watching, and that the policemen were there at his door for that purpose; whereas, on the contrary, they were serving as a guard for his protection.

And so we were settled in our new home, the last Papa was to have in this life. And there gathered around him a group of aristocratic female devotees, sitting at his feet to hear his simple, yet wise, teachings. Chief among them, and organizer of this circle, if "organizer" is the correct term for such an unorganized gathering, was Anna Aleksandrovna Virubova, his faithful Anyushka, who, after the royal family, was to be his closest friend and principal disciple. As word spread of these meetings, the gossips set to work, snickering as they spoke of nameless evil rites, including those of an orgiastic nature, that were conducted by the starets, although there was not then, nor was there ever, any evidence of such goings-on. Since I came and went at all hours of the day, I think I would have known of them, if there had been anything of the sort.

Among those who attended the sessions was one Maria Evgeniya "Munia" Golovina, a lovely, wistful young woman in her late twenties. A true devotee of God, she had been betrothed to Prince Nikolas Yussupov, Feliks' elder brother, but to her dismay, as she was preparing for the wedding, the news was brought to her that Nikolas had been killed in a duel defending the honor of another woman with whom he had been having an affair. The double shock of his death and the knowledge of his infidelity had turned her mind away from the world toward a spiritual life, and she was among the first to attach herself to my father, whom she sincerely believed to be "the word made flesh."

The elder Yussupovs maintained their warm sentiments toward the girl who had so nearly become their daughter-in-law, and she was a frequent visitor in their home. Thus, it was she who first spoke in glowing terms of the holy man and, strangely enough, it was Feliks who listened with the most attentive ear, noting not only her words, but what was even more convincing, her attitude of reverence and her radiant countenance.

On several occasions, Feliks had seen visions and heard voices, and these had served to draw him strongly toward a life of contemplation, but there were countervailing attributes, his overweening arrogance, his vanity, his petulance when his will was frustrated, his weakness of character, all of which conspired to endow him with a dichotomy of purpose, wavering between a deep yearning for God and his irresistible gusts of desire. Knowing, or at least sensing, the tumult that tore at his soul, Munia, like any recent convert, wanted to proselytize and Feliks became the target of her crusade. She was quite surprised when Yussupov expressed not only a willingness but an eager desire to meet my father, and so Munia, feeling as though the mantle of leader had fallen on her shoulders, arranged a meeting at her mother's home on the Winter Canal.

Papa was having a glass of Madeira when the resplendent Feliks arrived. He swept into the room with customary arrogance as if he were some sort of god paying a courtesy call to some minor prophet of his theology. But when he saw my father he deflated like the rupture of a hose under too much pressure. Overcome with some strange humility he did not understand, he approached Papa with head bowed as though he were the lowest menial in the land. No longer the pompous bon vivant with a thousand social graces and a wit as sharp as the Tsar's razor, he was not unlike a country bumpkin, or a schoolboy facing his headmaster.

Papa shook his head negatively. It was not his fashion to allow anyone to so abase himself in his presence. He therefore took the prince into his arms and gave him the familiar triple kiss on the cheeks which was my father's trademark to one and all, the high and the low.

Some years later when Yussupov, doing some of his own peculiar type of soul-purging, wrote in justification of his role as my father's murderer in chief, he noted that he had disliked Papa at first sight and that he instantly recognized him "for the fraud he was." Also, that he had known "the starets was not to be trusted, for he had a shifty manner."

Dear Munia, who was on the spot at the time, told me a different story, and I'm sure a more accurate one.

"Oh, Maria," she recounted at my urging, "you should have been there. You should have seen Feliks. He was like some shy lad from a secluded life, blushing and tongue-tied. I'm sure your father will make him a convert, but it will take some doing. He did try to ask some rather naive questions about the meaning of life, but he is not accustomed to asking and it was difficult. Just think of it, to convert a prince."

Munia, of course, was enraptured with the idea she had been the instrument that brought them together, my father and Feliks.

Feliks, she said, seemed to gain some confidence as the conversation progressed and even seemed to relax somewhat, speaking in his high and rather affected voice, employing the condescending manner with which he masked some inherent weakness.

Papa was not as gullible as Munia, yet he was fascinated by Feliks. He spoke to me about this young prince whom

138

he was both repelled by and drawn to at the same time. Papa had that amazing ability to read character that is so rare.

"What was he really like, Papa?" I asked during our short time together the following day.

"Who?" Papa asked, seeming to be thinking of more important things than a child's inquisitiveness.

"The prince, Papa—Prince Yussupov."

"Oh," he replied indulgently, "a frightened boy, frightened by the world around him, his own desires, which I doubt even he understands, frightened by the future and torn between many demons. He is as a man tied between two horses, each pulling in the opposite direction."

I knew Papa pitied him and saw him as a mockery of a man. But there was more. "Strangely enough," Papa said, "there is something quite engaging about the man. Some unspoken desperation, a silent crying in the wilderness for help, as if there were a real person imprisoned inside him, pleading for release. Maybe I can help him. Perhaps . . . but enough of this. There must be more interesting things on your mind than the strange pursuits of adults."

Papa ended our conversation with that but he had already, without revealing anything he knew, asked Munia to arrange another meeting with the young prince. Of course Munia was delighted and immediately complied.

In passing, to Munia, he made a strange remark about Feliks. "There is a beautiful quality in Feliks' nature but his weakness and self-indulgence are twisting it." He paused for a moment and left her with a final statement, "He needs help desperately, or the dyavol will gobble him up for dinner."

The meeting did not take place. Before Munia could arrange it, Yussupov had left St. Petersburg for London, en route to Oxford.

It was the wrong place, the wrong man and the wrong time. It was not a place to go for redemption when one was of Yussupov's bent. This was the land that remained as a legacy, not so much of Oscar Wilde, who had died, broken and penniless a few years earlier, but of Lord Alfred Douglas, who, though equally culpable, seemed to have suffered very little. As a result of this intellectual belligerence, homosexuality became almost obligatory among the young bloods and intellectuals of the time. It was almost unfashionable not to engage in such practices. Wilde and Douglas set a fashion which would be followed by many of the literary lights who would come after them; albeit, none seemed to have had Oscar Wilde's compulsion toward reputational suicide.

Any spiritual or religious feelings Yussupov might have had as a result of his initial meeting with Papa were lost in the swirl of fancy-dress balls and dinner parties during his years at Oxford.

Thus, the prince frittered away his time in England. Although enrolled in one of the world's greatest institutions of learning, he chose to major in the ancient and more inviting College of Sodom.

Just as Papa had predicted, Yussupov's weakness and self-indulgence won out over all else. He passed the point of being helped. The dyavol had, in truth, begun to gobble him up.

╳ELEVEN╳

Rasputin and Iliodor, the starets and the *monakh*,* made a strange pair as they conversed together; the one so full of gaiety and vitality, and the other so dour and humorless. The two had become good friends, although Papa hated the pomposity of most churchmen, and Iliodor was more pompous than most; but still there was something that drew them together, even though the priest squirmed when his friend teased him. I was never able to understand Papa's liking for Iliodor, and when he came to Pokrovskoye to stay with us during one of my father's visits, I avoided being in his company as much as I could.

Iliodor was inordinantly proud of his widely advertised celibacy, holding that none could enter the Kingdom of God except through that door. And this became the subject of one of their friendly theological debates, as Papa described it to me, sometime later.

"In our Father's house there are many mansions,"

* *monk*

141

quoted Papa, and added to the passage his own words, "and each of the mansions has many doors. Do not think you hold the only key to God's realm."

"I do not hold the only key," Iliodor replied. "There are many keys, enough for all who want them, but all the keys unlock the same door."

"Nonsense! If that were true, then all the eunuchs would go to heaven."

"Make a joke if you will, but it is nevertheless true that the spiritual aspirant must serve either God or Venus; he cannot serve both."

"This much I will grant you," said my father, "that a spiritual aspirant may become so filled with the presence of God, he will have no thought for the flesh. His spirit will soar upward, leaving all bodily thoughts behind; his physical being will be unnoticed and untended. He will not care for food or drink; he will not care for sleep; he will have no desire for sex. But his is a rare type. You will remember I said, 'he may become so filled'; there are others who cannot rise above the body." And here, as I learned later, he was remembering his own experience. "When he would free his spirit from its sensual bonds, the flesh presses in upon him more insistently than ever. His need is great, and he cannot overcome it. What is he to do?"

"He must pray the harder," said the intransigent monk.

"No, my friend, at such a time he cannot pray. The call of his passions is too strong. If he is to continue in the holy life, there is only one remedy for him. He must stop his prayers and find a woman with whom he can regain his peace. Then, fulfilled, he may return to his prayers. God will not condemn him for his momentary lapse, for many momentary lapses, if they become necessary. But a time will come when he will not need a woman; when such thoughts do not arise in his mind. And then he will be able to find his way to God."

"But you would make a mockery of the monastic vows. We swear to remain continent. How could we follow your way and still remain faithful to Mother Church?"

"I do not want to argue with the Church, but I say

that the vow is based on a misunderstanding. It does not profit a monk to kneel at his prayers while his very soul burns with desire. The early fathers knew that the vital energy expended in sex is the same vital energy used to carry us up to the feet of God. The yogis of India call this vital energy *ojas*, and they say that it is the ojas that carries the kundalini, the spiritual force, up the spine, from its base to the top of the head, where we find enlightenment. But if one cannot meditate because of his carnal needs, he had better satisfy those needs quickly, and then return to his meditation. The ojas is swiftly replenished, and a time will come when he is so taken by rapture that he will not feel the twinges of desire."

"But, Grigori Efimovich, that is almost heresy. We were discussing Christian spirituality, and you introduce some heathen teaching. I know little of these yogis you mention, but I do know they are not Christians. We are to follow the way of the Khristos; not the way of some barbarian."

Iliodor had become quite red in the face during this last outburst, and Papa hastened to calm him.

"Come now, Otyets Iliodor, it is not my wish to change you into a yogi; although, by the way, they are not barbarians. But if you read the teachings of our Lord, you know that he said the publicans and the harlots would go into the kingdom before those who had heard the word, but had not believed."

And so the argument continued far into the night, and neither of the friends could convince the other. Of course, there were many bones of contention between them. On one occasion, the talk turned on the subject of which sin was the greatest. Iliodor stated his thesis in no uncertain terms.

"There can be no question; the greatest sin is that which is forbidden in the First Commandment: 'Thou shalt have no other gods before me.' It is the most important commandment, because God put it first."

"Of course, it is important, but so are all the rest. We are not talking about commandments, but about sin, and I say that it is clear the Khristos considered hypocrisy to be the worst offense."

Iliodor squirmed uncomfortably in his chair, feeling

that the debate was becoming a shade too personal. He knew, and he feared that his friend also knew, that he had not always been scrupulously sincere and forthright. To defend himself, he moved to the attack.

"So, Grigori Efimovich, you speak of hypocrisy. But have you always been as pure as your reputation for holiness would make people believe? Have you not mingled a little dalliance in with your spiritual teaching? What of the noble ladies who sit in your court with such manifest devotion? What of them, I ask?"

Papa's rush of anger was quickly subdued. He knew the monk's insinuations were only an attempt to strike back, and so his answer was delivered in a most serene tone.

"Iliodor, you know me—or you should know me—better than that. You must also know that I do not lie, so that when I tell you I have had no relations with any woman since I last saw Praskovia Fedorovna, you may well believe that it is the truth."

And Iliodor, taken aback by the obvious integrity of his opponent, could only make the worst possible response under the circumstances: "So you tell me, Grigori Efimovich, so you tell me."

And he tried to restore the friendly atmosphere in which the conversation had begun with a smile, but this only added to his image of cynicism, as though he had not believed a word of it.

It was at this moment that Papa's eyes were opened to what he had sensed all along was the true nature of his "friend." Here was a man so steeped in worldliness, so lustful, so greedy for power, that there was no way by which he could be reached. Here was no friend at all, but a potential enemy. And yet Papa was always unwilling to see anybody as evil, as committed to the destruction of anyone he considered a possible rival for honor and fame.

And so, instead of withdrawing in order to keep the peace, he tried to save the monk by exposing him to his real nature.

"Look here, my friend, you do not understand yourself. Our greatest difficulties arise out of a lack of self-knowledge.

144

Was it not Solon of Athens who admonished us: 'Know thyself'?"

"I know myself as well as the next man, I should think. And I find nothing in my heart for which I need be ashamed."

"Iliodor, Iliodor, we all have something in our hearts, some incident that makes us wince when we recall it, something we might wish we had never done."

"You may have such memories, but I do not. I can think of no action of mine with which to mortify myself."

"Perhaps I can jog your memory. You do remember visiting my home in Pokrovskoye last year?"

"Yes, of course."

"And you remember, I should think, peeking at my servant Dunia as she made her toilette, and so were able to catch a glimpse of her body?"

"You . . . you . . ."

"Come, honest confession is good for the soul. Confess this lapse—a momentary lapse, if you will—I beg of you. It will cleanse your heart. It may be painful, but only for a moment. It is like pulling an aching tooth; a brief instant of pain followed by a wonderful feeling of relief."

"I have nothing to confess," and the unrepentant monk almost screamed. "You are lying; no such incident ever occurred."

But Papa could see the terrible confusion of emotions struggling within Iliodor, and hoping to break down his defenses in a last desperate effort to save him from his overwhelming hypocrisy, he made one final attempt.

"You know in your heart that I am speaking the truth; I can see it in your whole manner. Confess—confess and save yourself. Be not like the scribes and pharisees; confess!"

But now the monk's expression was one of unalloyed hatred. No penitent was here; there was only a man beside himself with anger, anger arising out of his fear that his secret might become known.

"Go! Leave me! You are no friend, but a vicious enemy—and a sinner. I would have no further communication with you. It is you who are the sinner, not I. My life has been

145

blameless. Who knows what yours has been? There is the door." He pointed dramatically. "Go!"

And with that, what had been a friendship of some years' standing came to a bitter end, and the bitterness was to follow my father to the grave.

In some ways, Papa was naïve; you can, so to speak, take the muzhik out of Siberia, but you cannot take Siberia out of the muzhik. His virtures of integrity and openness were somewhat offset by a lack of tact and diplomacy, and his determination to speak the truth, even the unwelcome truth, made him more than a few enemies. Such an enemy had Iliodor now become, and a deadly enemy he proved to be.

But there were also many friends and many devotees who came to hear him speak of God and the spirit. His "court," as these disciples were called, flocked to our apartment, hoping to spend the day under his religious instruction, listening to him expounding the Gospels, absorbing his simple, yet profound, philosophy based on his knowledge that God was within and must be sought there. I believe that many of them came merely to bask in his presence, to feel the emanation of his supernal power. And, as with almost every holy man, there were a few whose love was of a more physical nature. I have heard it said that the teacher must be very careful with such disciples, for they set a fatal trap into which he may fall. He must walk the razor's edge between total acquiescence, which will end in their mutual ruin, and total rejection, which will send the poor would-be disciple off, perhaps to fall under the spell of some less ethical teacher, one of the many who put themselves forth as holy men in order to capitalize on the fascination for exotic religions. But, with Papa, this hazard was increased, for he radiated a potent animal magnetism, an almost aphrodisiac aura that enveloped those who were susceptible; but of this he was quite unaware. One such devotee who fell hopelessly in love with him was a former nun, Sister Akulina.

During his days of wandering, he had come one night to the convent of St. Piton, in Okhits, and the good Sisters had welcomed him to stay the night. As they set a simple meal before him, he heard an unearthly sound, enough to make his skin crawl with apprehension. It sounded like the scream of a soul in torment, one who was burning in the eternal fires of hell. And there followed more screams and shouting, a veritable harangue of coarse and guttural sounds. When he questioned them, the nuns told him that one of the younger novices was suffering from periodic convulsive attacks, and that no doctor or priest had been able to help her. He asked to be taken to her, and the abbess and one of her assistants led the way to a barred cell from which the anguished cries and fearsome howls poured forth in an unending torrent. The abbess invited him to see for himself through the small grating in the door, and he was truly shocked by the sight. The novice was lying with her face to the wall, but her whole body was writhing about, and a deep masculine voice was issuing from her lips, punctuated by an even more convulsive movement, her hands extended before her as though to ward off a blow, and then an unearthly scream, as though a blow had been dealt her.

The abbess said, "To see her now, you would never believe that she is usually a beautiful and serene girl, dedicated to the Virgin and to the convent. It must be the work of the dyavol; we are sure he possesses her, but only at certain times. It is sad, but no exorcist has been able to help her."

But Papa was not so certain as was the abbess, and turning to her, he said, "Reverend Mother, permit me to enter her cell; it is possible I can help her."

Feeling that the case was hopeless in any event, and that nothing would be lost by permitting him to enter, she unlocked the door. He stood on the threshold and made the sign of the cross, praying inaudibly for a moment. Then he strode to the girl's bedside and spoke in an authoritative voice.

"I order you," he said, "to be silent."

The girl turned her startled eyes toward him, and the countenance she presented was bloody and bruised, distorted by snarling, animalistic hatred. He knelt beside her as the astonished nuns looked on, and prayed aloud, as though calling to One far off, and he prayed that God would forgive her grievous sins. Astonished, the good Sisters looked at each other, for they knew of no sins the unfortunate girl might have committed. But the starets knew; although unaware of the details, he could sense that there was a heavy burden on her

147

soul. And as she calmed, it seemed as though an invisible hand were washing away her hatred and fury. Then he prayed that God would restore her to health and grant her forgiveness, and as he prayed, her face took on a glow of serenity. After some moments spent in silent thanksgiving, he rose and turned to the abbess.

"My prayer has been answered. She is healed; the Virgin of Kazan, the Holy Mother of God, has granted her absolution."

The miracle, for the good Sisters knew not what else to call it, was recorded in the convent register as an act of God's mercy, and there it remained until the Communists took over all the holy establishments, driving the inmates away, the more submissive ones to work on the *kolkhozi** or in the factories, and the rest to suffer the slow death by combined cold and starvation in the prison camps of northern Siberia. And the convent record, as but one more example of the "opiate of the masses," was, of course, destroyed.

Not long after her healing, Sister Akulina asked to be relieved of her vows, feeling that the quiet convent life did not afford her sufficient opportunity for expressing her gratitude to the Lord. She determined to go out into the world and devote her life to caring for the sick and the needy, and had been happily engaged in her work, which she saw as both an atonement for earlier sins and a service to God, when she learned that Rasputin, her healer, had come to St. Petersburg, and felt an overwhelming desire to be with him. He was not difficult to locate, and upon discovering her identity, he welcomed her into his circle of devotees, his "court." It soon became obvious to all the members of that court that hers was more than a devotion of the spirit; Sister Akulina was, in fact, openly and unashamedly in love with her master, always taking a place at his feet and ever ready to serve him, running to fetch a glass of water or a piece of fruit, lovingly stroking his hand or kissing his cheek. And in recognition of this love, it was Akulina who was singled out by the Tsarina for the sad honor of bathing and laying out the corpse that had been my father, prior to its burial on the grounds of the Royal Palace at Tsarskoye Syelo.

The attempt of the Bolshyeviki to charge him with

*collective farms

148

having raped the young nun during the time he spent in her cell at the Convent of St. Piton, healing her and exorcising the evil spirit that possessed her, was as ludicrous as most of the other charges leveled by the cold-blooded killers of the revolution. The abbess and another nun were present in the cell during the entire incident, as was the rule of the order; no man was ever permitted to be alone with a nun. But truth, according to the definitions of dialectic materialism, is that which serves the Communist cause, regardless of fact, and fact was never permitted to stand in the way of Communist "truth."

Although Akulina's love for the starets was never consummated, another member of the court was more successful. The lady in question was the wife of a minor nobleman, who had first given Papa lessons in reading and writing. Olga Vladimirovna Lokhtina was a rather pretty and provocative blonde, of no particular intellect, and rather shallow and self-centered. She became a part of the court more through her physical attraction to Papa than through any devotion to religion. However, he fended off all her efforts toward a liaison until one day, lingering behind while the others left, she asked if he would come to her house that evening to see her husband, who was ill, and unable to go out. Believing her story, he arrived at the Lokhtin door at the appointed time, only to be greeted by Olga Vladimirovna clad in a sheer peignoir. She hurried him into a small drawing room, and as he was about to ask for her husband, she dropped the single garment around her feet, and embraced him. Overcome by the unexpected assault, his resistance weakened by many months of celibacy, he yielded to her.

After her coup, since hers was an unstable nature, she went about preaching her new gospel; Rasputin was the Lord God of Hosts, and she was the reincarnation of the Holy Virgin. Papa ended the affair as quickly as she had begun it, and pleaded with her to stop broadcasting her ridiculous statements, but even when he commanded her in the strongest terms possible, she continued promulgating her doctrine. At last, his patience worn thin, he banned her from the court. At this, she flew to Iliodor, her worst possible choice for a confessor, since he had conceived his own desire for her some months earlier, in spite of his protestations of celibacy.

Throwing herself at Iliodor's feet, the distraught young woman acknowledged her transgression and pleaded for his help in overcoming her unrequited passion. If she had looked into his eyes at that moment, she would have been horrified to see the naked hatred that had suddenly shone forth, but her gaze was lowered and she did not see. His enemy, in fact, had thrust upon him the prize that Iliodor had sought without success and then added coal to the fires of his abomination for the starets. And then he laughed to himself; so Rasputin has called him a hypocrite. Well, who was the hypocrite now? He did not stop to consider that he, and not the starets, had lusted after the girl, and that the affair had come about as the result of entrapment—a well-planned ruse—and not of his seeking.

Motivated by what must have been a confused mixture of emotions, he suddenly seized the girl and began an attempt to force himself upon her, and as she tried to protect herself, she screamed. All at once there were footsteps in the hall outside the cell door, a clamor of excited voices, and the door was flung open. Iliodor threw Olga Vladimirovna from him into the arms of the first monk to enter, and assuming an outraged look, informed them that she had tried to lure him into violating his vows.

Dragging the terrified and screaming woman out into the courtyard, the monks tore off her clothing and whipped her. And then, as had been done to the woman in Siberia, they tied her to a horse and sent it on its way out into the countryside. After being dragged for some distance, she was found by some farm people who cut her free and took her badly torn and bleeding body in. They cared for her and sent for a doctor who treated her wounds until she recovered, but her recovery was only physical, her mind having been shattered by the dreadful experience.

Learning of the vicious subterfuge employed by Iliodor to shift the blame for his actions onto the sorely scarred shoulders of the misguided Olga Vladimirovna, Papa was outraged, and he vowed to see that justice was done. He took his complaint to the Holy Synod, but sufficient time had elapsed for Iliodor, realizing his vulnerability, to go to see Episkop Hermogen with a charge against Papa. Unfortunately, Hermogen had undergone a change of heart, due to Papa's discovery of a shortage in the funds of the Union of True Russian Men, and had insisted on having a full hearing even though the bishop had tried to quiet the scandal. The result was the finding of two of Hermogen's friends guilty of embezzlement, and the bishop had never been able to forgive his former friend. Still smoldering over this incident, Hermogen had been more than ready to listen to Iliodor's complaints and made little effort to verify them.

A hearing was held in the episkop's monastery at Saratov, and Papa found himself ringed about by hostile faces, including those of Iliodor and his protégé, Mitia Koliava, the dwarf prophet; Hermogen, of course; and two men he did not know.

Hermogen took his seat at a table facing the others in the room. He said, "Grigori Efimovich Rasputin, you are charged with serious offenses of the flesh by our Reverend Brother. He has told me of your many sinful acts, acts which you have not denied."

"But, Your Reverence," he protested, "it is not I, but the archimandrite, who is charged with an offense."

"*Tishye!** I will tell you when to speak. Remember your station; you are only a muzhik."

Thus rebuked, he became quiet and awaited Iliodor's attack, which was not long in coming.

"This man, Your Reverence, this upstart is a known lecher. Using his power over women, he has seduced I do not know how many of them. One of his poor victims came to me, seeking my assistance, and she told me that the accused mesmerized her and that she was powerless to resist him. And then, the poor demented creature tried to seduce me, me of all people. Of course, I had her sent away to an asylum, but I fear her mind is gone beyond all hope."

Thoroughly outraged by Iliodor's twisted assault, my father arose: "Your Reverence!" And as the bishop started to interrupt, he continued, "No, I will be heard. Iliodor has told you a pack of lies."

But that was as far as he could go, for Iliodor gave an almost imperceptible signal to the two anonymous men, and

*silence

they came up behind the starets and forced him back into his chair. Before my father could gather himself to renew his defense, Iliodor began to speak in the stentorian tones that had brought him fame as a preacher.

"Behold this man, Your Reverence. He is afraid to let me speak. He knows that my truthful words will condemn him. Although the unfortunate woman had her mental breakdown in my cell, his was the sin that brought it on. His is the guilt, and to him must be meted the punishment."

As the others nodded in agreement, Hermogen turned a stern gaze upon the accused. "How can you answer this just accusation, when it must be obvious, even to one so steeped in sin as yourself, that the archimandrite's words are true?"

So invited, my father rose to speak in his own defense. "I can show you that he has told you nothing but lies, trying to place the yoke of his own foul deeds upon my shoulders. Who was it, he or I, who had Olga Vladimirovna whipped and dragged through the streets tied to a horse? And yet he claims that I drove her mad. But if her madness was of my doing, why did he order so brutal a punishment for her? If she was mad when she entered his cell, he should have provided care and treatment for her. But if she was not mad when she entered his cell . . ."

But Iliodor was not about to permit such damning evidence to be pursued, and he leaped up, shouting, "The muzhik lies. Anyone can see that he lies; it is written all over his face. Enough of this; seize him and let his punishment be carried out."

Already on his feet, my father turned to see the two strange men advancing upon him. Taking up the chair upon which he had been sitting, he swung it in an arc around him, causing the pair to step back in surprise. As they came on again, he swung once more, and when they stopped, he ran toward the door. Safely below the menacing chair, the dwarf Mitia ran in and wrapped his arms about my father's legs, but Papa was too sure of foot, and kicking backward, he dislodged the little prophet, sending him flying halfway across the room. With nothing to stop him, Papa got to the door, pushed it outward, and slammed it shut behind him, just as they all came up

152

to force it open. But in the moment before the conspirators were able to mass their full strength, he had time to wedge the chair under the doorknob, thus effectively locking them in for at least a little while, time enough for him to get free of the monastery grounds. However, far from feeling exhilarated by his escape, he was saddened to learn of the bitterness of his enemies, a bitterness that would drive them to such lengths, even to perjuring themselves, to bring him down.

The plotters, foiled in their first attempt, retired to plan their future course of action, and Papa was left to pursue his usual activities in peace. But not so the Tsarina. When she heard of the disgraceful incident, as she did from the indignant lips of Anna Aleksandrovna Virubova, her immediate reaction was to summon all parties, accusers and accused, to appear before the Tsar. In this far more equitable court, it soon became obvious who was telling the truth and who had lied. But the evidence was not easily come by at the outset, for Papa was loath to testify against such eminent churchmen, and such recent friends.

Finally, the Tsar, his patience worn thin, addressed the starets: "Grigori Efimovich, I want no more of this equivocation. I order you to tell me what you know of this affair, and everything that you know."

So commanded by his beloved sovereign, he recounted the whole sordid tale, while the two churchmen fretted at the restraint under which they were forced to await their turns to speak. At last, the truth was out, and when he had finished, the Tsar turned to Iliodor.

"What have you to say? Can you deny the account we have just heard? But, before you deny it, be warned. Agents of this court are gathering evidence. They have already spoken to the people who took the unfortunate Olga Vladimirovna Lokhtina in, the doctor who has her in his care, and others. Now speak!"

Thus confronted, Iliodor was for once at a loss for words. The smooth tongue was still, and there was silence throughout the room for a long moment.

"Iliodor," the Tsar finally said, "have you nothing to say in your own defense?"

The monk glanced furtively about him, like a trapped

animal seeking a way of escape. But there was no escape from the trap he had set for himself, and at last, speaking with a humility born of fear, he pleaded, "Have mercy, Little Father, have mercy on me."

And Hermogen echoed, "Have mercy, Little Father."

The Tsar stood, and his Tsarina stood beside him, as he pronounced his sentence: "You, Iliodor, and you, Hermogen, are herewith banished from this court and from this city. You are to retire to monasteries of your choices, at a distance of not less than one hundred versts from St. Petersburg, and there you are to live out your lives. Tak i bit."

The two disgraced churchmen stumbled from the room taking their first steps on the road to exile, and Papa went forward to thank the Tsar for his decision. The Tsarina turned to her husband with a smile.

"I think," she said, "that we should invite Otyets Grigori to join us for dinner. Do you not agree?"

The Tsar's face lit up. "Yes, yes, of course, dear Aliks. Tonight, I have to entertain several of the ambassadors, but tomorrow night I am free. Would that suit you?"

Papa laughed. "You know, Little Father, that my time, as well as my prayers, is at your service."

"Tomorrow night, then. And bring the little one."

When Papa told me that we were going to the Royal Palace for dinner, I was so excited I could hardly speak. While he had been there many times, and I had been there with him, this was to be my first dinner with royalty. Immediately, everything was in confusion. I had nothing to wear. How did one act at the palace? Would they like me? What would I say to the Tsar and Tsarina? How would I get along with the royal children? A million questions ran racing through my head, but there were not a million answers to go with them. Fortunately, Dunia, who was always poised, took me under her wing. A very suitable dress was brought out; my hair was brushed and combed until I felt like a horse being curried; I was scrubbed till I feared there would be no skin left to cover my bones. And then we were ready. A footman in royal livery knocked at the door; the carriage was waiting below, and we were off to Tsarskoye Syelo.

The imperial family lived at the Aleksandr Dvoryets,* which was built by Ekaterina Vyelikaya† for her grandson Aleksandr I, preferring its more moderate size to that of the Great Palace, which was used only for state dinners and receptions. We were driven to the palace in a drozhki which bore the royal crest on either side. The coachman and footman wore the blue velvet livery of the Romanovs, and sat with such stiff dignity that one might have supposed they were aristocrats in their own right. We swept up the driveway to the palace through wrought-iron gates, past sentries of the Royal Guard, and arrived at the great entrance in regal style. A footman sprang forward to open the drozhki door and help us alight, and another swung open the door, while two others stood by to help us off with our coats and hats. From that point, a page took over and conducted us down a hall paneled in mahogany to a reception room into which he ushered us. Rising to receive us was the Tsar of all the Russias, the Tsarina and their five children. As Papa embraced first the Tsar and then the Tsarina in his familiar style, I could not help thinking that she was one of the most beautiful and gracious women I had ever seen. Of course, I was overwhelmed at standing in the presence of such, as it seemed to me, almost godlike personages. But the warmth which they displayed in responding to my curtsy, a curtsy that Dunia had made me practice for hours, soon put me at my ease. In fact, the Tsarina caught me in mid-curtsy and embraced me and gave me a most motherly kiss. Then I was introduced to the tsarevich and the young grand duchesses, who left off crowding about Papa and hugging him and made me at once feel as though I were part of their family. They drew me to a small *zakuski* table laden with caviar, both black and red, prawns, anchovies, herring, *bitki*‡ and bottles of vodka and wine. The grand duchesses stood to one side, waiting politely

*Alexander Palace
†Catherine the Great
‡small meatballs

155

for their parents and guests to serve themselves first, but Aleksei, with an impudent grin, picked up a bitki by the toothpick upon which it had been impaled and popped it into his mouth. The Tsar shook his head in mock reproof, and sighed.

"After I am gone, Russia will be ruled by a Tsar who will go down in history as Aleksandr Uzhasniye."[*]

The royal children wanted to know all about me, where I went to school, what I did in my spare time, and what it was like to be the daughter of so great a man. It was difficult at first to realize they were talking about my father, for to my young mind, he was just my father, loving and kind, wonderful at healing bruises and sprains, but then weren't all fathers like that? As we talked, I had an opportunity of examining the room with its walls of rose damask, its furniture of some light-colored wood that I later learned was maple, paintings and photographs hung all about, and a handsome sort of cabinet whose top was a recess in which stood a large crucifix. But my inspection of the room could not be too thorough, because the grand duchesses spoke over each other in their inquiries. I found myself drawn most closely to the one nearest my own age, and strangely enough, with my own name, the Grand Duchess Maria, and we were to become fast friends.

At last, our conversation was interrupted by the butler, who announced that dinner was served. We moved into the large dining room, with long windows hung with red velvet draperies trimmed in gold braid. The pile of the rug was so deep that I almost tripped when my heels caught in it. The table was covered by a fine damask tablecloth, upon which were plates of golden china bearing the royal crest, and at each place there were three goblets also crested in gold. Almost everything, the linen napkins, the knives and forks, and the silver serving trays, were marked with that crest. Behind each of the red velour chairs was a footman resplendent in blue livery and wearing white gloves. At each side of every plate there were crystal racks to hold the various knives, forks, and spoons, and something Dunia had failed to mention was that if one was not finished with a dish, but merely wanted to lay one of these implements down, one was supposed to return it to its rack.

[*]Alexander the Terrible

Unfortunately, after taking two bites of the salad, I laid my fork down on the plate and the salad was promptly whisked away by the footman behind my chair. It is likely that I would have starved if the Tsarina had not noticed my plight.

"Was the salad not to your taste?" she asked.

"Oh, yes, Your Highness, it was delicious, but the waiter took it away."

"Ah, yes, I see. You placed your fork on your plate, which is a sign that you have finished."

And then she told me about using the racks, and I was able to eat my fill of the rest of that delicious dinner. I also learned that the man behind my chair was not a "waiter," but a footman, and so, in no time at all, I was an initiate in the way of royal eating. After the meal ended with servings of a wonderful home-made ice cream, we retired to the drawing room. I later secured the recipe for the ice cream, and it will also appear in a book of Russian recipes I am working on. Here it is:

ICE CREAM ROMANOV

2½ pounds sugar
10 egg yolks
1 quart light cream
1 large vanilla bean
½ pint whipping cream

Beat sugar and egg yolks in a saucepan until the mixture is ribbonlike in consistency when swirled from a spoon. In another pan, combine the light cream and vanilla bean and bring to a low boil for a few minutes, stirring constantly. Add a little of the cream to the egg mixture, stir, and continue to add a little at a time, until all of it has been stirred in. Continue to stir over a moderate flame until the mixture coats the spoon, but do not allow to boil. Strain the mixture into a large bowl and stir occasion-

ally until it has congealed. Whip the whipping cream lightly and fold into the mixture. Place in the freezer until ready to serve. NOTE: For a smoother texture, after the ice cream has been frozen, remove it from the freezer, spoon it into a bowl, beat it thoroughly, and return to the freezer. The more times this is done, the smoother the ice cream will be.

Other Flavors
Any flavor of ice cream can be made by substituting chocolate or any fruit for the vanilla bean. However, in making chocolate ice cream, it is desirable to use about half of the vanilla bean in addition to the chocolate. In making any of the fruit flavors, substitute ½ pint of the fruit juice for an equal amount of the cream.

In the drawing room, a huge silver samovar, also bearing the royal insignia, was wheeled in on a cart. The very strong tea from the little pot at the top of the samovar was ready, a few drops of that dark brew were poured into each cup, the rest of it being filled with hot water from the samovar, and we sat down to the cozy hour that Russians love so well, when the talk is good and hearts are warm. Between carrying on a conversation with the royal children and trying to listen to what the grown-ups were saying, I was kept pretty busy. The Tsar never mentioned Iliodor.

Papa could not stand the total omission of the incident. He said to the Tsar, "Mark my words, we will be hearing more from Syergyei Trufanov. It is not his nature to remain behind walls of an ancient monastery while the world turns outside."

When we left we were kissed by each member of the Royal family, and Maria put her arm around my waist as we walked to the door. We were helped into the drozhki, and they all stayed in the doorway to wave good-bye to us as we started down the drive.

I babbled constantly all the way home and Papa must

have thought how silly children are. But Dunia didn't. I stayed up half the night reliving the event for her benefit. She wanted to know the seating arrangements, what kind of silver and crystal, and her eyes grew large when I described the lavishness of the palace. It had been my first royal dinner, and the many dinners that would follow would never shine in my memory as bright as the first one. The war would rage, the palace would fall, and everything would pale by comparison to that happy occasion.

Papa's vision that night was of the future and oh, how right he was. Hermogen, old and beaten now, obeyed his ruler and retired permanently to a monastery to study and perhaps to pray for remission of his sins. Iliodor, as Papa pointed out, could not long be contained. He went through the motions of bowing out, leaving St. Petersburg where it was patently unsafe for him to operate. But it was not his nature to be silent for long.

He traveled about the country, speaking wherever anyone would listen to his venomous lies about Papa and the supposed or imagined orgies conducted in our home.

Country people are often ready to believe the worst about their government. It takes their minds off their own problems, failing crops, floods, drought, etc. So, when Iliodor told the populace that Papa was sleeping with many noble-women—even the Tsarina—they ate it up like borscht. Those opposed to the Romanov regime could not have concocted a better minister of propaganda for their cause. Iliodor led the pack, however naïvely as to purpose, in the bringing down of the Russian Empire.

Russia was like a woman in labor. There was too much pain to pay attention to rabble-rousers like Iliodor; consequently he was able to spread venom about the countryside. And as he continued to go about unmolested by any authority, he became braver and more confident in his position. He was now beginning to believe himself totally invulnerable. His lies, therefore, grew in proportion.

He was able to convince a large part of the country that there was unbridled immorality throughout the capital city and that the palace, even, had become nothing more than an aristocratic whorehouse.

I can recall one evening that Papa and I spent with

the Tsar and his Empress. Papa was not unaware of the forces against him. As long as they were only exerted toward him, he did not give a piffle. "No man," he once said, "is physically capable of performing all that I am accused of in one day—not in a year—not in a lifetime. Any fool can see that."

I sat on the floor on a large silken pillow at the feet of the Mama for all of Mother Russia—my Empress. As Papa and the Tsar discoursed on events of the day, the Tsarina caressed my tresses. I felt so comfortable, knowing that such a wonderful woman loved me—and she did. She was constantly after Papa to let me come and live at the palace. "Reverend Father," she would say, "she is like my own daughter. My children adore her—especially Maria. It is like fate brought our families together. It was destined to be—so why not allow her to live here with us—let me mother her while you go about your important work."

Papa always threw his head back and roared. Perhaps not the most social thing to do in the presence of royalty, but he was no respecter of station. "My dear child," he said to the Tsarina, his eyes wide and twinkling and filled with humor, "without this one"—he motioned to me—'by my side, I would be only half a person. Remember, my family is miles from here." Papa's smile vanished when he spoke of Mama and home.

I had been in St. Petersburg for quite some time before I found out why there was such a gulf between Papa and my mother. Mother seldom burdened me with her problems. On the farm Mitia was always out of the house doing the men's work that was necessary to maintain things just as father and his father before him had done. My sister was too young for Mama to confide in—and I just had too much to do, helping her, to be further encumbered. Consequently it was Dunia who finally told me what had happened when Papa brought my mother to St. Petersburg for surgery. A tumor and its complications brought about the removal of the tumor, and a complete hysterectomy was performed.

Afterward, my mother, being of the old school which felt sexual relations had one purpose—procreation—confronted Papa with the facts of life. "You are a man of God," she told him. "Go. Do what you have to do. I can no longer give you children, and perhaps that is a sign from God that you should abstain from such things. During my stay in the hospital and on the return trip, I have seen how revered you are. I have seen the power you have over people. It is a sacred trust. One you must fulfill. You have already given of the flesh—now you are destined to a spiritual life."

Dunia told me that Papa protested, but only because of his great concern for his family. Papa was always a family man first.

But it troubled him. It was our custom, if I was awake when Papa got up in the mornings, to have some time together. He arose about six and I tried to wake up in order to spend that precious time alone with him where I would read from the Bible as he had his meager meal and we would discuss home and the farm, my school progress, and, of course, a certain amount of childish gossip.

Shortly after our visit to the palace, we had such a time together and it was then I learned I would be without Papa for quite some time.

"You know, Maria, that the Tsar spoke privately with me for some time when we were at the palace."

"Yes, Papa." I had wondered what went on, but I thought it was some matter of state and that was one place I didn't try to pry. The royal family constantly called Papa in to ask about such things and sometimes he would tell me what was asked, often humorously because some of the things they asked, he told me, could have been figured out by a small child.

This was different. "The problem with Iliodor and Hermogen is causing some embarrassment to the Tsar."

I could hardly understand why. It had been a clear-cut case of conspiracy against my father. "But Papa, why should that be? It was proven to everyone's satisfaction that you were innocent."

"Ah, my child, you do not understand politics. And it is political."

I did not understand and looked askance.

"You see, the Tsar banished both Iliodor and

Hermogen, and that, on the surface, should have been the end to the matter. But no, Iliodor cannot be quiet. He is spreading his venom and malicious lies about the countryside. Russia today is in a turmoil. You do not see it because it has not surfaced, but unless there are some changes it will come to the top like a deal fish and stink up the place.

"The Tsar must show some sign that he takes a certain amount of heed to the stories being spread about me—and his court—by a disgruntled priest. Therefore I am to take a journey away from the capital for a while."

I felt the tears rising, and a lump formed in my throat. I knew from the tone of his voice that I was not included in his plans.

Papa tried to spare me the real reason for his own banishment from court. Dunia related the most pressing reason for Papa's trip out of the country after he had departed for a pilgrimage to the Holy Land amid much sobbing on my part (and Dunia's) and an equal amount of consolation from Papa.

Papa boarded a train for the Crimea where he would transfer to a ship to complete his journey. Dunia and I departed the same day for Pokrovskoye and a long visit with Mama.

During our journey, Dunia, who could not contain what was in her heart, revealed the entire story to me as Papa had told her and what she had seen for herself. She was a very loyal and faithful woman who loved Papa with all her heart.

Iliodor was not alone in his endeavors to destroy the House of Romanov; there were others, powerful men whose financial interests gave them overwhelming power; men with no real love for Russia, except to further their own powerful financial base. Shrewd men, they thought they saw in my father, knowing his opposition to their plans, someone they could buy off with bribes and power. But they understood nothing about the man. He had all the power he would ever need—and power was not his goal. They found him incorrupt-ible and were driven to seeking other ways of rendering him harmless to their cause.

So Papa was the target of both Left and Right, since he maintained a middle-of-the-road stance politically.

Once the news of Iliodor's banishment reached them, they made quick to use him for their own purposes.

From Iliodor they learned more of Papa's habits and

movements. They had plotted before but without any success. This time their plan was to be more elaborate. It was no secret that Papa liked to visit the Villa Rodye, with its resident band of Gypsy singers and dancers, where he could relax away from his work and even join in the dancing.

Being of a gregarious nature, he soon became part of a circle of friends who were also habitués of the place.

Into this circle, there came one night a former ballerina named Lisa Tansin. She was a Finnish woman who was teaching in a ballet school. It was not difficult to get next to my father, and she engaged him in conversation about his love for dancing. It was an equally simple matter to challenge him to dance with her—because he loved dancing and could not resist a challenge. He found her an altogether delightful dance partner, her fine sense of rhythm and lithe body inspiring him to perform at his best; and quickly the time passed.

Lisa Tansin first prevailed upon Papa to join her and a few friends at her house where she challenged him to toast her in vodka. After several such toasts, he was quite drunk, having imbibed throughout the evening at the Villa Rodye.

The party turned into an orgy, so Papa told Dunia afterward. He was caught up in the festivities. In the midst of it all, somebody took a series of photographs, showing Papa surrounded by a bevy of enticing nude women—a fallen saint shown in the act of falling.

Much later that night—actually just before dawn—two sturdy fellows delivered Papa to our doorstep, bawling out at the tops of their lungs, so all the neighbors were sure to hear, the bawdiest of songs and the raciest of anecdotes.

They banged loudly on the door, and Dunia answered the knock and took charge of Papa, slamming the door in the face of Papa's escorts.

Whatever damage they had intended was done.

Dunia's first concern was that I should not be awakened to discover my father in such a drunken condition. She did her best, she said, to calm him. I had already been awakened by the shouting and loud knocking at the door. However, I had stayed up late the night before and soon drifted back to sleep.

Dunia managed to get him into his bedroom and began the task of getting him ready for bed. As she was removing his clothing he looked at her quizzically, as though trying to focus on the woman who was now taking liberties with him. And, at last, he saw who it was.

"Dunia," he asked, "what are you trying to do to me?"

"Hush! I'm only getting you ready for bed. Don't make a sound or you'll wake Maria."

"Oh, yes," he nodded groggily. "Mustn't wake Maria."

It was inevitable now. Papa was still tipsy, most of his clothes had been removed, Dunia was in her nightgown; they were together in his bedroom. He suddenly lunged toward her, took her in his arms, and pulled her down onto the bed. With any other man, she told me, she would have struggled to free herself. But not Papa.

"I had loved your Papa for such a long time. It was because of that love that I left the Kubasovs to work for him. So I submitted, gladly."

From that night on until the end of his life, she was his mistress. I loved her as a mother and found the new liaison delightful.

Her concern now was that my sister Varya, who would be coming to live with us, should not learn of the relationship, and it was so successfully concealed during the remaining years that it came as a tremendous shock to Varya when she finally learned about it after Papa's death.

However, a few days after Papa's night on the town, while he was entertaining the ladies of his court around the long dining-room table, a man came to the door of the flat. Upon admittance, he handed a small package to Papa, who opened it, presuming it to be one of the many gifts of money that were constantly coming to him by messenger. But he took one brief look at the contents and quickly closed it.

Dunia explained what was in the package. "Your father was stunned to find a set of photographs that had been taken while he was indulging himself with Lisa Tansin and her friends, and although he had been in the center of the activity, he had not been aware that such events were taking place for the benefit of a camera."

His guests—mostly ladies—noticing his seriousness,

164

looked at him quizzically, wondering what could cause such a pleasant session to turn so solemn.

Papa, without explanation, excused himself and locked himself in his bedroom, together with his male messenger.

"I sensed something was wrong," Dunia said, "and so I stationed myself at the entrance of the hallway to prevent anyone who might be curious from intruding while the two men talked. Their conference was brief."

I remembered the day because I came into the room to replenish some food and saw the two of them come out of Papa's bedroom. The man left quickly and Papa was grim as he resumed his seat in the circle, but I never questioned Papa about anything in the presence of company. It was absolutely forbidden.

That night, after I was fast asleep, Dunia confronted Papa about the incident.

"He seemed almost glad that I asked," she later told me. "I could see it was a great burden on his shoulders."

"What was that all about?" she asked him.

Papa, slumping down in his chair, told her there were some photographs of an obscene nature.

"Let me see them," she demanded, already trying to think of a way out.

"But Dunia, they are not fit for your eyes."

"What can you show me that I have not already seen?" she said, challenging him. "Let me be the judge of whether they are fit or not."

Papa resisted. "Oh, no. They are much too horrible."

"Grischa," she said, her patience thinning, "be sensible; how can I help you if I do not know what is at stake?"

His resistance broke down completely when she put the question to him: "Have I not earned the right to share in your problems?"

Silently he passed the package to her, and hung his head as she examined the explicit photographs.

"So that is what you were doing all night. A trollop— but a pretty trollop." Quickly compensating for her jealous instinct, she said, "But of course you were drunk."

As miserable as he was feeling, he was amazed at

Dunia's commonsense attitude. He would perhaps have expected it if their relationship had been as it had before. But now that she was his mistress he expected her to be outraged.

"Inside I was laughing at his frustration," she told me. "I told him not to expect me to feign a gasp as most of the women at court would have done. I was made of sturdier stuff and he might as well accept that. I wanted to get right to the point because it was obvious we must devise some plan to counter this covert operation."

"So now," she asked him, "what is it that they—whoever 'they' are—want?" With some humor she asked, "I'm sure they don't want you to paste these in your family album—or do they?"

"The man said I have but two choices: I must leave St. Petersburg forever, or these will be shown to the royal family."

Dunia observed her lover for a long minute. What had happened to him? He had been so strong, so vibrant, so much the master of every situation; a giant, unafraid of any man, perhaps even of the dyavol himself. And now he had lost all confidence in himself; he seemed to be crumbling before her very eyes. And she knew, as if some heretofore hidden font of wisdom had begun to flow through her mind, that she had to do something to restore that confidence, or he would be destroyed; and not only he, but his mission. God's work must be done, and Grischa was the one He had chosen to do it.

"Grischa, *lyubovnik,** look at me. No, don't turn away. Yours is not to be a life of shame, but to be sure that it will not, you must act."

"But what can I do? Either I leave St. Petersburg voluntarily, or the Tsar will banish me when he sees these pictures."

"If you do as your enemies wish, your life's work, the work given you by God, will be finished. But there is still a third way—if you have the stomach for it."

"I do not have much stomach left, my Dunia," he smiled ruefully.

But she would hear none of that. Her Grischa was a

*lover

166

hero, larger than life. He could do it; he must do it. And she explained what she had in mind.

"There is a story my father used to tell, of a woodcutter who was coming home from the forest one night, when he was seen by a wolf. Now this wolf had been driven out by the pack, for one reason or another, and he had been hunting alone, and because he was alone, without the pack to help him, his hunting had produced very little in the way of meat. But here was a lone man who should prove easy prey, and so the wolf began sneaking up behind the man, hoping to bring him down with one surprise leap. But just as he was preparing to spring, the woodcutter saw the wolf's shadow, for the moon was low in the sky behind him. The man was frightened, you may be sure of that, but he knew that if he tried to run, the wolf would have him in the time he could take two steps, and so his only hope was to use his wits. He turned suddenly upon the wolf with a terrible roar, and curving his hands so that in the dim moonlight they would look like claws, he made as if he wanted to catch and eat the wolf. The dismayed wolf yelped in terror and, tucking his tail between his legs, he ran off howling for mercy.

"Sometimes, *balovyen*,* one must turn on his attackers, and by facing them with a show of strength, he may force them to run away. Do not yield to their demands, but attack."

"Yes, you are right." His back was straighter now. "Of course, I don't know who these people are, so I cannot attack them. But I can move first; I can go to the Tsar with these pictures, and show them to him. I believe the Little Father will be sympathetic. If he is not, well, that will be God's will."

"Now, there's the Grischa I know. The Tsar will understand that they are only trying to hurt him through you."

With confidence renewed, he went to see the Tsar, taking a drozhki to Tsarskoye Syelo. Telling a footman that he wanted to see the Tsar privately, he was soon admitted to the study. As soon as the door was closed, he told Nikolas what had occurred at Lisa's house, and as he finished, he laid the package of obscene photographs on the handsomely carved

*darling

167

desk. The Tsar looked closely at each of the pictures, a frown creasing his usually smooth brow, and at last fixed Papa with a perplexed gaze, shaking his head sadly.

"You did well to bring these to me, instead of waiting for these people to send them. They might even have given them to Aliks, and I am afraid the shock would have been too much for her. It is easy to see that they are using you as a pawn in their filthy game, in order to weaken my position and to destroy the Romanov line. You have been foolish, very foolish, but, no doubt, the temptation was great. Well, no damage has been done, but they will try again."

The Tsar thought for a moment, and then went on: "You have mentioned your desire to make a pilgrimage to the Holy Land. I think this would be a good time for it. I will, of course, give you the journey as a token of our esteem. The Lord knows you have earned it through your many services to the crown."

Within a week it was done. Papa's affairs were wound up, Dunia and myself were packed aboard the train to Siberia, and Papa was off to the Holy Land.

As the broad plains passed in panoramic beauty through the windows of the train, I thought how much I loved my father and nestled close to Dunia, resting my head on her shoulder, thankful that he had chosen such a wise and sage lady to be his mistress.

✖TWELVE✖

As much as he had dreamed of this pilgrimage and the opportunity it afforded him of walking upon the sacred soil the Khristos had trod, the reality was not measuring up to his expectations. It was not the fault of Jerusalem, for the Holy City was much as he had envisioned it from the engravings and paintings he had seen. But his heart was heavy, and the burden proved most difficult to bear. How could he have been so weak as to have fallen into the trap set for him by the Little Father's enemies? True, the temptation had been great, yet each step leading toward the denouement had been so gradual and so well camouflaged that he had not realized where that path was leading. However, that was no excuse. A man of purity cannot be tempted beyond his power to resist, and for all his prayers and meditations and visions, he was not pure. His every instinct called for him to lay the blame at the door of Lisa and her employers, but he would not permit himself to yield to such an obvious attempt at avoiding his responsibility. He had sinned;

with his eyes wide open, if somewhat blurred by drink, he had sinned, and until God saw fit to forgive him, a sinner he would remain.

He roamed the streets and the narrow cluttered byways of the Holy City under a blazing sun, visiting the sacred and historic places, the Church of the Holy Sepulcher, the Via Dolorosa, the Pool of Siloam; he mourned the Khristos at Golgotha, but it was in the Garden of Gethsemane that all his defenses were finally swept away. There had been a residual clinging to his own self, the "I" that it is a part of our natures to defend, even against the onset of illumination, but a combination of strict fasting and other forms of penitence, and an increased awareness of those gifts that had been so casually thrown away, brought him to the lowest point of despair he had ever known. He had lost his powers of healing and prophecy, and he acknowledged the justice of his punishment. He had earned every strike the Lord had laid upon his flesh, earned them by engaging in vile practices, and worst of all, earned them by forgetting God. He who had received such blessings, enough to have sanctified any man, had turned his back upon his Benefactor, as though those gifts and visions had been mere playthings. Oh, he had stood in the midst of corruption, but what excuse was that for entering into corruption? And he shed bitter tears of remorse, his soul stripped bare of its successive layers of armor, until it stood alone, where his Lord has stood, in the garden where his Lord had prayed for his persecutors. He who was not fit to pray even for forgiveness, or so he felt at that moment, could only weep for grief and shame, and with a love for the Khristos whom he had betrayed.

And, as he told it, of a sudden he looked downward, surprised to find he was no longer standing upon that hallowed ground, but had risen a little and was watching the corpse of a man stretched out as if in death. What was even more astonishing was that the corpse seemed to bear an uncanny resemblance to himself. He felt a certain lightness, as though he were disembodied, and looking at his hand, found there was no hand to see. Had he died, then? It appeared so, except that he was still somehow connected to that quiet body, and the invisible cord that held him to it was beginning to draw him back. His first thought was that he did not want to return, and he tried to pray that his release might be permanent. But even as he formulated the words of that prayer, he knew that it must not be uttered. And he prayed, as his Lord had prayed on this very spot: "Not my will, but thine be done."

And then, he was back in his body, but its weight was such that he could not rise. There was something wrong; he was ill, very ill. He, who had never suffered any ailment except as the result of an injury, was too weak to rise. His whole body felt hot, and there was no strength in his muscles. After a time, he was able to stagger to his feet, but would have fallen again had not a small group of pilgrims noticed him and half supported, half carried him down to the city. They took him to an inn, and put him to bed, and there he lay with a raging fever, he knew not how long.

In his more lucid moments, he knew he was on the ragged edge of death. At times he would slip out of his body and watch the lifeless shape sweating in the heat and from its own fever, and then he would slide back into that body and watch the fever-induced images flash before his eyes. They were all there: Irina Danilova and her servant girls; Natalya Petrovna, her nude form dragged by a horse; the hypocrite Iliodor and his minions; Praskovia Fedorovna, so loving and understanding; Olga Vladimirovna; and Lisa, wooing him, mocking him, pinching his flesh with hot irons, bathing his head with boiling water; all of them talking to him, their words overlapping, so that he could not hear what they were saying. For a brief moment, he caught a glimpse of the Virgin of Kazan, but the others were between them, blocking his view, and in another moment she was gone, although he cried out to her. And he continued to cry for her, until sometime later—was it a day, or many days?—she came to him, and standing at the foot of his bed, smiled at him with sweet compassion. At the first sight of her, he slipped out of his febrile body, but she made the sign of the cross and indicated by a gesture that he was to return.

As she faded from view, he donned his body as a diver puts on the ungainly dress of his trade. The fever had broken, although he was still quite weak, but he knew it had

171

been God's will that he should resume his mission and he vowed that he would be true to his appointed task. And, suddenly, he was alive again, his spirit revived, and he took this as a sign that God had forgiven him. In a few days he was able to travel and anxious to return home. By the time his feet were planted on the decks of the outbound ship he felt as strong as ever. He gained even more inner strength when called upon to minister to a sick woman, a pilgrim, on board the ship. As he prayed over her, he felt the surge of healing power within his body and she was healed. All who witnessed the event called it a miracle, but Papa declined to take any credit. "It is God and God's will alone that cures the sick," he proclaimed.

His modesty brought about even more comment. Surely, many said, he must be a saint.

"My friends," he said, "you know what is written in the Bible: 'It is not I, but the Father who is in me, He doeth the works.' I am no miracle-worker, but a humble servant of God. Give your thanks to Him; He has healed this woman."

Papa's return to St. Petersburg was triumphant at least at the palace, where the Empress embraced him and welcomed him back to the fold. "I have told them all," she confided to Papa, "that you have been maligned and they shall all pay for their misdeeds. I am certain God will not let them go unpunished. It is they who are in the clutches of the devil, not you."

Papa's trip to the Holy Land was ample proof of his holiness and dedication to God and God's work. He risked everything by leaving the country. It doesn't matter that the Tsar and Tsarina believed in him. Those were terrible times, and detractors were busy encouraging the throne to banish him forever. But, as the Empress told Papa, God works His way.

But Papa was not to be able to stay in St. Petersburg for the moment. The Prime Minister, Kokovtsov, saw Papa as a threat to his position. He was jealous of the "power over the throne" that my father was supposed to have had. Kokovtsov was indeed a dangerous adversary. He was no priest jealously jockeying for position in the realm—he was the number-one adviser to the Tsar and held in high esteem.

He had kept silent because he knew of the attachment the royal family had for Papa and did not want to displease the Tsar—or so he told the Grand Duchess Maria who, being the closest of the royal family to me, related in detail a conversation he had with the Tsar upon my father's return from his pilgrimage.

"Kokovtsov offered your father a fortune to leave St. Petersburg and never return," she later related as we walked on the palace grounds. "I have heard all sorts of figures. Some say close to a million rubles, but one cannot believe everything one hears these days."

I agreed. Gossip was rampant.

"Your father laughed in his face. I've never seen a man so angry as Kokovtsov—he's so stuffy anyway."

We both laughed.

"But I'm not sure your father should intimidate a man so close to Papa. It could be difficult in the future."

What had happened was that Papa made an enemy for life when he refused to take a bribe and laughed at Kokovtsov. Heretofore Kokovtsov had been reluctant to take his complaints directly to the Tsar, although I'm sure they filtered through to his ears—nothing was ever secret in the palace if you intended it to be a secret.

Maria, the grand duchess, related the meeting Kokovtsov had with her father.

She said, "I pretended to be busy with my needlework, but I listened closely."

The conversation seemed to have gone something like this:

"Your Majesty," Kokovtsov said, "this man is a charlatan and dangerous to your reign."

The Tsar brushed his seriousness aside. "Please, Kokovtsov, are you not forgetting the great service he has given to the throne?"

"If Your Majesty will allow me, may I ask what great service you are talking of? I know of the miraculous recovery of the crown prince, but even Rasputin declines to take credit for that. Even he says it was an act of God."

"Ah, yes, but why did God choose to act *through* Rasputin? Can you answer me that? Why did he not act through the other doctors with all their nostrums and herb teas?"

It was a question Kokovtsov could not answer and

was sorry he had brought up. If there was one way to lose his point, it was through the link between Aleksei and Papa. Neither the Tsar nor the Tsarina would bear any political chicanery that would come close to their beloved Aleksei.

He changed his tack. "But Your Majesty, the halls are filled with stories of his orgies and disgraceful conduct."

"Mere gossip. Do you believe in gossip, Kokovtsov? You, who have on my orders created gossip and rumors to confuse my enemies?"

"But this is different, Your Majesty. Even the newspapers call him a thief and swindler."

"Since when do you place importance on what is printed in the newspapers? Can you verify the charges? Can they?"

"No, that is true, but what the papers say cannot be discarded. It molds public opinion and public opinion is important to you and the realm."

Again the Tsar brushed aside his logic. "The public does not run the country. It is run for their benefit and best interests and I will be the one who decides what is best. What is best in my judgment is what is best for all—whether they know it or not."

The argument went on into the night, and the Tsar, fearing an open revolt in his own Cabinet, promised to send Rasputin away.

Papa took the decision as he took all decisions from the Tsar. Whatever the Tsar wanted, he would do. "I live to serve Your Majesty," he said, "and to bear you any pain or cause any reproach to come upon you because of the lies of my enemies would be the last thing in the world I would ever want."

"I know that," the Tsar said, as he placed his arm about Papa's shoulder.

Papa's face suddenly darkened. "Let me tell you something—a warning—there are dark forces about to do you no good. If I am away too long, I fear for the life of your son— even for the stability of the crown."

The Empress asked for and received Papa's blessing before he departed for home, and promised him his stay away from court would be short. "I will talk to the Tsar. He will listen

174

to me. It is your detractors who should be sent away. Not you, Little Father."

It was the fall of the year and winter was just around the corner. Papa came home to us in Pokrovskoye and the royal family prepared for their annual journey to Poland so the Tsar could indulge in one of his favorite sports—hunting the rare aurochs in the deep, dark forests.

It was a delight to have Papa back again. I had missed him so much. Even Mama seemed to have more color in her face, and everyone tried to make his visit a happy one.

He was soon his old self again, filled with confidence, unconcerned about the palace, the court, or his political enemies. Just a family man having a good time with his children.

I asked him when we would return to St. Petersburg.

"In due time, my child. In due time. But don't you enjoy being home with Mama and your brother and sister?"

"Oh, yes, I do, but I cannot understand why the Tsar would allow you to stay away for long."

He looked deeply into my eyes, his eyes so penetrating, so knowing—and at that moment I saw a certain sadness there. Then he spoke. "The Tsar has willed that I stay here until he sends for me. When I return is his and God's decision. Not mine."

But, in any event, here he would stay and here he would work, laboring in the Lord's vineyard.

Many gifts of money and jewels and other valuable objects had been showered upon him in St. Petersburg, and of these he kept only enough to maintain himself and his household. The rest he sent home to be used for the benefit of the village, to restore the crumbling church and to furnish it with a fine new ikona of the Virgin of Kazan. However, in spite of all he could do, he retained the enmity of Otyets Pyotr, whose jealousy was such that he continued to preach against the starets, hurling imprecations, like Jove's thunderbolts, down upon the head of his hated rival. But now that Papa was back in Pokrovskoye, the people who had filled the church during his absence began to drift away again, coming to listen to the teachings of their local saint. And he told them of the divine spark within each of them, housed in a body that God had created to serve as its temple. He told them it was the spark of life, but it could only be known through meditation. Once known, it would purify the knower and give him that knowledge that would make him master of himself and his destiny. It was, he told them, the only reason for existence; the man who did not realize his own soul, his own true nature, would have lived his life in vain. Only this knowledge had value; all the rest was dross. Whether wealth or power, it was as nothing compared with realization.

And as the people listened to him, they could see— some of them for the first time—that there was truly a divine purpose behind their lives. He told them to seek the Kingdom of God within themselves, in their own hearts, and not to look upward, as though heaven were in the sky. And they did look within, and if they did not find the precious knowledge, they did find a degree of peace.

Adjusting to the life of the village, and happy to be doing the Lord's work in such peaceful surroundings, Papa began to hope that he would never have to return to St. Petersburg, with its hustle and bustle, its corruption and venality, its self-serving men and libidinous women. But he could see the storm clouds gathering on the horizon. If they were permitted to grow and spread, he foresaw only sadness and misery ahead. But it was in God's hands; His plans would surely bear fruit, whether sweet or bitter.

In the meantime, he worked and preached, and sometimes he took us children fishing down by the river, as he had done so many years before with his long-dead brother, Mischa. And as we fished, he made good use of the time, questioning us on our *katekhisis** and telling us Bible stories. For a special treat he took the whole family and a few friends for a boat trip down the Tura, all the way to Tobolsk, and there we were able to view the relics of a revered saint, Ivan of Tobolsk, who had been a Metropolitan in the time of Pyotr Vyelikie. On most evenings friends would drop in and we would gather around the samovar, with Papa leading us in singing psalms. It was a happy time.

But fate intercedes where man's plans have been

*catechism

made. While vacationing with the royal family, the tsarevich fell and hit his knee against a rock. The inevitable happened—severe internal bleeding. Then, for some unknown reason, the bleeding seemed to stop. The Tsarina thanked God for his quick recovery. Later in the week she took him riding in a carriage, and the jolting about over the knobby roads brought on another bleeding spell. This time it did not subside.

He was in great pain and had to be carried to his room, his leg and groin swollen beyond comprehension, and the doctors were certain he would die. Some of the doctors shook their heads sadly while others made random diagnoses—blood poisoning, gangrene, etc. In any event, it was evident to those learned men that the tsarevitch had finally suffered a fatal accident.

On the afternoon of October 11, 1912, I was walking with Papa along the river. He suddenly clutched his heart and said, "Oh, no!"

It frightened me. I thought he was having an attack and we were alone, quite some distance from any help.

"What is it, Papa? What is it?"

Seeing the fright on my face, he shushed me. "It is not I, little one. Do not fear for me. It is the tsarevitch. He has been stricken."

There was no possible way for Papa to have known anything about the accident, since it didn't happen until the following day. But I did not question his vision, and that is what it seemed to be.

However, the next month we received the first bulletin in Siberia. Routine messages were not sent out to the villages, but something of so serious a consequence was posted immediately for all to read and offer up their prayers for the safety of the crown prince.

During the bedside vigil the Empress spoke Papa's name to Aleksei, and he said, "Please, Mama, please send for the Little Father. Please!"

It mattered not to the Empress that Papa had been banished. Therefore, she didn't even consult her husband when she sent the telegram to Papa.

We were just sitting down to our midday meal when the telegram arrived. Papa read it and at once left the table and knelt before the ikona of the Virgin of Kazan, praying fervently and with all his devotion.

Mama motioned us to silence, not wanting the slightest noise to distract him from his prayers. She even made a hand signal to Dunia not to clear the dishes away from the table. And so we were all frozen like statues in our places as Papa prayed, his face streaked with perspiration. Finally, he made the sign of the cross.

Rising from his altar, he immediately hurried down to the village, where he sent off the following wire to the Empress: "Have no fear. God has seen your tears and heard your prayers. Do not grieve; your son will live."

By the time Papa's telegram was delivered to the Empress, Aleksei's temperature had gone down, the pain had subsided, and he was sleeping soundly.

The physicians busily patted each other on their backs, claiming a delayed reaction to the drugs they had prescribed surely cured the tsarevitch.

It was a thin facade, however, because no one in the household doubted for a minute that a miracle had been brought about through Papa's prayers. From the Empress down, the name of Rasputin was whispered in reverence once the young prince showed definite improvement.

Papa's enemies had anticipated the reaction and were now dreaming up an explanation that would be palatable to those fringe-area doubters who were not certain who had helped the prince, but leaned a little toward Papa's prayers.

According to his enemies in the court, the tsarevich had been administered small doses of poison by Dr. Badmaev, Papa's friend and (next to the Empress) chief exponent in the palace. This, they claimed, was the cause of Aleksei's illness. Then, they implausibly suggested, Dr. Badmaev had left off the dosage when the Tsarina sent her telegram to Papa, thus permitting normal recovery. To their way of thinking it was indeed not a miracle, but the crushing of a diabolical plot.

Much later, after the Revolution, the pieces were put together by a special commission to investigate the incident. The facts were that Dr. Badmaev was in St. Petersburg at the time and had never been Aleksei's physician. It was the bumbling of Dr. Botkin that allowed the condition to go so far, and Botkin failed miserably to make a case against Papa or the miracle that happened. His hatred for Papa was well known, since Papa, a man without formal education, always seemed to succeed in healing where he failed.

At one of their last meetings, they had argued about the soul, and Botkin had said, with an air of having completely routed his opponent: "I have performed many autopsies over the years, but I have never located a soul."

To which Papa had replied, "And how many emotions or imaginations or memories have you located?"

Once the tsarevich was back on his feet, the royal family returned to St. Petersburg, but Aleksandra Feodorovna insisted on a straight answer to her question: Why was Rasputin still in Pokrovskoye? Always before, the Tsar had put her off with some remark as, "It has been considered best for all concerned." But this time, such an answer would not do, and so Nikolas Aleksandrovich, the Tsar of all the Russias, yielded to his wife's demand, and told her the story, excluding, of course, all mention of the orgy or the content of the photographs, but making it clear that his enemies were attempting to use the starets as a vehicle for their attack. This she could understand, and she accepted his explanation. But there was a consideration of greater importance. What if Aleksei should have another attack when Rasputin was beyond their reach? The Tsar could only agree; the tsarevich's life could not be risked, could not be made hostage to their enemies' treasonous attempts. And so, with some reluctance, he wrote to Papa, asking him to return to the capital. And this time, along with Dunia and me, Papa included Varya in our little St. Petersburg family, convincing Mama that she, too, would profit from an education in the big city. So off we went, Papa, Dunia, my younger sister, Varya, and myself.

No sooner had we arrived at the capital than the telephone rang in our flat at Number 64 Gorokhovaya Ulitsa. It was the Tsarina.

Although Papa preferred servants or Dunia to answer the phone, I was impetuous. I had to know who was calling. I answered the phone when the Empress called.

179

"Mama," I exclaimed excitedly, "I have missed you—we all have missed you." Some of my father's lack of decorum certainly seems to have asserted itself with me at a very tender age indeed.

"Maria! How wonderful to hear your voice. Is your father well? How nice to have him nearby where I can have benefit of his counsel." She went on and on and finally said, "Oh, yes, you must come to dinner—tonight. You and your father."

I explained that Varya was also with us.

"Bring her. By all means, bring her, too."

Papa, of course, was delighted that he was in such good graces again with the palace and that he would once again be consulted when all else seemed to fail.

Varya was as excited as I had been on my first dinner at the palace and I went on and on about it, naturally exaggerating for her benefit. Her eyes were like twinkling stars.

Dunia and I coached her with great enthusiasm as to what was and what was not proper protocol at court. Papa laughed and said, "Child, just be yourself. That is all that counts. Being yourself."

Once more, with regal elegance, the drozhki came for us. We enjoyed the ride out to Tsarskoye Syelo in the early winter twilight of an evening that was quite balmy for so late in the year. It was good to renew old acquaintanceships with the royal family, and I took great pride in introducing my twelve-year-old sister, who looked like a china doll that evening, to their Imperial Highnesses and my dear friends, the tsarevich and the grand duchesses. Varya and Anastasia, who were of an age, hit it off at once, as my namesake Maria and I had done. The royal children plied us with questions about what we had been doing since last we had met, and our happy babble continued all through dinner, interrupted only by Aleksei, who, because of his ill health, had been badly spoiled and could get away with all sorts of pranks. This night, he amused himself by flipping a few drops of his soup with a spoon at Anastasia, who cried out in resentment at this outrage. The tsarevich was gently reprimanded, and quiet was restored. As far as I was concerned, the good old days had returned in all their glory.

But my father knew that the good old days were not

back, and he feared that they never would be. He could see that the Tsar's policies for dealing with the nation's problems were hopelessly inadequate. If Nikolas had moved firmly in the direction of the new liberalism, there might have been opposition from the Right, but aligned with the moderate Left, and with the support of the workers, his rule would have been secure. Conversely, if he had rigidly suppressed the radical Left, he would have gained the support of some of the workers and peasants, the moderate conservatives, and perhaps the far Right, and this would have provided the necessary backing for his reign. But his policies, or lack thereof, leaning first to one side and then the other, infuriated both and left him without any strong faction at his back.

My father, who realized the urgency of reform, knew also that the restoration of law and order had to be the first item on the agenda, and that only after this had been achieved could reforms be instituted. He advised the Tsar to follow such a course, adding that it was essential for the imperial family to emerge from its protective isolation and appear before the people. Instinctively, he knew that if the Tsar and Tsarina were to let the people see them as decent individuals, rather than the monsters the revolutionary propagandists were painting them, their popularity would rise, and the crown made more secure. But the Tsarina, ever of delicate health, had built up a phobia about the risk of public exposure. Nikolas had once been the target of an assassin's attack, and she feared further attempts on his life. In her mind, safety existed only within the palace walls, surrounded by the Imperial Guards. In the world outside, there were savage beasts who were lying in wait, prepared to fall upon them and tear them to shreds. She could not bring herself to risk it; even her faith in Papa was not enough. When violence is on the rise, bold measures are necessary to maintain order. Neither Nikolas Aleksandrovich nor his beloved Aleksandra Feodorovna were capable of being so bold and aggressive.

Papa set about with plans to save the dynasty. He did not want the blood of the House of Romanov on his hands, nor did he wish to spend a lifetime feeling a sense of guilt from lack of action. He was sure God had sent him back to St. Petersburg on just such a mission.

Although the Tsar spent more and more time with

his generals and military advisers, the Empress spent more time covertly with Papa, seeking his guidance, information she could pass on to the Tsar—a word here, a phrase there. "He doesn't always listen to the things I tell him you have advised. But sometimes he overrules the generals with your good common sense. We mustn't give up the fight for peace, Little Father."

Papa sensed that time was short. Shorter for Russia than anyone else seemed to know or care about. So he threw himself into the quest for a quick peace with all the fervor he knew. Our flat became the nucleus of his activities in that direction and I had a feeling of exhilaration knowing that I was in the midst of history being made, rubbing elbows with the participants and feeling caught up in the onrush to wherever it took me.

Papa spent less and less time with his court, for now the petitioners were flocking to the door, most of whom were, as they had always been, seekers of position and wealth, and, for the most part, they were turned quickly away by Papa. He wanted only dedicated people around him now. He had no more time for the nonsensical, flattering women who flitted about like social butterflies with nowhere to light.

Occasionally, however, one would come along who understood his aims and the plan—these he did not turn away, but quickly recruited them to his cause and sent the appropriate note to the appropriate official to get them on the "common-sense road to peace" bandwagon.

One man came with ideas to improve our long-decadent transportation system. He certainly fit into Papa's plan. If he could better the railroads in any way, or the highways or waterways (many were not being utilized properly), then he was indeed a lucky find. Papa would see that all doors were opened to him. Prior to this feeling of urgency coming over Papa, he had not taken full advantage of the power he had in court. Now he used it to the utmost and many mistook it for a power grab on his part. Nothing could have been further from the truth. He was, in fact, with the Empress' help, trying to save the realm. If some petty official tried to put an obstacle in the way of an appointment, Papa saw to it that he was soon sacked. In this fashion, Papa created an informal club, the members of which were unaware of their membership, consisting of those who could further his purpose of restoring tranquillity to the nation.

So ruthless was his campaign that he began amassing new enemies at an alarming rate; enemies, in some instances, who had banded together without regard for class barriers: bureaucrats and merchants, aristocrats and manufacturers, all thwarted by one or another of his activities. One of his leading foes was the Grand Duchess Elizaveta Feodorovna, the sister of his best friend, the Tsarina. The sisters had become alienated, and since the grand duchess' only information came to her in a distorted form from those in the anti-Rasputin faction, she could rely only on rumors and scandal. She had never met my father, and thus was unable to judge him for herself. An even more powerful enemy was M. Rodzianko, the new president of the Duma, a tall, stentorian-voiced man, who was also a relative of the Yussupovs. Feliks' mother had been among the first to resent the fact that a muzhik could have so great an influence over the Tsarina, and she, in concert with Rodzianko, set to work to turn the prince away from Papa. Feliks found himself, upon his return from England, cast into a vortex of hatred for Rasputin. Rodzianko told Feliks little could be done legally about my father when he was in such close contact with the Ministers and the Royal Family. There was only one out, he reasoned—assassination. Yet he doubted there was anyone around capable of such a feat. He considered himself too old to accomplish the physical deed, although he had often committed the crime in his heart.

Although the prince had been very close to the Tsarina in his youth, the connection had been broken off, due principally to the influence he had gained over the Grand Duke Dmitri Pavlovich, who was two or three years younger than Feliks. Dmitri had been a favorite of the imperial rulers; in fact, he had lived with them at the palace and had been considered as one of the family. When the Tsar and Tsarina learned of what was going on between them, Dmitri was forbidden to see Feliks again, and the Okhrana was ordered to watch the prince, and to act as an inhibiting force by making their presence obvious. Although their effort was successful in keeping the boys apart for a time, Dmitri finally took a house in St. Petersburg, and Feliks came to stay with him there. Whatever course their relationship followed at that period could not have been a smooth one, for Dmitri, consumed by jealousy, tried to commit suicide, and Feliks came home one night to find him, apparently lifeless, on the floor. However, he was alive and recovered quickly. But the incident had a sobering effect on Feliks, and for a time he permitted the religious side of his nature to take the ascendancy.

Giving up his errant ways, he went to visit the Grand Duchess Elizaveta Feodorovna, who had been like a mother to him. The Tsarina's sister had built a convent in Moscow, and was its Mother Superior. Noted for her piety and good works among the sick and the poor, she was everywhere hailed as a saint, yet this woman was to write Feliks' parents after he murdered my father and congratulate them for the dastardly deed committed by their son.

Later, she would confide to Feliks that after my father's murder several Mothers Superior from various convents had come to visit her to relate some unexplained incidents in their various communities on the day of the assassination. Priests, for no logical reason, had become insane, creating havoc and destruction and any number of the good nuns had become sex-crazed, offering themselves to the priests in wanton abandon.

The grand duchess was shocked at Feliks' confession of numerous transgressions, but his tears of repentance moved her heart, and she gave him her blessing. She understood that his better nature had been buried beneath a mass of maternal indulgence, and that he was not entirely to blame for his flawed character. And so, to determine whether or not his repentance was sincere, she set him to work in caring for the poor. And for the first time in his wasted life, he became productive and turned his thoughts to the needs of others beside himself.

Feeling purified and spiritualized, he fell in love with the Princess Irina Aleksandrovna, daughter of the Grand Duke

184

Aleksandr Mikhailovich. Innocent and unaware of the sometimes bitter facts of life, the princess saw only Yussupov's handsome face, his gay wit and sparkling personality, his charm and engaging manner, and she returned his love tenfold. Having taken the road toward decency, he felt impelled to tell her of his nature and the details of his scandalous life, concealing none of the dark corners of his life to that time.

She seemed not to care at all, seeming to even understand his interest in other men and, as too many women are wont to do, blamed other women in his life for his gross indiscretions.

But Feliks had another barrier to overcome, the opposition of her parents to the marriage. However, he persisted, as he always did when he wanted something badly enough, and in the end he won out.

Princess Irina was the granddaughter of the Dowager Empress Maria Feodorovna, and so it was quite natural that the wedding would take place in the chapel of the Anichkov Palace, the Dowager Empress' home.

The guests accompanied the happy couple to the railroad station, where they boarded the Yussupov private car for the honeymoon trip. And Feliks adds a pathetic note in his memoirs: "As the train moved out, I saw Dmitri standing on the platform, by himself—a lonely figure."

Ж

The year 1913 marked the three hundredth anniversary of the founding of the Romanov Dynasty. Nationwide celebrations were planned. It was hoped that three hundred years of rule could be turned into a popular cause and help the Tsar garner the support of the populace. But it was during the celebration that an outbreak of strikes took place and many people were killed in the name of change, reform, or revolution—whatever label one cared to give the turmoil that existed in Russia, and the turmoil existed on a widespread basis. Unrest, indeed, hung over our country like a black and ominous cloud.

The Balkan War was now a full-fledged conflict.

185

Greece, Bulgaria, and Serbia, along with Montenegro, were revolting against their Turkish masters. The Montenegran princesses, Grand Duchesses Militza and Anastasia, were staunch patriots, and employing the not inconsiderable influence of their husbands, they attempted to force the Tsar into entering the war against the Turks. There might have been several benefits to be realized by Russia if she had entered the conflict; she badly needed to restore her military prestige after the humiliation of the loss to Japan; she needed a warm-water outlet into the Mediterranean, a longtime goal of the empire; she would have gained some territory; and there would have been full employment in the munitions plants and other factories. In addition to these reasons, the Grand Duke Nikolai Nikolayevich, who was soon to be the commander in chief of the army, was goaded into favoring the war by two determined females, only one of whom was living. The first was his wife, Anastasia, and the second was Joan of Arc, who had apparently developed a strong taste for bloodshed since her *auto-da-fé*, now that she was communicating through a spiritualist medium.

The Tsar also had a need for the unification a small and successful war could bring to his country, and he was strongly tempted to listen to these arguments, which were, in varying forms, bombarding him from all sides. Arrayed against these, and working almost alone, two voices were raised, those of Count Witte and my father. They were an oddly assorted pair, the aristocrat and the muzhik, but each respected the other and they worked well together.

Believing that God's kingdom existed in all men, regardless of ancestry or nationality, Papa considered wars as mockeries of God's will, a madness that attempted to set God against Himself. And with that philosophy to bolster his argument, he went to see the Tsar. Once more, as on so many times, Papa sat across that ornate desk from His Majesty.

"Vyelichyestvo, you must not lead Russia into war."

"But, Otyets Grigori, I think it would be good for the nation, and most of my advisers agree. It would help the economy, and it would quiet the discontent of the people."

"No good can come from evil, and killing is evil." The starets was beginning to get a bit hot under the collar.

186

"Even Nikolai Nikolayevich thinks the war would benefit the country."

"I admire the grand duke; he and his brother have been very kind to me and my family. But this is not a time for personal feelings. I say again, war is evil." He was even more emphatic.

"Yes, yes, I agree, of course. But think of what it would do for Russia." The Tsar was becoming a little less certain of his position.

And now, Papa was thumping the desk with each word, each syllable, driving his point home. "War inevitably brings disaster; this war would be the end of Russia, the Russia we have known and loved."

"Very well, my friend; you may be right. I promise you this: I will not go to war before speaking to you again."

Papa felt that he had carried the day, and retired after expressing his gratitude to the Tsar. And a few days later, Nikolas issued a statement to the effect that Russia would not become involved in the Balkan War, after which, and probably to avoid attempts to change his mind, he took the imperial family on a hunting trip to Poland.

But those who stayed behind, those who were privy to the inner workings of the government, knew that Papa had been the one mainly responsible for the decision, and their fury descended on his head. The grand duke and his Anastasia had been his first aristocratic supporters in St. Petersburg, and his brother, the Grand Duke Pyotr, had been most kind and generous during Mama's operation and recovery, and they were incensed. Nikolai Nikolayevich had a particularly low boiling point when he felt he had been betrayed, and he most emphatically believed that he had been betrayed by Rasputin. He stormed into the study at 64 Gorokhovaya Ulitsa, and began berating Papa in front of Varya and me, calling him an ungrateful *svinya** after all he and his wife had done for him. Although maintaining a calm exterior, I could see that Papa was shaken by this unfair accusation; how could one's gratitude to a benefactor be requited by agreeing to the performance of an

*pig

evil act? But the grand duke was far from finished with his diatribe; he merely veered off in another direction.

"As everyone knows, the Tsarina is quite mad, and the only proof of this anyone needs is that she listens to you. She should be removed from the palace, away from your influence, and placed in an asylum."

As he continued, Papa's face began turning white, as had the knuckles of his hands with which he was gripping the arms of his chair.

"What's more, Nikolas Aleksandrovich should be forced to abdicate. It would not be difficult to replace that spineless weakling."

It was quite plain to me, and I am sure that it was even more plain to Papa, that the grand duke was not only uttering treasonous thoughts, but that he was more than willing to offer himself as the man best suited to wear the crown. The grand duke spouted a torrent of such vituperations for some minutes more, and then, like a Roman candle sputtering out after its pyrotechnic display, he fell silent, stood up, glared at Papa, turned on his heel, and, without any signal of farewell, slammed out of the room.

Papa stood there for a moment, not saying a word, and we remained silent as well. Then he spoke, as much to himself as to us. "Pray for those who despitefully use you."

He knelt before the ikona and prayed aloud for guidance. He had done God's work, but in following His will, he had lost good friends and endangered the success of his mission. He prayed that God would show him a way out of the dilemma. He prayed for the salvation of Russia from its enemies, both those that were within, and those without.

And he prayed, "Dear Heavenly Father, save these, your unhappy children."

188

✖THIRTEEN✖

Papa has been described as a man with powerful influence in high places. It has been written that he kowtowed to dukes, duchesses, bankers, businessmen. To some degree that might be an accurate statement—but only to a very small degree. My father's power, if in fact he had all that much power, was through the peasant, the common man with whom he had such great rapport.

I saw the royalty, the bankers, and the businessmen, with their large bundles of money and expensive fur coats on my father's doorstep, not out of great belief in my father as a religious man, but with thinly disguised bribes for what they were seeking at court: an appointment, a favor, a friend or family member on the verge of scandal (hoping that Papa could squash it). They came, and Papa took their money.

But he took bad money and put it to a good cause. For every banker there were a hundred or more common folk with real need. They never asked for anything. They came with their country cheeses, Madeira wine (which Papa loved more dearly than any other spirit), and humble little gifts of affection for their starets.

Papa sensed their needs just as he despised the greed of the wealthy. It was not unusual for my father to have to spend hours with some peasant whose family was desperate. Hours spent trying to get the man to accept help. My father, like the Robin Hood of storybook fame, gladly took from the rich to help the poor.

That was the basis of much of the hatred against my father. People like Iliodor could not understand why Papa, with all those opportunities, did not strive for personal wealth, and through wealth, power. That certainly would have made more sense to them and they would then have been able to compete with him on a common ground—personal greed.

That he was indeed a man dedicated to God and country flabbergasted them. Consequently they were against him.

Iliodor was not one to be contained. And he decided that he would bring down Papa and the House of Romanov because of the crown's support of my father. Traps were being set, and Papa's remaining time on this earth was to be an obstacle course of treachery.

Even from prison Iliodor had some influence. During his solitary confinement he managed to concoct a plot to commit a mass assassination. His target date was October 6, 1913. It was the Tsar's name day. His plan was to murder sixty high government officials and forty bishops.

It is amazing that when a man is popular in one area, he can be despised in another. Papa was a man loved by his Tsar and the royal family, and by the common people of his country. But love creates jealousy and from jealousy comes hate and the will to destroy.

Iliodor had no trouble assembling enough of Papa's enemies to plot. One hundred and twenty high-explosive bombs were obtained, along with other tools of the assassin, and one hundred radicals were trained in the use of the weapons. The plan was to throw the missiles of death into crowds of

190

people as they emerged from churches. It did not matter that innocent people would die.

When that many people get together in a plan, someone always leaks information—either intentionally or accidentally, often in a tavern where beer and wine loosen the tongue. And so, one of Iliodor's compatriots, who hated my father but loved money more (Wealth before martyrdom!) unfolded the entire scheme before the Okhrana, whose budget was unknown, but probably unlimited. Once again Iliodor was taken into custody, and this time the Tsar turned his back on him.

However, intrigue continued. The Grand Duke Nikolai Nikolayevich had vowed to get even with Papa—yet he had to be careful not to incite the anger of the crown. Through Iliodor he found a means to accomplish the dream in his heart —riddance of the hated starets—without anyone pointing a finger at him. Hadn't Iliodor already stated his avowed purpose?

Being a grand duke, he had influence—even within the secret police. There was a small opening at one end of the underground passage beneath the house where Iliodor was being held prisoner. The grand duke offered Iliodor freedom through that passage—if he could assure him the demise of my father.

Iliodor, of course, couldn't do the deed himself. But he could engineer it. When the right amount of money is placed in a greedy hand, that hand may be bound to protect country and emperor, but . . .

And so it was. Iliodor had a female follower, Chionya Guseva, who had never met my father and had no personal motive to kill him, but she was under Iliodor's spell and would do his bidding.

Upon her solemn promise to follow his wishes, she was armed with a sharp knife, a sum of money for expenses, and orders to strike on command.

Ж

Having arrived at the advanced age of fifteen, I felt quite mature.

School was a bore and the boys more interesting than grammar or algebra. Particularly the handsome young men of the aristocracy, or the dashing army officers that I had met when I had accompanied my father to an affair at one of the city's many palaces.

I was receiving invitations from some of these young men to go to the theater, but Papa laid down some very strict rules: There must always be a chaperon, and I must be in by ten o'clock.

As any young girl can tell you, I found ways in abundance to circumvent my father's rules.

Accompanied by Marusa Sasonova, whose room I had shared when I first arrived in St. Petersburg, I went window-shopping along the Hyevski Prospekt, using the shop windows more as mirrors than frames for the dresses and furs displayed, mirrors to reflect the images of any boys that might be following. There was one large store directly across the street from the Gostinitsa Evropa* that provided an excellent arena for the sport, but, of course, the strict protocol of that day prevented us from meeting any of the young men with whom we slyly flirted. It was all innocent enough, and probably good practice for the future, when we would play the game in earnest, acting the role of reticent maiden, while charming some young man into the rash adventure of proposing marriage.

We also discovered the fun that could be had with a telephone, calling numbers at random, until a man with an attractive voice answered. We took turns in carrying on innocent, but nonetheless seductive conversations with him, holding out the promise of nameless delights, nameless because one cannot name the unknown, until the poor fellow was completely under our sway. And then we would make an appointment to meet him, taking the simple, everyday precaution, however, of giving false descriptions of ourselves. After ringing off, we would station ourselves across the street from the trysting place, where we could watch the inflamed swain as he looked up and down the street for a sinuous redhead and a statuesque blonde, who, of course, never appeared.

And then, one day, the tables were reversed. Instead of telephoning some unknown, I received a call from a man

*Hotel Europe

192

who said he had been following me for several days, enraptured by my breathtaking beauty. We could not be certain as to which of us had so captured his admiration, for he had not named either of us, but I rather thought that he must have been referring to Marusa, for she was far more beautiful than I. He had promised to call again, and we waited in eager anticipation for that call. It came the next day, and at intervals of one or two days thereafter, and he finally revealed that he had been following me all the way home, which is how he had discovered that I was Rasputin's daughter. His conversations were always filled with flattery, and I was already half in love with him, when I had to tell him that I could not see him as he had requested, because I was accompanying my father back to Siberia in a few days. And in the excitement of preparing for the journey, I hardly noticed that he did not call again.

Taking the train from St. Petersburg to Tobolsk, we transferred to a river steamer for the remainder of the journey to Pokrovskoye, and it was during this last leg of the trip that I was approached by a dark man who introduced himself as a newspaper reporter, named Davidsohn, who said that his had been the voice at the other end of our recent telephone conversations. I did not care much for his appearance, but I was flattered to learn that he had followed me, and somehow neglected to tell my father about it. And this was a tragedy, for what I did not know was that, once we had docked, he went at once to join Chionya Guseva at the lodgings she had taken, there to make the final preparations for the assassination attempt.

The next day was a Sunday, one of those balmy early summer days that belie the notion of Siberia as a dark and cold land. The date was June 28, 1914, and although no one in Pokrovskoye knew it, an event had taken place some one thousand miles to the west that was to change all our lives. Returning from church on that bright, sunny day, the family and friends, all but Varya and I, who had been invited to a neighbor's house, gathered at the table for the Sunday dinner. Feeling renewed, as he always did when he came home to the quiet of the village from the hurly-burly of the big city, Papa expanded in one of his happier moods, telling stories of his experiences in St. Petersburg, of his successes in throwing the police off his trail when he wanted to go about his private business, and of the way in which he invented bits of spurious information to pass along to them—once it was a nonexistent Chinese with whom he carried on mysterious conversations—and of how he liked to offer raw country vodka to overly pompous officials who had come to spy on him, a drink that tasted like petroleum, which he named, with some pride, "Rasputin's Revenge."

It was an altogether delightful gathering, as I was told later, Mama laughing with the rest at his tales, until there came a knock on the door, and Dunia went to see who it was. She came back in a moment to say that the village postman had brought a telegram from the Tsarina. In it, she asked him to return to St. Petersburg at once; her reason was most compelling. Although she was not more specific, all the nations of Europe had been thrown into turmoil by the news that the Archduke Ferdinand of Austria had just been assassinated at Sarejevo, Serbia, along with his archduchess. But the tone of the Tsarina's message was sufficiently serious that it demanded an instant and affirmative reply. Papa drafted his telegram and took it down to the post office for transmission. As he came out into the street, he found it filled with villagers, decked out in their Sunday finest for their customary after-dinner stroll. And just before he arrived at his destination, he came face to face with one of those who strolled.

Chionya Guseva had been idling about the street with a seeming casualness she was far from feeling, hoping that her intended victim would appear. She had carefully studied the photograph furnished by Iliodor, and she was certain that she would have little difficulty in recognizing him. And now her patience was about to be rewarded. There he was, that man with the beard, the terrible sinner whose death had been decreed by God. She waited until he was quite close to her, and then stepped out of the stream of townspeople and came to meet him, holding out her hand, begging for a coin. As he reached into his pocket for a kopek, she withdrew her other hand from beneath her shawl, and in that hand she held Iliodor's knife, and she thrust it into Papa's lower abdomen, drawing it upward with all her strength. When it had cut its deep gash from his navel to his sternum, where it was halted by the bone, she withdrew it for the purpose of striking again. But before she could stab him a second time, Papa, staggered by the shock and pain, managed to fend her off with his hands. He did not have to protect himself for long, for the people nearest to him clutched at her. She dropped the knife and turned to flee, but the angry crowd caught her before she had taken a half-dozen steps, and began beating her and tearing at her until she was rescued by the local konstabl and dragged off, semi-conscious, to the tiny one-room jail.

Bent over in agony, clutching his abdomen to prevent his entrails from falling out onto the dirt street, the blood pouring out between his fingers, Papa was helped back to the house by his anxious neighbors, although, by the time they had reached the door, he needed more than their help, for he would have fallen if they had not caught him and carried him into the house. Both Mama and Dunia were stunned by the sight of the men and their burden, but neither of them was the sort to faint at the sight of blood. Mama did not take time to clear the table, but merely swept dishes, serving bowls, and silver off onto the floor to make room for her wounded husband. She began to examine the long incision, and Dunia remembered to send one of the men to bring Varya and me home. She turned back to help Mama in the grim work at hand. Removing his clothing, they sponged away the blood, so that they could determine the extent of the damage, and it was extensive, his abdominal wall having been slashed clear through, and even some of his intestines having been cut. Mama's cool command of the situation, and her refusal to break down and weep over her husband's still form, were undoubtedly the decisive factors in saving his life.

Dmitri was sent to the post office to wire a summons to the nearest doctor, who was at Tyumen, and Mama and Dunia commenced the fearful task of trying to staunch the bleeding. They knew that they had a long night before them; it would be many hours before the doctor could arrive. And as this work progressed, Davidsohn appeared at the door, seeking information about Papa's condition, claiming that he wanted the story for his newspaper. I was the one who answered his knock, and as I looked at him and heard his question, I realized in one horrifying flash that I had been duped by this man. Like the burst of a skyrocket, the knowledge came to me: why he had called me on the telephone, why he had flattered me until he extracted the information he wanted about our trip to Siberia, why he had been on that boat, and most despicable of all, why he had come to our house. He had, of course, wanted to find out if the murderous attempt had been successful. I was plunged into my own Slough of Despond, having seen in that instant that I had unwittingly led the assassin to my father, and, unable to bear the anguish of that realization, I could only scream at the conspirator to leave.

"Haven't you done enough?" I shrieked at his back. But, of course, he did not reply. There was no need.

As the door closed behind him, I sank to the floor, sobbing in my misery. But I was not permitted to wallow in grief for too long, for Mama called me to come and hold Papa's hand and comfort him during his brief lucid moments, while she and Dunia wound him around with wet sheets in an attempt to stop the bleeding. Even as far as we were from medical help, they knew the effects of peritonitis, and although they did not know it by that name, they had seen the results of severed intestines, and knew that once the infection had set in, there was nothing any doctor, no matter how skilled, could do. No one in the family slept that night, and sadly, though we would not admit it, even to ourselves, each of us was convinced that he would not live to see the dawn.

It was well after midnight when the doctor arrived, driving his *troika*,* behind totally spent horses. Papa had re-gained consciousness, and although in great pain, he had clung to life by virtue of his powerful physique and an immense store of vitality. Examining his wound, the doctor could see that priority must be given to preventing the onset of peritonitis, and performed a preliminary operation to cleanse the abdominal cavity and to patch, as well as he could by candlelight, the torn parts of the intestines. For reasons of his own, which I believe were spiritual in nature, Papa refused to breathe the ether, and clasping a cross given him by Episkop Theofan, prayed for the

*three-horse carriage

strength he needed to endure the knife. Mama, Dunia, and I stood by as nurses, and I held his hand to encourage him. As the scalpel began to do its work, I felt him shudder and was horrified at the realization of the agony he must be undergoing, although mercifully not for long, as he relapsed once more into blessed unconsciousness.

As soon as it was light, the doctor bundled up his delirious patient and had him placed in his springless troika. Although his horses were fairly well rested, it was thought that a fresh team would make much better time and would not tire so quickly, so Dmitri selected the farm's three fastest horses to hitch up. The doctor had a most difficult decision to make: whether to drive at full speed over the rutted roads, thus risking the life of his patient by bouncing him to death, or to go more slowly, taking a chance of letting him die because of the delay in treatment. He chose the former, a judgment that proved to be the correct one. Dunia and I sat on either side of Papa, holding him against shocks and cushioning his body with ours. During the more than six hours of the journey, he emerged from his coma only once. Seeing me as I hovered over him, he tried to speak.

In a daze, he could only mumble, "He must be stopped. . . he must be stopped. . . ."

I could not understand what he was trying to tell me, for in the confusion of that long night, no one had stopped to read the Tsarina's telegram, and even if they had, they would not have understood who it was that had to be stopped.

As the month of July wore on, and Papa hovered between life and death in the hospital, the actions and counteractions that would inevitably lead to war went forward. In retaliation for the assassination of the Austrian archduke, Austria issued a strongly worded ultimatum to Serbia. President Raymond Poincare of France went to St. Petersburg to arrange for an invitation to England to join in an effort to bring pressure on Austria not to attack. Conferences were organized, but Austria refused to permit foreign nations to decide questions of her "national honor." And on July 28, 1914, Austria declared war on Serbia. The German Chancellor Theobald von Bethmann-Hollweg urged negotiations between Russia and Austria,

197

and Russia limited its mobilization to the Austrian frontier alone. But the war faction prevailed—and here is where Papa's influence might have prevented the cataclysm—mobilization was made general, extending along the entire western frontier. On July 31, the Germans issued an ultimatum demanding the cessation of all military preparations along her front with Russia, and at seven o'clock on the evening of August 1, declared war on Russia, as the Grand Duke Nikolai's faction had known they would. And so, while Papa was still helpless and incapable of bringing any influence to bear, the curtain was raised on the final act in the tragedy of the Romanovs, the Empire, and the Russian people. Toward the end of July, able at last to sit up, Papa wrote a letter to the Tsar:

> *My friend:*
> *Once again I repeat; a terrible storm menaces Russia. Woe . . . suffering without end. It is night. There is not one star . . . a sea of tears. And how much blood!*
> *I find no words to tell you more. The terror is infinite. I know that all desire war of you, even the most faithful. They do not see that they rush toward the abyss. You are the Tsar, the father of the people.*
> *Do not let fools triumph, do not let them throw themselves and us into the abyss. Do not let them do this thing. . . . Perhaps we will conquer Germany, but what will become of Russia? When I think of that, I understand that never has there been so atrocious a martyrdom.*
> *Russia drowned in her own blood, suffering and infinite desolation.*
> *Grigori*

Once it was known that Papa would recover, the family returned to Pokrovskoye, and I was left behind to comfort him. So I was not present when a strange event occurred. Dunia, although not a particularly religious woman, had prayed all during the long hours before the doctor arrived, and she had continued to pray while he was in the hospital. When it was known that he was out of danger, she took to offering a daily prayer of thanksgiving before the ikona of the Virgin of Kazan, which hung on the dining-room wall. Kneeling before it one day, she noticed that a drop of moisture had appeared below the Virgin's eye, and as any good housekeeper would do, she brushed it away. To her amazement, it was replaced by another drop, and then another. She again dried the painting, but try as she would, she could not keep it dry. Awed, she called Mama and the rest of the family, and when they saw what was happening, they knelt before the ikona and prayed, overwhelmed by the knowledge that they were witnessing a miracle. Word of this was sent to me at Tyumen, and when I read the message to Papa, his face turned white.

"The Holy Mother weeps for Russia," he said somberly. "It is a sign that a great misfortune is about to strike us."

And within the week, the whole world knew what that misfortune would be.

Ж

For the first few months after Germany's declaration of war, the Tsar was certain that he had been wise in following the counsels of the war faction, and that his fortunes had at last taken a turn for the better. Not only were his armies advancing on all fronts, but the nation was giving him the kind of support he had not known during the twenty-five years of his reign. The nationwide strikes had come to a halt, the male citizens were flocking to the mobilization centers to enlist, and patriotism had replaced the apathy of the people. The flag of Russia flew in every street, every theater played the anthems of the allied powers, that of Russia followed by those of England, France, and Belgium. And when, on September 3, the Russian army won a great victory at Lemberg, everyone was in a frenzy of zeal to help the war effort. It was at this time that the name of the city, St. Petersburg, was thought to have too Germanic a flavor, and it was renamed Petrograd.

It was to this scene that Papa, ill and in constant pain, made his return. Everything had changed; the sale of liquor, long a state monopoly, was banned altogether, although the wealthy had no difficulty in satisfying their requirements. Even though he had opposed the war, he felt it his simple duty to do what he could to ameliorate its effects. Corruption must be fought, the condition of the soldiers must be made tolerable, and the wounded needed prayer. Known for his outspoken opposition to the war, he found himself with few friends; the line of petitioners now consisted of those seeking news of their prisoner of war sons and husbands, or the release of the only son from the service so that he could work on the family farm. All the rest seemed to know that he was out of favor, and they avoided the flat. His enemies, having failed at bringing off his murder, now felt they could ignore him. He realized, more than ever, that in a time of madness, the sane man stands alone and unheard.

Basking in the warm glow of public approval, the Tsar failed to realize that it was not his personal popularity, but the fever of war that had ended his domestic problems, and he was convinced of the rightness of his position.

It was the only time I can remember that the Tsar was actually cold to Papa. I went to the palace with my father for that last visit with the Tsar. It would be the last time the two old comrades would sit together in conversation. The Tsar would soon leave to take over the leadership of the troops at the front. He always felt that Emperor or no, a leader's place was with his troops, leading them into victory—or consoling them in defeat.

The Tsar welcomed Papa formally. I sat quietly at the Tsarina's feet. However, this time there was a difference. The Tsarina did not interrupt with commentary during their discussion.

Papa's aversion to war was well taken by many and well known by all. But as an American general said during World War II, there is no substitute for victory, and the Tsar's troops were winning great victories—it was only the beginning and he was grossly misled by those meager gains in the overall picture of the war.

However, the Tsar pictured himself as the victorious

200

king who would unify the country and be popular throughout his lifetime, leaving the realm to Aleksei without fear of his being deposed by any popular uprising.

"Your Majesty," Papa begged, his voice strained and tired from his recent illness, "you must understand that I have nothing to gain—not even your favor—by my opposition to this useless war. Russians are dying in this war, and when it is over, win or lose, the victory will belong to the specter of death, to the hospitals for the blind and infirm, the crippled, blighted, and hated veterans who will roam about our countryside, infest our cities and ghettos—only to be resented and eventually despised by those for whom they fought—and yes, eventually also, even by those who fought side by side with them— those who return whole in body."

Papa shook his head sadly, tears streamed down his face. The Tsar sat and listened, sipping a drink slowly. The Empress' face was pained, but she said nothing.

Finally, when Papa had expended himself, the Tsar set his glass down carefully on a side table, got up and walked across the room and back, and came face to face with my father, looking down at him where he sat, for Papa did not get up just because royalty felt like taking a walk. He truly felt all people were equal.

"Little Father," the Tsar said, wearily and with some impatience, "there is a time to listen and a time to do something. This is our grand opportunity to save the realm and the good name of Romanov. You have served us well, and we know that. But what more can you want of us? Would you be Tsar?"

Papa was stunned. His face paled and his piercing, hypnotic eyes seemed to have lost their power. His spirit was broken with one question from the one man he most respected and loved in the world.

The Tsarina dropped her eyes. She, too, was pained. She, like Papa, had opposed the war. After all, wasn't her own brother in the German Army? But her twenty years as the Empress of Russia had set her loyalties. Her husband was the Tsar and her only son would succeed him. Fate had set her as the wife of and in the future the mother of a Tsar. She would

201

not openly oppose her husband now, who looked at the war as almost a religious undertaking.

"Perhaps, my friend," the Tsar said, placing his hand on Papa's slumped shoulder, "perhaps there comes a time when we must all step aside for the future. The old ways must give ground to the new. It happens to us all at one point or another. Death is the prime motivator, of course, but sometimes age or ideas—ah, yes. Especially ideas. They change. I have been out in the field. I have seen the great masses of my people supporting the war. It has brought us all together again—like a family.

"I must beg of you not to condemn this effort public-ly. It cannot help our cause—it can destroy your own."

The Tsar bade my father farewell and left the room.

The Tsarina patted me on the head, then rose from her chair. I, too, stood. Papa's head was bowed and I saw tears streaking down his weathered face, running in rivulets which lost themselves in the tangle of his beard, which was like a forest supporting his face.

The Tsarina put her hand to Papa's cheek and he took the hand in his own and kissed it.

"Do not despair, Little Father," she said. "Your time is not through. There is much work for you on this earth. We need you, now as always."

It was a gesture, but I knew, as did Papa, the Tsar, and the Tsarina—it would never be the same for Papa. My heart cried for him. He could have supported the hostilities and continued to be the second most popular man in Russia. He chose conscience instead.

The Empress did not desert Papa completely. For a time, Papa visited her in Anna Aleksandrovna Virubova's little house, which was on the palace estate, and she telephoned him at least twice a day to inform him of the tsarevich's condition. She did not want her "Little Father" too far away from her son—war or not.

But the relationship with the royal family was on ice.

Ж

Varya was still attending school. I had forsaken that establishment in favor of French lessons from a private tutor. Had Papa been more healthy in spirit and body, I'm sure he would have given me a lot of argument about that decision, but he was not the same man he had been.

I couldn't be kept away from the excitement that was everywhere about the capital. The soldiers marching off to the front, the handsome young officers of the allied nations, the flags flying from every post and window and from atop buildings. And the bands, those wonderful military bands. The martial atmosphere was ever-present.

The theater, the ballet—with Marusa I went once or twice a week to these marvelous productions. It was good to be alive in the effervescence of the city with gaiety around every corner.

But a cloud was forming over my happiness. I was young and it was expected I would be caught up in the spirit of the war, but I couldn't help notice that Papa was not the same man he had been before. His recovery from his wound had been retarded, I was sure, by the final thrust of the Tsar. Sometimes I felt that Papa had no desire to recover. I'm equally sure that the Tsar's words cut deeper than any knife. All I could do was give him lots of love and attention.

I did not learn until later that Papa's condition was more serious than I had known. It was more than the physical pain, or the humiliation the Tsar had imposed upon him. But he had lost his powers of healing.

In an attempt to overcome his pain and shame, he began to drink. His relief was only temporary. The more he drank, the more he had to drink to ease the ache. His spiritual and psychic powers became dulled by his excessive drinking.

Though I could hear him praying with all his former intensity, he had again entered what he called the dark night of the soul. There was no response to his prayers. He was like a strong runner who has suddenly been crippled; a man with perfect vision who has lost his sight.

Outside of myself—and he never liked to burden his children with his problems—there was only one to whom he could turn for solace and understanding. The loyal and loving Dunia realized the turmoil that bedeviled him better than anyone else, and it was her feeling that, since it was virtually impossible for him to fulfill his mission, whatever that might be, in his present condition, he would be better off if he were to go back home to Pokrovskoye. But, as sick as he was, he doggedly refused, clinging to the command to do his Master's work in the capital. When Varya and I were out for the evening, Dunia, who could see that her beloved Grischa was fast becoming a habitual drunkard, would sit with him and try to distract his mind from his torment, but there were times when its intensity would not permit him to sit still, and he would rise and walk the floor. And when that did not give him surcease, he would storm out of the flat, to go she knew not where. Sometimes, she could lure him into bed, soothing him with her body, as only she could do, and afterward, when his agony had subsided for the moment, she could distract his mind by encouraging him to speak of the past, to reveal his experiences in his search for God, and to dredge up the very depths of his soul. In so doing, Dunia came to know more of the real man than any other person, more than father or mother, more than any intimate, more, even, than his own wife.

And thus she managed to keep him somewhat in check, preventing him from utterly destroying himself in his mad quest of some nostrum that might relieve the awful agony. But even this comfort was to be taken from him, as though God had determined to put him to the final test, for a telegram arrived for Dunia, informing her that her mother was dying in Siberia. It was arranged for Katya to come to Petrograd as her replacement, but, of course, while Katya was an excellent cook and housekeeper, she was not the one to provide a safety valve for her employer. And so there was no one to restrain him, and he began seeking relief from his torment in the sort of wine, women, and dancing that were to be found in some of the less inhibited cabarets.

The news from the front, in the last half of 1915, was bad, and grew steadily worse. Lemberg had been lost, and, hampered by a lack of adequate weapons, the army was driven out of Warsaw on August 7. By the latter part of September, all of Poland had been captured by the Germans and Austrians. Anxious to do what he could to help the Russian cause, and knowing that, after their terrible defeats, the soldiers' morale would be at a low ebb, Papa sent an offer to Grand Duke Nikolai Nikolayevich to come to the front and to bless the men and pray with them. It was a journey that would have entailed great sacrifice, because of his health, but the grand duke saved him the trouble, in a message which said, "Come and I will hang you."

The grand duke could never forgive my father for his opposition to the Balkan War; but Nikolai Nikolayevich had, in turn, an enemy in the Tsarina. In one of her letters to the Tsar, she wrote:

> The prayers of your Friend rise up to the skies for you day and night and the Lord will hear them. Here begins the glory of your reign. He has said so and I believe him. May the replacement of Nikolaska take place rapidly. No beating about the bush.

The "Friend" was Rasputin; and "Nikolaska" was the familiar name for the grand duke.

Following the advice of the Tsarina (it was God's will, he said), the Tsar removed the grand duke, blaming him for poor leadership, and assumed the role of commander in chief. But this move only served to worsen conditions on the home front, for the grand duke had the confidence of the people, and what little the Tsar had gained in public support at the outbreak of the war had been eroded by this act, and by his refusal of the Duma's requests for changes in several of the ministries. Between the military defeats and the mismanagement of the government, much of the patriotism and enthusiasm of the populace waned perceptibly.

As the armies withdrew from Poland, they uprooted the local Jewish communities, dispersing them over many sections of Russia; all in the mistaken belief that the Jews were pro-German. Once inside Russia, they were looked upon as German spies and attacked by disorganized mobs, although what assistance these poor homeless and hungry people could have given to the enemy was never made clear. But here was

205

a cause for my father, and despite his pain, he threw himself into the effort with a total commitment that raised him out of the dark mood into which he had fallen. And, for a while, life was pleasant in the flat at 64 Gorokhovaya Ulitsa. He was powerless to stop the war, but he could do something to save the Jews.

Because of this campaign, Papa created a whole new set of enemies, consisting in the main of those who wanted a scapegoat upon whom they could load the consequences of their own shortcomings. But he was enured to enemies by then, and a few more could not prevent him from doing another of God's tasks. After some struggle and a good deal of maneuvering, he managed to have a bill presented in the Duma that protected the rights of the Jews, including the right to receive an education in the state schools. And the bill was passed; the first such in the history of Russia.

While he was busily engaged in this cause, he spent less time in nightclubs. And then one day, an old woman came to our door. She was so bent and crippled by arthritis that Papa described her to me as appearing "like the branch of a burnt tree." Suffering from intolerable pain, she pleaded with him to heal her, adding through her tears that no doctor had been of any help. He took her into his study, held her poor gnarled hands in his, and began to pray. Since his youth, whenever he had prayed for a healing, a light had appeared in his head, as though an electric lamp had been turned on by some invisible hand. But now, all was darkness, the lamp would not light. He tried to concentrate, changing his prayer to one beseeching God for the return of his power, and when this did not help, he attempted to will a healing for the woman. But the will, when employed with some force, creates tension, and tension has a way of negating healing through the generation of a fear that there will be no healing. And so the woman was not helped. At last, he admitted defeat.

"I am sorry, babushka, I cannot do it. The Lord has seen fit to take the power from me."

"Can you do nothing for me, Otyets Grigori?"

Papa sadly shook his head. "The power was never mine; it was always the Lord's. If He will not do it, I am helpless." He gave her a slip of paper and sent her to his old friend

Dr. Badmaev. "He is a skilled physician. Perhaps he can help you."

This seemed to be the final blow; first the knife attack, and the wound that would not let him rest; his inability to keep Russia out of the war; the Tsar turning away from him; and now this. God had forsaken him. He had failed.

But he was not alone to blame for his doubts. He had not wielded a knife against himself. Was he to blame for the act of another? In his anguish he cried out the last seven words of the Khristos. And in despair, rushed out the door and made his way to the Villa Rodye. There he would find companions and drink; there he would dance and hear the wild, yet strangely quieting Gypsy music.

Weakened by months of debauchery, it was a gaunt and cadaverous figure that greeted Dunia on her return from her mother's funeral. It was Christmas, but little of the spirit pervaded our land, and even less in our flat. Papa was too weak for any celebration of the Nativity, and he was also too weak to resist Dunia when she put him to bed, although he made a few feeble attempts to assert himself, only to surrender finally to her will, which could be quite strong when the occasion required. She nursed him and fed him regular and nourishing meals, she gratified the desires that still flamed up at times, and she prayed for his recovery. She had taken over all his care, now that Katya had returned to Pokrovskoye.

Under her firm, but tender rule, he began to regain his strength; his color improved and he began to fill out. But he was still convalescing when I brought him some shocking news. I had been at the Sasanovs' house with Marusa, when we heard that Anna Aleksandrovna Virubova, Papa's only true friend remaining at court, had been in a terrible railroad accident. She had been on her way from Tsarskoye Syelo to Petrograd, during a heavy January snowfall, and, due to the limited vision, the train had run into another on the same track. There had been a horrendous cacophony of sounds, the grinding of metal on metal, breaking glass, screaming people, escaping steam, and then, as all movement ceased, the groans and cries of those who had been injured. Anna Aleksandrovna had been struck in the head by a falling girder, and her legs had been trapped and crushed in the wreckage, and she had lain in that condition for some time until found by a rescue party. She was dragged from the train and laid out with the other injured passengers in a nearby waiting room. Before long, a few doctors were brought to the scene, and they began a systematic examination of the crash victims, but there were not nearly enough of them to attend to everyone who had been injured.

A cursory examination of Anyushka led them to believe she was so near death that any time spent on her would be at the expense of someone with a chance of survival. Consequently, she was left to die and went without treatment for many hours.

Mercifully, her periods of consciousness were brief, and took her away from the pain of her suffering.

Of course when word reached the palace an ambulance was immediately dispatched to the scene and she was brought back to the royal fold, where doctors hovered over her, ministering as best they could.

I broke the news to my father. "Papa, Papa," I cried, "Anna Aleksandrovna has been in a terrible accident. The doctors hold little or no hope for her. Actually the words they used were 'totally hopeless.'" I began to cry, for she had truly been a great friend to both my father and all of our family. She was our last link to the palace.

Papa did not even wait for me to finish. He struggled out of bed and called Dunia to help him dress. Despite her protestations about his own condition, he ordered that a hired car be brought to drive him to Tsarskoye Syelo.

His rift with the Tsar meant nothing to him. He strode up the palace steps as if he owned the place and was directed to Anna's sickroom. He brushed past the Tsar with only a slight nod of recognition. The Tsarina stood by as he knelt beside the bed of his dear friend and took her hand, speaking to her in a gentle, but insistent voice.

"Anyushka, Anyushka, look at me."

When there was no response, he called again, his voice stronger and louder: "Anyushka, look at me; I am here."

Her eyelids fluttered open. "Otyets Grigori, thanks be to God." And she relapsed into her coma.

I, having accompanied Papa to the palace, thought she had gone to meet her maker and began to cry softly. The Tsarina put her fingers to her lips as if to shush me.

"Hush, child," Papa said, as he rose with great effort to his feet, uncertain on his suddenly tired and rubbery legs. He turned quite formally and addressed the Tsar and Tsarina: "She will live, but," and he shook his head sadly, "she will always be a cripple."

He seemed to want to say something else to them, but lacked the strength. "Come," he said to me, and we left the room, I walking behind him, seeing how disheveled and ill he himself was.

As the great door closed behind us, Papa faltered, wavered, and his knees buckled. He was too large for me to handle, but I reached for him—too late. He fell headlong, crashing onto the corridor floor. I screamed.

Servants rushed to pick him up and I held his hand. It was like ice, as though he had been crawling in the snow, and his face was ashen—drained of all vitality.

"Get a doctor!" I was shouting.

"No, no!" Papa said weakly. "Take me home."

The servants carried him to our car where Dunia was waiting. We bundled him up and she ordered the driver to take us back to our flat quickly.

He was immediately put to bed by Dunia, and I waited in the kitchen with a cup of warm broth. Once Papa was made comfortable and Dunia was assured for herself that he was sleeping and resting, she came to me in the kitchen. Her face was solemn. "I think he has not long to live. Come, sit with me."

Together we watched over him, saw that his breathing was shallow, face drawn and only slightly darker than his white pillow, the skin tight and almost parchmentlike. His body continued cold as if in death.

When she returned from school, Varya joined us and

we watched him, although there was little we could do but keep him covered to conserve his bodily heat.

I was complaining to Dunia at the shabby treatment he was and had been receiving from the palace when the phone rang.

"Go, see who it is," Dunia said.

"Hello?"

It was the Tsarina. "My dear, dear child. I have only just heard from the footmen of your father's collapse. How is he now?"

"I don't know, Mama, he looks terrible." And I couldn't help but add, "Just as he has been going downhill ever since..." I couldn't go on. It was not my place to chastise the mother of all Russia. My voice faltered. "I'm sorry...."

"You have nothing to be sorry for, dear. We have all made mistakes, wrong judgments. But the important thing is that your father get well." She said she was sending some flowers, and asked me to assure Papa of her deep affection for him. She was as good as her word; the flowers came in a massive bouquet, and there was an enormous basket of fruit, so heavy that one of the secret policemen had to help the messenger carry it up the stairs. The rift with the imperial family was healed, but that healing had nearly cost him his life.

But Papa said that if he had been in a condition to make a choice, he would have preferred things as they now were, for he had entered the sickroom not knowing whether or not he could heal a cut finger, let alone Anna Aleksandrovna's broken legs and crushed skull. But even as he had risen from kneeling beside the bed, he had felt a warm surge of gratitude, for the light had come as he prayed for her, and he saw this as a certain sign that God had forgiven him and restored his healing powers. He had wanted to embrace the Tsar and Tsarina, and to tell them of his unflagging love, but the room had begun to spin about him, and he had felt a strong need of fresh air. He had started for the door, hoping to reach the outside and restore his balance, only to fall. But his last conscious thought had been one of gratitude; the Lord had relented and his penance was at an end. His communication with the Khristos within had been reestablished.

✕FOURTEEN✕

During his long convalescence, Papa had an abundance of time in which to review the last two years of his life. His recovery was due to two factors: his magnificent physique and Dunia's loving care. She was nurse, mother, mistress, and confessor, all rolled into one, and she served him day and night. As he lay in bed, he realized that while others had had to work long and diligently for powers such as his, he had been born with them. And, since they were not the fruits of his own efforts, he had not placed as high a value on them as had those who had struggled to attain them. And he also realized that having frittered away his gifts, he would now have to toil to regain them, toil as any beginner would. And he began to pray and meditate, and to repeat passages from the Bible to himself. He determined to live, as one Master had put it, "in constant remembrance of God."

With the war going so badly for Russia, the people set out to find scapegoats upon whom to vent their rage. Ironically, they were incited by the very groups that were really to blame for the deteriorating situation: the munitions profiteers, the inept civil servants, the self-seeking military and government leaders. Like the sheep that an aroused mob most closely resembles, they began looting and burning shops owned by those with Germanic names, caring little that the vast majority of these were loyal to Russia. The real target of their instigated hatred was the Tsarina, and rumors about her were circulated as fast as they could be manufactured. She was a German spy; she had erected a secret wireless transmitter at Tsarskoye Syelo, over which she sent coded details of Russian military plans to the Kaiser; Rasputin was an agent in the pay of the Kaiser; the Tsarina and Anna Aleksandrovna—poor crippled Anyushka—were Rasputin's mistresses, and while working for the German victory, were indulging in three-way orgies on the side. When the Tsar removed the egocentric and inept Grand Duke Nikolai Nikolay-evich from his command, it was seen as a victory for the Tsarina, the hated Germanskaya,* who would now use the Tsar as her puppet. But even if they had known of her many rebuffs to Wilhelm's overtures, it would have made no difference; their minds were closed to reason. They did not want facts; they wanted scapegoats, and in the Tsarina and my father they found a symbolic cause of their frustrations, the proxies for all the inept public servants who had led them into the quagmire.

Now that the Tsar was in command of the armies, the home front came under the management of the Tsarina, an indirect management, to be sure, for she had no such authority under Russian law, but she exercised power through her letters to her husband.

In many of these letters, she gave greater weight to her suggestions by saying that they had been offered by my father, who might never have heard of the particular idea. The revolutionaries declared that he was the real ruler of Russia. The Mad Monk, as Iliodor called him, although he was neither mad nor a monk, and Anna Aleksandrovna Virubova were

*German (fem.)

conspiring with that well-known German spy, the Tsarina, to destroy Russia.

But there never was a more unlikely cabal; the "plotters" were all in poor physical condition: Rasputin barely able to be up and about, Anna Aleksandrovna still on crutches and in pain from her crippling accident, and the Tsarina confined almost entirely to a wheelchair because of her weak heart. All were too ill to do more than the minimum amount of work in line with what they considered to be their duty. But, in spite of his infirmities, my father kept one thought uppermost in his mind: He must do what was best for his country. And his plans, if not always in the highest tradition of statecraft, were still, to him, an improvement on the current policies of the government. It was plain to him that the monarchy must be preserved; if it were to fall, all Russia would fall with it. He had seen the aristocracy, decadent and concerned only with position; the venal industrialists, striving only for unreasonable profits; the revolutionaries, bent only on tearing down the whole fabric, and he knew that there was not one shred of patriotism in the lot. The liberals, impractical as ever, cried out for a democracy under a parliamentary form, like that of England. But the Duma —as an example of how such a system would have operated in Russia—was a welter of endless debate, deciding nothing, accomplishing nothing, the members indulging themselves in invective and diatribe. He could see no other way than that of placing himself under God's will and guiding the Tsar according to that will. And although his contact with the Lord was fitful at best, his way might well have succeeded if Nikolas Aleksandrovich had not been vacillating, weak on major issues, and stubborn on minor ones. On one occasion, when the Tsar had failed to carry out one of his suggestions with the necessary vigor, Papa exploded at the dinner table, giving a terse, but accurate description of him: "No guts."

Ж

The sad plight of Russia did not seem to have much effect on Prince Feliks Feliksovich Yussupov, who had been doing his level best to fit into the pattern of a normal husband. In March 1915 Irina Aleksandrovna bore him a daughter, and at the christening in the family chapel, the Tsar stood as her godfather, and the Dowager Empress, the child's great-grandmother, was the godmother.

Not long after this happy event, Feliks' father was made governor-general of Moscow, where he soon found himself in difficulty because of his dictatorial rule. He had always been an insecure man, having become a prince by marriage, and was, therefore, more jealous of his position than if he had been to the manner born. He came to consider any opposition as a personal affront and an act of treason, and became convinced that those in disagreement with him were in league with the so-called German party, that nonexistent organization supposedly headed by the Tsarina and Rasputin. Everything that went wrong was their fault, and he avidly joined in a plot to depose the Tsar, place the Tsarina in a convent, and exile my father back to Siberia. It was a year for plots; they blew in on every breeze, and floated out on every tide, and like most of them, this one came to nothing. It did, however, set Feliks' emotions to working. He, too, was obsessed with my father, but his obsession, at least at the outset, was not that of his father.

He had tired of a strictly heterosexual diet, and wanted nothing so much as to be with another of his persuasion. Dmitri, or an even more titillating notion, that strange and magnetic man, Rasputin. Requiring a confidant, he went to see Munia Golovina, at whose house he had first met Papa, and poured out his desire, although obliquely, into her sympathetic ear. But she was as innocent as his wife about such matters, having no conception of what he was talking about, and so gave him the only advice she could: to see the man whom she still regarded as the resurrected Khristos. He was surprised, as well as amused, by her suggestion; here was a man who was occupying more and more of his thoughts, despite his feelings of class distinction, and here was Munia, telling him to see the healer who was to cure him of the very affliction that he, the healer, was exacerbating. It was laughable, in a grim sort of way.

"What is there to lose?" she asked. "You can meet him at my house. I will arrange an appointment."

The meeting took place, and Feliks, not wanting to speak of his real problem before Munia and her mother, made an engagement to have a subsequent meeting at our flat. And a week or so later, when Varya and I returned home from shopping, we found an exquisitely tailored young man, with rather delicate features, sitting with Papa in the dining room, and were introduced to Prince Yussupov. At that age—I was sixteen, and Varya two years younger—we were attracted by any handsome man, but there was something about this one we found faintly repellent, a languid manner that was not usual in young males. Any normal girl in her middle teens, upon first meeting an acceptable man, immediately and unconsciously resorts to her instant inner computer, a far more complex device than any that has gone with the astronauts to the moon, and she assesses him in the role of a potential lover, even if she does not know exactly what that means. Neither Varya nor I could think of Yussupov in that light. And when we compared notes after leaving Papa and Feliks alone, we each found that the other had suppressed her laughter with great difficulty when the prince had picked up the wineglass that Papa had just set down, and had turned it so that he could drain the last drop from the very spot on the rim that Papa's lips had touched. We had also sensed a certain coldness when he said good-bye.

As Varya observed, "He's got ice in his eyes."

I added, "And in his veins, too."

After the prince had left, I asked Papa: "Why did he come?"

"He has a problem, and he needs me."

"Will he come again?"

He nodded in assent, and from that day forward, Feliks was an almost constant visitor at Number 64 Gorokhovaya Ulitsa. I noticed that he always came in by the back way, but when I asked why, Papa refused to say.

Although the war had been going on for almost two years, it became clear that Yussupov was not one of the great patriots of his time. There was a law enacted to provide for the needs of farming families, thereby maintaining an adequate food supply, to the effect that an only son could not be drafted into the army. But the law did not specify that it applied only to farmers, and thus it provided a nice escape for Feliks. He was

215

indeed an only son, now that his older brother was dead, but he was not what one might classify as an essential worker for his family, which had hundreds of workers on its several estates. Nevertheless, he took advantage of the law, until the Tsarina summoned him to the palace and told him of the adverse comment his refusal to serve his country was causing.

She may have shamed him into going through the motions of becoming involved in the struggle, but it was strictly superficial on his part. He enrolled in the Corps of Pages, a training school for young officers—and at the age of twenty-nine he was the senior in the school, most of his classmates being in their teens. With his age and education he should have led his class, but he spent a great deal of his time seducing his classmates rather than devoting himself to becoming a good officer.

The school only served to amuse him sexually and keep him out of the war because he continually failed to pass examinations and had to go through the whole thing all over again.

When Papa and Feliks had their first meeting at our flat he came straight to the point: "You must know, of course, that I have homosexual desires as well as heterosexual, and the former is interfering with my marriage."

In fact, it was ruining his marriage, but Papa saw some hope, since he was genuinely concerned for his wife. He must have had great affection for her because they continued to live together until his death in 1967. It was because of his love for his wife that Papa thought he could help him.

And there was another reason for my father's willingness to help the prince, one that was in the interest of the crown. Knowing that Princess Zenaidye Nikolayevna Yussupova, Feliks' mother, was close to the Tsarina's sister, the Grand Duchess Elizaveta Feodorovna, and that both were leaders of one of the most virulent groups opposing the Tsarina, Papa hoped that, by gaining their friendship, or at least their neutrality, through helping Feliks, he could lessen their hatred and curtail the plotting that was tearing Russia apart.

Although the prince's visits were a well-kept secret, Anna Aleksandrovna Virubova came to learn of them. Having known Feliks all of his life, she was well aware of his changeable nature, and warned Papa that the loving friend of today could turn overnight into tomorrow's implacable enemy. But Papa believed he was making some progress, presuming that there were few born homosexuals, that most homosexuals had been turned aside from normal ways by some incident, or series of incidents, in their early childhood. If this were true, one could be returned to a socially acceptable life from what Papa conceived to be a bad habit. It is quite likely that modern psychologists would disagree with this view, but the answer to the problem, if answer there be, is still undiscovered.

In any event, the prince's main concern was that no one should overhear his confessions. But there was one who did hear, with whom he was not concerned. He had been reared in a life-style in which servants were deemed to be something less than human; intelligent animals trained to serve their masters, but otherwise of little account. Brought up in such an atmosphere, he completely ignored Dunia, and as she said later: "He looked at me with blind eyes."

But Dunia was there, and she heard much of what was said, things that shocked the simple woman from Tobolsk Province at first, but which she later repeated to me in all their strange detail. And when I heard her account, the reason behind my father's murder became a little clearer.

For a time, it seemed to Papa that he was justified in his hopes for Feliks' cure; the prince was more relaxed, less mincing in his mannerisms, less furtive, and even I began to relent a little in my attitude toward him. But not so Dunia, who remained unconvinced, unable to see more than a superficial alteration in him.

Papa laughed at her misgivings: "He may be weak, but basically, he is good."

At which Dunia sniffed: Grischa thought everyone was good.

However, it was not long before he was forced to agree, at least in part, with her estimate. Princess Irina Aleksandrovna left with her in-laws for a holiday in the Crimea, and with the last inhibiting factor removed, and a plenitude of time on his hands, Yussupov returned to his old ways. The next time

217

he came to the flat, he displayed every sign of having been drinking steadily, and his eyes were bright with a glitter that made Dunia uneasy as she showed him into the study.

Addressing her directly for the first time, he said, "How strange it is, Dunia, that you never married. A crude sort of man, perhaps some muzhik, could find you quite attractive."

And when Papa entered the study a few moments later, he found Feliks lying stark naked on the couch. There was no doubt what he had in mind, and Papa was dismayed to see that all his efforts had been in vain. The very idea of what he knew was in Feliks' mind filled him with disgust. He could only contemplate with nausea the idea of contact between those of the same sex. And when the prince rose from the couch and came toward him, Papa could stand no more. With a revulsion that he could in no way suppress, he placed both hands on Feliks' chest and thrust him backward until he fell onto the couch. Struggling manfully to swallow the gorge that rose in his throat, Papa gave the prince a dressing-down that would normally have been reserved for a disobedient stable boy. In a cold fury, Feliks threw on his clothing and stormed out of the flat, swearing never to return. And although Papa did not know it, more than hurt feelings were at stake; the die had been cast.

Sentiment in our little household was one of relief. "Good riddance," said Dunia, "I'm glad to see the back of him."

Varya and I, too, were pleased, although curious. But when we asked Papa why Feliks had not returned, he told us that the prince was busy elsewhere. And he cautioned all of us not to gossip about the matter.

"People come here as they would to confession," he told us.

Ж

Not the oldest living Russian could recall a harder winter than the one of 1916. From the western border clear to the Urals, blizzard followed blizzard. While the people suffered, the troops nearly froze in their trenches. Ill supplied, ill fed, and ill armed, their morale diminished to the vanishing point, they began

218

deserting by the thousands. Some of them had formed into roving bands, still bearing their arms, and terrorized the countryside, stealing what little food they could find, and thereby contributing to the shortages in the cities. In Petrograd and Moscow, women queued up for bread, standing all day long in shivering lines at the bakeshops, only to find, on moving up to the door, that there was no bread. Electricity was rationed, and so was wood and coal, so that the people spent a good part of their time huddled in bed under every available blanket, and whatever pieces of clothing they were not already wearing.

Papa was in a state of profound depression; he would have accepted any suffering to have spared the nation. But his inability to cure Feliks gave indisputable evidence of his waning powers, and if he could not heal one poor human of his sexual aberration, how could he hope to heal an entire nation of its conflicting states of lunacy?

In all his forty-five years, my father had, with very few brief lapses, been an optimist. His feeling had always been that where there was evil, there was good to overcome it; where there was suffering, there was always comfort and consolation; the Good Lord stood at the side of those who turned to Him in their need. But, of course, it was necessary for them to turn to Him, and it appeared that the people of Russia were not, with few exceptions, placing themselves at His feet. And if they would not, there was no hope for them; death and destruction would be their lot. Always, in his mind, it was "their" lot, never his own, for somehow he knew that he would not be there to undergo the final torture of defeat and chaos with them. And this further increased his sorrow, for he had always seen himself in the role of comforter and healer. But of what use was a healer shorn of his powers? Perhaps it was time for him to make his exit. Alas, poor Russia, poor people, and poor Romanovs. What would their future be? The fragmented images, all that remained of his once-potent clairvoyance, showed him a scene of unalloyed misery, and he went about the flat overwhelmed with the burden of his foreknowledge.

With little work to do on the farm, now that everything was deep in snow, Mama permitted my brother, Dmitri, and Katya to visit us, and having his son with him brightened

Papa's outlook for a while. But when the vacation was over and it was time for Dmitri to return, Papa, still seeing dimly into the future, begged him to stay on for Christmas, saying that it would be the last they would spend together. But Dmitri had promised Mama to bring Dunia back before the New Year, and he felt it necessary to refuse. Papa was right; he never saw his son or Dunia again.

In an attempt to restore his physique for the work that he knew was ahead, Papa started taking long walks alone, followed only by his guards, too steeped in gloom to chat with them as he had previously done. One afternoon, after trudging along the banks of the Nyeva, he told Katya that he had seen the river running red with the blood of the grand dukes, and turning from her, he stumbled into his study. There, he wrote a long letter to me, which he sealed and placed in my bureau, as I watched him in wide-eyed wonder.

He admonished me: "Don't open it until after I am dead."

Unable to conceive of a world without my father, I laughed uneasily, certain that he was joking, and thinking it was a pretty poor joke.

Ж

Even as my father was trying to formulate some plan that would save the empire, in his palace by the Moika Canal, Prince Feliks Feliksovich Yussupov was plotting his revenge. And it was not long before he found others to fall in with his plot. The Grand Duke Dmitri Pavlovich, with whom he had reinstated his former relations, was easily convinced of the rightness of Feliks' thinking; anything that Feliks wanted must be right. And they set about finding others who would join forces with them.

And these were by no means my father's only enemies. There was the Grand Duchess Elizaveta Feodorovna, who had left her convent to visit her sister, the Tsarina, and had given vent to a violent outburst against him. There were the members of the Duma, the most virulent of whom were Maklakov and Vladimir Mitrofanovich Purichkevich, who inveighed against him in speech after speech. And there were churchmen, high in the councils of the Synod, who believed the rumors that he was wooing the tsarevich away from Orthodoxy, and preached against the "heretic." The total impact of the combined animosity further served to sap his vitality; as the pain of his wound lessened, the mental anguish of watching Russia follow its downward path caused his health to fail. He began frequenting the Villa Rodye once more; there, dancing and listening to the wild Gypsy music, his thoughts could be pushed into the background for a time.

It was after one such all-night carousal at the Villa Rodye that he returned to the flat exhausted, hardly able to navigate the stairs. Falling into bed, he had just dropped off to sleep when there came a telephone call from the Royal Palace. I answered the phone and found the caller to be the Tsarina. She was frantic. The tsarevich had been on his way to the front with his father in an effort to bolster the morale of the troops, and he had fallen ill. Grigori Efimovich was the only one who could help the boy. Would he please come at once?

I ran to tell Papa, only to find him lying on his back, staring blankly at the ceiling, apparently unable to hear what I was saying. His face was ashen, and he felt icy cold when I touched him. Because of the urgency of the occasion, I persisted in trying to rouse him, and finally I broke through his near-catatonic state, but he could only raise a blue-tinged hand in a weak gesture of refusal, and whisper, "Not yet. Not yet."

Frightened, for he seemed to be at the point of death, I ran for Katya, and we sat beside him, wondering what we could do to restore his vitality. He was struggling to collect his forces, and some energy began to flow through his body. He began to pray, but no answer was given him. And he wept for his lost powers, because he was unable to help those who needed him. I had never seen my father cry; he had always been the strong anchor that held my life's craft from drifting onto the rocks. He had been my citadel, but the walls had been breached, the anchor chain had broken, and I felt very lonely indeed. And then the telephone rang again.

It was the Tsarina, and in panic, she cried out: "Aleksei is dying. Tell your father he must come."

The Tsar took the phone: "Where is he? Please get him."

"Just one moment, please, Vyelichyestvo."

I hurried back to Papa's bedside and asked him what I should say.

He replied, "Tell them to send a car."

After relaying his message to the Tsar, I helped Katya get him up and into his clothing. By the time we had made him ready, the car was at the door. Katya took one of his arms and I the other, and between us he managed to negotiate the stairs. It occurred to me that he was not warmly enough dressed, and I wanted to go back and get another coat, but he waved to me and told the chauffeur to drive on. His eyes were closed, and I knew he was praying.

Whether it was his prayer or some other power, Aleksei responded as he had always done under Papa's ministrations, and again, the royal parents were grateful for his efforts. As Papa prepared to leave, the Tsar caught him by the coat.

"How can we ever thank you, Grigori Efimovich?"

"It is not I you must thank, Vyelichyestvo."

"Then, Otyets Grigori, give me your blessing."

"This time, Little Father, it is I who need your blessing." He embraced the Tsar and Tsarina, and left the room.

Aleksandra Feodorovna put her fingertips to her face, and said to her husband with some surprise: "Why, Grigori Efimovich left a tear on my cheek."

Even in the attenuated state of his clairvoyance, he had seen that which he could not recount to his dear friends. They were never to see each other again.

Ж

On the following day, Yussupov telephoned to say that he wanted to see my father again. I took the call and relayed the message with some reluctance to Papa, at the same time pleading with him not to renew their meetings. But he discounted my fears, having received renewed faith in his powers after the tsarevich's healing. He went to the telephone and arranged for the appointment. But his yielding to Feliks' persuasion was but further proof of his waning powers. In previous times, he would have instantly perceived the hatred and revenge seething within Feliks' brain, but now he was as a man deprived of sight. And lacking any forewarning, he trusted the prince.

✕FIFTEEN✕

By the afternoon of December 16, 1916, the snow that had been falling so heavily stopped, although there was every likelihood that it would not remain clear for long. Taking advantage of the lull in the blizzard, Anna Aleksandrovna Virubova climbed the stairs to our flat. Still limping, she used a cane. The climb was difficult for her, and she had not been to Gorokhovaya Ulitsa for quite some time. But now, she was on an errand for the Tsarina, who had sent her to ask his opinion of a pain in Aleksei's leg, as well as to take some gifts for Papa, Varya, and me.

I led her to the dining room, where Papa was sitting, having a glass of his favorite Madeira, and I offered a glass to Anna Aleksandrovna. As she sipped it, she sighed.

"We have changed, you and I, dear Grischa," she said, "and I do not think for the better."

"All things change, Anyushka."

"Of course. But I was just remembering when I first

saw you as you strode into the tsarevich's sickroom, like a giant; so confident in your powers, you seemed to tower above the Tsar."

She sighed again, and gave us our presents from the royal family. And then she proceeded to the second reason for her coming.

"The tsarevich has developed a pain in his leg," she said. "Her Majesty does not think it sufficiently severe to require your going to him. What do you think?"

"You are right, Anyushka, it is not serious. Just keep the doctors away from him and he will be all right. I can tell you this much: Throughout the rest of his life, Aleksei will not be seriously ill again."

I was surprised to see a look of infinite sadness cross Papa's face, for what he had just predicted should have been most welcome news. I did not realize that he had seen how tragically short that lovable little boy's life was to be. Anna Aleksandrovna had not seen that look of sadness, and took his words at face value.

"And what about you, Grischa? You do not seem to be in very good health."

He mustered up a characteristically crooked grin. "I am like a horse; nothing affects me."

Katya, coming in with more wine, looked at him as a reproving mother might. She said, with her usual bluntness: "He should get more sleep."

Making an attempt to appear his old jovial self, he raised his glass, and with a laugh less humorous than he had intended, replied, "Who needs sleep when there is wine?"

But his weak sally of levity did not impress any of us, and Katya persisted: "Tonight, at least, you should have your rest. Do you not agree, Anna Aleksandrovna?"

"Of course, I agree."

But Papa replied, "You know that is impossible, Katya Ivanova; I have an appointment at midnight."

"Where are you going so late at night?" Anna asked.

"Out by the Moika Kanal, to see Feliks' wife."

Anna Aleksandrovna would have stayed to question him further about what seemed to her a peculiar circumstance:

that he was making his first visit to the Yussupov Palace at such a late hour, but guests were soon coming to her house, and she had to get back to greet them. She arose, and taking his hand in hers, bent to give it her customary kiss. But a chill swept over her as she held it, and she looked up at him, her eyes full of pleading.

"What more can you ask of me?" he asked gently. "You already have all I can give."

Upon her return to Tsarskoye Syelo, she first went to the Tsarina's boudoir before going to her own house. Seated in that delicately decorated room, all ivory trimmed in gold, Anna Aleksandrovna made her report, repeating what Papa had said about the tsarevich's health, and adding that it was a shame that the starets had to go out in his weakened condition to the Yussupov Palace to see the Princess Irina.

"I think it most unwise for him to be going at so late an hour. It's so cold out."

Hearing this, the Tsarina looked up quickly. "But there must be some mistake, Anyushka; Irina Aleksandrovna is still in the Crimea." She looked thoughtfully up at the ceiling, as if to find the solution there. "Surely, there must be some mistake."

Making a mental note to call the starets and straighten out the matter, if only to satisfy her own curiosity, she went back to talking about Aleksei and her thankfulness that his condition was not serious. If she had realized what was actually at stake, she would have rushed to the telephone and ordered Papa to stay home.

When it was time for dinner, we found Papa in a better mood. He had been drinking steadily, and although he was not drunk, he was in good spirits, joking and playing with us. Katya served him a light meal of fish, black bread and honey, his favorite diet, and feeling quite content, he appeared to be his old self again. After we had eaten, he took me into his bedroom and showed me a pile of bank notes, amounting to some three thousand rubles, that he had kept in his bureau drawer, set aside for my dowry, when the time came for my marriage.

After the dishes were cleared away, he sat for a while

with us, chatting away, until, around seven o'clock, Katya answered the door and admitted the Minister of the Interior, A. D. Protopopov, who was a constant visitor and had become a close friend. He seemed quite depressed and melancholy, and asked Varya and me to leave the room so that he could speak with Papa in private. But even though we did as he requested, we could still hear most of the ensuing conversation through the door.

"You know, Grigori Efimovich, that there is a plot—in fact, several plots—being hatched against you."

"Yes, I know."

"Well, then, I would advise you to stay inside for the next few days. You will be safe here."

"But, Gospodin Ministr,* that is impossible. Already, I have an appointment for later tonight."

"Oh, no. You must cancel it."

"It is too late to cancel it."

"Well, then, at least tell me where you are going."

"I cannot, my friend. It is confidential."

"Perhaps you do not appreciate the seriousness of what I am saying. You know, do you not, that I have ways of obtaining information, ways that are reliable?"

"Of course; after all, you are the Minister of the Interior."

"So, you will see that what I now tell you, in the strictest confidence, is that there is a plot by some of the aristocracy, including members of the imperial family, who are planning to kidnap the Tsar and Tsarina, and place the tsarevich on the throne, under the regency of the Grand Duke Nikolai Nikolayevich. You will either be exiled to Siberia or put to death. I even know the names of the conspirators, but I cannot mention them at this time. They are so highly placed that I dare not move against them until they take some action."

"That is terrible. To think that they would do such a thing to that kind and good man. Terrible." He mused for a moment. "What about the guard at Tsarskoye Syelo? Is it sufficiently strong?"

"Oh, yes. As soon as I learned of the plot, I had the

*Mr. Minister

226

guard doubled, and every man is loyal to the Tsar." He arose. "I am already late for an appointment. Won't you reconsider your decision and stay home tonight? Think over what I have revealed to you. Your safety is vital to Their Majesties, and to Russia, you know, and I think you owe it to the Little Father to take care of yourself."

"Do not worry; I will be all right."

Varya and I were called back into the room to say good night to the Minister, and we all stood at the door to see him off.

Protopopov looked very serious as he turned to me and said, "Try to persuade him not to go out tonight. I cannot." He sighed, and descended the stairs without looking back.

I picked up the protest where Protopopov had left off, trying with every argument I could think of to convince Papa to stay home. But he was adamant, turning a deaf ear to my pleas. Finally, to prevent further discussion, he said, "I shall die when God wills; not one second before, or one second later. And there is nothing that I could do to prevent it."

Katya joined us for an hour or so around the dining-room table, and Papa had me read aloud from the Gospel of St. John: "In the beginning was the Word, and the Word was with God, and the Word was God. . . ." And he explained to us what John meant by "the Word."

"And the Word was made flesh and dwelt among us. . . ." And again came the explanation, so clear, so easy to comprehend, that for the first time I could feel the beauty and the truth in those mystic passages, and I also had more under-standing as to why Papa so impressed his followers.

That our evening together should be spent in Bible reading has given me strength all these years that I have been alone.

The clock in the hallway struck ten. Papa kissed Varya good night, then me—then sent us off to bed. He stayed talking with Katya of the old days in Pokrovskoye, of swimming and fishing in the Tura, of the farm and how it had prospered under Mama's management.

But I was unable to sleep. Protopopov's serious plea to keep Papa home was like an alarm that wouldn't shut up, keeping me awake. Dread was building up inside me. I was still awake when the clock struck eleven, and I heard Katya going up to her own room and to bed. Soon the house was silent, except for the ticking of the clock, as it ticked off the last hour of my father's residence at 64 Gorokhovaya Ulitsa.

Unable to sleep, I got up and wandered about our third-floor flat. Large, it was filled with nondescript furnishings that cast shadows like gray, ghostly grave markers in some far-off country cemetery. I stood in the doorway to the main reception room. There was the large round table, laden with gifts—fruits, jewelry, clothes, many packages as yet unopened —given to my father by his disciples and guests. I moved about the room, touching my hands to the backs of the many chairs, the sofa—and thought how often with all this sitting space, many had to stand, for the visitors were countless.

But tonight there were no visitors.

I recalled, earlier in the evening, the hushed conversation between Papa and Feliks. It sounded somewhat to me as if Papa was trying to get out of going. Feliks looked so tall and handsome in the dim light of Papa's study. He wore the elegantly cut clothes of a gentleman which clearly marked him as a member of the nobility. He wore a fur coat and cap with large earflaps pulled down on either side and he carried a heavy guitar case.

Although Papa seemed buoyant and it looked as if a gay party were in order, I heard him say to Feliks: "Why must it be *this* night?" and Feliks mumbled a reply I did not catch.

"So be it," Papa replied. "Wait here my little one, while I change into a fresh shirt."

I remember Papa picked out his most handsome shirt—a blue silk embroidered one with cornflowers which the Tsarina had made for him with her own hands. His favorite. For a poor muzhik who had once lived for a whole year in rough dirty robes in his native Siberia, my father's wardrobe for Petrograd was quite splendid. Most of his expensive shirts were made for him by the Tsarina. His needs, as he often said, were simple and he rarely gave thought to what he wore. This night he seemed so particular.

One thing that had always made me curious was that my father and Feliks' meetings were always so clandestine,

228

so secret. I could perhaps understand why Feliks would want them secret. It was no secret about the court that Papa was not exactly a close friend of the Yussupovs—to the contrary—but Papa was always so outgoing and unsecretive about his activities. I never could put my finger on his desire to keep their meetings from being known.

Finally, I, too, was overcome by drowsiness and went to bed, unaware it would be my last peaceful night's sleep for a long time.

Ж

Papa was now beyond any help from any of us. He was in the grip of an oddly assorted group who, under normal circumstances, would have had very little in common. And although Prince Feliks Feliksovich Yussupov had brought them together, their reasons for being there were quite different, for he had played up to the particular hatred that each had for my father. His own reason was a mixture of revenge (the hated muzhik had spurned his advances) and misguided patriotism, fed by his relative Rodzianko, leader of the Duma; the Tsarina's sister, the Grand Duchess Elizaveta Feodorovna; the Dowager Empress Maria Feodorovna, his wife's grandmother; and others of the aristocracy.

The Grand Duke Dmitri Pavlovich had a very simple reason for being one of the plotters, his feelings toward Feliks. Whatever Feliks wanted, he wanted. If Feliks thought that Russia would benefit from the starets' death, Dmitri could only agree.

Captain Ivan Sukhotin, a cavalry officer, was the sort of military man that believes any act committed in war, however base, was acceptable; and this was war.

V. M. Purishkevich was one of the more important members of the Duma, and one of the most vocal among those who wanted to dethrone the Tsar. He believed that my father was destroying Russia through his influence on the Tsarina, and holding that the end justifies the means, was willing to employ any means, even criminal ones.

Dr. Stanislas Lazovert's reason for becoming involved in the crime was somewhat obscure. He was serving as a

229

surgeon on the Red Cross train commanded by Purishkevich, and was eager to please his leader, as well as a wealthy prince. It was he who was to prepare the poison with which my father was to be put to death. Yussupov later said they had all agreed to give Papa a sufficient dose of potassium cyanide to kill him instantly.

But that raises a question in my mind: Why, if he was really poisoned, did my father not die? I know he had a superb physique, but he was not a fictional character, not some super-man that inhabits today's comic books. When Chionya Guseva stabbed him, he bled, and nearly died. And at the time of his murder, he was not, by any means, in his best physical condition. Based on the facts I could collect afterward from Yussupov, his servant Ivan, and his sister-in-law, I came to the conclusion that it was more likely Dr. Lazovert substituted some opiate for the potassium cyanide he was supposed to have used.

Prior to his appointment with my father that fateful evening, Feliks had already prepared a room in which to commit the act of murder. The room, in the basement of the Yussupov house, had been completely redecorated under Feliks' personal supervision. He had particularly insisted that the room look as though it were constantly in use, rather than newly arranged. He feared Papa might become suspicious if the room were less than comfortable and lived in.

Originally the room had been part of a wine cellar. The room was divided by a low arch; one section was rather expansive, the other small. From the small section an entrance led to a spiral staircase, the top of which opened onto the courtyard. Above that Feliks maintained his own study.

The furnishings included carved antique chairs, elegantly upholstered in time-ripened leather, other chairs—massive oak with high backs—diminutive black cupboards. Scattered about were small tables draped in brightly colored materials, atop which sat ivory goblets and Italian art objects. On top of one of the cupboards was a seventeenth-century crucifix of rock crystal and silver, most likely Italian. A large open fireplace formed out of expensive red granite dominated the dining room. Above it gilt cups and old majolica plates stood side by side with some ebony carvings. A large Persian carpet covered the floor. There was also a large casual white bearskin rug.

Thus was the setting.

Ж

As Papa closed the door behind him at our home, he made the sign of the cross and pulled his collar up tighter about his neck. A large black limousine was waiting at the curb for Papa and the prince. Dr. Lazovert, disguised in a chauffeur's uniform, was the driver. Papa entered the car first, followed quickly by Feliks, who quietly closed the door. The car pulled quickly away and into the black night.

The snow was starting to fall again and Papa thought it unusual that the car was moving so rapidly.

"Why the hurry?" he asked Feliks.

Feliks did not answer. Instead he gently pressed his hand against Papa's thigh. Papa was uncomfortable, never enjoying that close a proximity with a male companion. Feliks was more like a son to him.

Papa was quite fond of Feliks—had always been. That he didn't approve of Feliks' behavior was one thing, but it did not deter his liking the young prince. Feliks had usually been somewhat detached, and not so familiar, and it puzzled Papa, who quickly drew his knee away from the prince's advances and began a lively conversation.

"Tell me again about the headaches your wife has been having."

Feliks, slipping into a strange mood, did not reply. No longer nervous, Feliks' mood became dark and somber. He appeared to be put out that Papa had withdrawn from his unwarranted gesture.

Feliks continued silent as the car careened at excessive speeds around corners in the ever-deepening snow. The car made an awful racket in the night as the tire chains beat a rapid rhythm against the icy roads.

Papa asked once again: "Why the hurry?"

231

Yussupov, not wanting to alarm my father, thought he better come up with some sort of explanation for what was already a strange set of circumstances.

"My wife is having a party but the guests will be leaving very soon, I'm sure. We'll go to the game room and wait for her there." He added, "She *insisted* I bring you tonight." Realizing his statement wasn't making a lot of sense, Feliks, as an afterthought, said, "She somehow manages to get through even though her headaches are painful."

"Well," Papa said, "it certainly seems an odd hour for such a meeting, but perhaps you know best." Papa pulled out a gold pocket watch, a recent much-treasured gift inscribed to him from the Tsarina. The tiny gold hands said 12:30 A.M. He sighed as he slipped it back into his pocket.

Both men cringed as the car bumped along the wintery street. The car finally came to a stop, though, alongside the Moika River, at the side entrance of the imposing and magnificent Yussupov Palace.

The palace was three blocks long and considered the most elegant in all of Russia, save for the royal residence. At a side door the two men alighted hurriedly because it was still snowing and a crust of slippery ice covered the trodded ground.

They banged the huge brass knocker on the door, and as they waited, their breath made smokelike steam billows in the cold night air. Papa shivered, as though he was pleased the journey was at an end.

Yussupov conducted Papa down into his prepared "game room." The sounds of a Gramophone came from upstairs, playing "Yankee Doodle Went to Town," and some voices, which the prince told Papa were the sounds of a party his wife was giving.

The room looked as though it had been occupied recently. There were empty teacups and on one table a chess set with chessmen poised in their play on the board.

Papa felt comfortable. After removing his greatcoat he moved to the area of the fireplace and sank down into one of the big hearth sofas facing the glowing flames. He put his feet out, resting them on the bearskin rug.

The prince offered him a glass of port.

232

Papa refused it. "You know I prefer my Madeira."

Yussupov excused himself and said, "Oh, how silly of me. Of course." He excused himself and went to get the Madeira.

Papa moved closer to the blazing fire to warm his frozen fingers, pressing his cold hands together to stir up circulation. Feliks had gone upstairs for the wine and Papa was alone in the room. For some unknown reason, he picked up the glass of port and drank it. Perhaps it was the cold; perhaps Feliks took longer than necessary to return. In any event, he drank the port—and Papa never drank port.

Papa, becoming impatient, and hearing the music filtering down from upstairs, started up the staircase to see what was taking Feliks so long. Just then, Feliks appeared at the top of the stairs, with a bottle of Madeira.

"Ah, Father Grigori," he said, "forgive me. I have been trying to persuade my wife to leave her guests. It will only be a moment more. Meanwhile, why don't we relax."

With a bottle of wine in one hand, Yussupov gently took Papa's arm with the other hand and backed him back down the stairs.

Feliks led Papa to the sofa, where, on a coffee table, a feast was prepared. There were several wineglasses, rum cakes, bonbons, and other sweetmeats. Papa, who never cared for sweets, declined them, but relaxed with a glass of wine.

Yussupov sat down next to Papa and they both sipped the heavy wine. Papa said he felt a strange headiness, unusual for him. Yussupov assured him it was probably the heat from the fireplace.

"Perhaps," Papa said, expelling a large sigh. "Perhaps I am more tired than I thought."

Feliks again and again filled Papa's glass, ever moving closer to Papa and saying in a soft voice, "Grigori . . ."

Suddenly, Papa jumped to his feet. "I've got to leave. Obviously she isn't coming." He walked toward the clothes closet for his coat.

Feliks, not to be denied, followed closely behind him. "Oh, no! Grigori, don't go. She'll be here in a minute—I'm sure."

Feliks nervously drank down the remaining contents of his glass, his heavy breathing close to the back of Papa's neck.

Suddenly, the coconspirators, waiting in the upper study, began to make some noise.

"You see?" Feliks almost shouted. "You hear? That is probably the guests leaving." He tugged at Papa's arm. "She will be here now. Wait, let me go and get her."

Feliks went rapidly up the stairs, in order to quiet his friends. Dmitri gave him a revolver to take back with him, when he told them Rasputin would not wait much longer.

Yussupov returned to find Papa admiring the crystal crucifix, and as he examined it, Feliks said, "Grigori, you had better look at the crucifix and say a prayer before it."

Papa turned and there was a look of tender surrender in his eyes, as if he knew the trap had finally slammed shut on him.

Papa looked up, and suddenly two strangers appeared from the upper part of the house. At first Papa couldn't tell who they were, and then he recognized Dmitri and Dr. Lazovert.

Just as my father was about to speak to the grand duke, two other men, Captain Sukhotin and Purishkevich, entered the room from the landing above. They all moved swiftly into the lower chamber.

Papa, trying to collect his thoughts, stood in a daze. Paul Stepanoff approached Papa and grasped his hand, as if in a tender display of affection.

"What's the matter? Afraid to have a little fun?" He almost fell at Papa's feet in his overanxious movement to grasp Papa's hand.

"Holy Mother," Papa stammered, recognizing the intent of the gesture.

Suddenly his tormentors came for him en masse, as he desperately tried to push them away. But it was useless. He caught sight of Feliks, whose eyes were glassy and set, and said, "May God forgive you!"

Having used him sexually, Feliks finally pulled forth the gun and fired a single shot into Papa's head as he was struggling back to his feet. Papa fell backward, onto the bearskin

234

rug. Blood began to spread across the white fur from the wound in Papa's head.

"Is he dead?" asked Yussupov.

"No, a little wine will fix him up," volunteered one of the men as he grabbed a half-filled glass and promptly threw it into Papa's face.

"What do they want of me," Papa mumbled half-consciously, "what do they want?"

Suddenly things began to happen more swiftly. As if programmed for this very moment, the men moved in unison and with precision over my father's body. There was much kicking, punching, and gouging at the inert body lying on the now blood-soaked rug.

One of the men drew a dagger and, pushing aside the man who was still straddled across the lower extremities of my father, rapidly tore away the remains of his trousers. Some say it was Feliks who wielded the knife; others say differently.

In any event they all hovered close, watching as the deed was committed. With the skill of a surgeon, these elegant young members of the nobility castrated Grigori Rasputin, flinging the severed penis across the room.

No one ever knew whether the sharp pain in his groin was felt by the victim. He never uttered a sound.

Yussupov, seeming to come out of a trance, seized at Papa's body and began to shake it violently. Then, as he let it drop back on the blood-wet rug, he was amazed to see an eyelid quiver and then open. And in another instant both eyes were open, and he was horrified to see increasing signs of life. Papa suddenly jumped to his feet with some new God-given strength and grasped Feliks in a grip of steel, one hand on each of the prince's shoulders. Feliks responded with occult hysteria.

"I suddenly realized who Rasputin really was," Feliks later related. "It was the reincarnation of Satan himself who held me in his clutches and would never let me go until my dying day."

But with desperation born of terror, Yussupov pulled himself free, and my father fell back, apparently giving up the ghost, lifeless, onto the floor.

The conspirators left the starets on the floor and went

up the stairway to the study, to further carry out the plot—disposal of the body. In the middle of the discussion they heard noises in the hallway. When they opened the door they saw my father, who had crawled up to the first landing, surge forward through the door out into the open courtyard.

"My God," Yussupov cried, "he's STILL ALIVE!"

Purishkevich rushed out with his drawn revolver and fired two more shots, and then two more. Papa fell into a mound of snow.

When a policeman came to investigate the shots, Feliks met him at the gate, and explained that a drunken guest had fired off a few rounds.

Satisfying the policeman, Feliks returned to the house to find that his servant had moved the body back indoors and placed it on the landing. Feliks looked at his handiwork.

"My head," he said later, "was bursting asunder. My thoughts were confused and I was beside myself with rage."

It was told by Purishkevich that Feliks launched an attack of physical abuse on the silent body of my father, that it "was such a harrowing sight I doubt I shall ever be able to forget it."

Sukhotin, in the meantime, had donned my father's greatcoat and cap, and had been driven by Dr. Lazovert back to our flat, with the idea of throwing anyone who might have followed the car on its first ride to the Moika Palace off the track, and Dmitri went along as a substitute for Feliks. Upon their return, they found Purishkevich alone, he and Ivan having put Feliks to bed. Fearing that his present unstable condition might undo them all, they let him sleep, wrapped the body in a piece of cloth, tying it securely with a cord, and placed it in the back of their car. They drove to the Petrovski Ostrov,* and there, from the top of the bridge, they threw it through a hole in the ice into the river. Their hope was that their grisly package would be carried downstream, under the ice, and so out to sea, thus ensuring that it would never be found.

Ж

And thus passed Grigori Efimovich Rasputin, who died not of

*Petrovski Island

236

bullet wounds or mutilation, although either of these would have eventually resulted in his death, but of drowning. For it was found that his wrists, which the plotters had bound when they tied him in the cloth, were badly scarred by the ropes, evidence that he had struggled to free himself once the cold water of the river had revived him.

Gone was the starets, the strayed Holy Man, the fallen saint, my loving father, and with him went his God-given powers of healing and clairvoyance, employed solely for the benefit of his fellowman. Gone was Rasputin—and who was there left to pray for the unfortunate people he had loved so well?

⚔EPILOGUE⚔

It was long past midnight when I finally fell into a fitful sleep, disturbed by dreams that contributed little to my rest. I was in the toils of another nightmare as the gray dawn broke over the city, one filled with flitting images of a sneering Yussupov, a threatening Chionya Guseva, knife raised, prepared to strike again, and a worried Anna Aleksandrovna. Into this confusion of visions, a bell intruded with an insistent ring, and, glad to be awakened, I ran to the telephone. At the other end of the line was Protopopov, apologizing for calling so early.

"What time is it?" I asked.

"Just seven. I wanted to know if your father is home."

"I'll see if he is in his room. Please hold the phone."

Finding his room empty, and his bed unmussed, I returned to the telephone. "No, I'm sorry; he isn't here."

"Thank you. I must go."

And without any explanation, the Minister hung up.

The sense of foreboding that had overcome me on the previous night now returned tenfold. I had to know what had happened to Papa, and yet I dreaded what I might learn. Putting my fears behind me, I called Munia Golovina, and asked her if she had seen him since midnight.

"No, dear, I haven't. Isn't he at home?"

"No, he isn't. He went off with Prince Yussupov at midnight, and I haven't seen him since. I'm worried."

"Perhaps he is still with Feliks."

"Oh, Gospozha Golovina, would you please call the prince and ask him?"

"Yes, Maria, I will. Don't worry; I am sure that he is all right. I'll call you as soon as I've talked to Feliks."

But although I waited for the return call, it never came. Katya had meanwhile prepared our breakfast, a breakfast that none of us could touch, although Katya tried to eat a little of it as an example to Varya and me. And, finally, unable to wait any longer, I called Anna Virubova at her house in Tsarskoye Syelo.

"Oh, Gospozha Virubova, I'm so worried about Papa." I told her what little I knew, and asked, "Do you think you could find out what has happened?"

"I will see what I can learn. In the meantime, do not worry. No harm can come to him; of that I am certain."

The lady in waiting stopped only long enough to make herself presentable before rushing over to the palace to inform the Tsarina. And hard on her heels came a flurry of telephone calls. The first was from Protopopov, who phoned from his office to furnish a summary of the few facts known to the police; the pistol shots, Feliks' statement that a drunken guest had fired them, but little more. Then the Grand Duke Dmitri Pavlovich called to ask the Tsarina if he could come to tea. When she refused him, he gave every evidence of being quite disturbed. And no sooner had he rung off than a call came from Yussupov for Anna Aleksandrovna, asking to see her.

The flood of telephone calls had only added to her uneasiness, and so she replied, "No, Feliks, I cannot see you, at least not today."

"Well, then, I must speak to Her Majesty. Please tell her that I want to give her an account of what has taken place."

"What has taken place, Feliks? Have you something to tell me of the whereabouts of Grigori Efimovich?"

"No, no." His voice had a decided tremolo. "I know nothing of that." There was no question but that the murderer had not recovered from his panic of the previous night, in spite of the statements in his books to the contrary.

"Well, then, what is it you have to tell?"

"I will call later. Good-bye."

At ten that morning, the police, who were scouring the whole city for some clue, went to see Yussupov. The police chief, General Grigoryev, questioned him, and he related the version of the story concocted by the plotters on the previous night, that the shots were fired by a guest.

"Wasn't Rasputin among your guests?"

And Yussupov writes that he replied, "Rasputin never comes to my house."

Just as the chief was leaving, Munia Golovina telephoned and waited impatiently on the line while Feliks saw the policeman out.

When he picked up the instrument, she asked, "What have you done with Grigori Efimovich?"

The prince, his heart sinking, replied in a quavering voice: "I have done nothing with him. I have not seen him in several days."

"Feliks, do not lie to me. You called for him at his flat last night around midnight."

"Oh, that. Well, I only spoke to him for a few minutes."

All at once, she was alarmed. Why had he lied to her about not having seen the starets, and then reversed himself, admitting that he had? There was something afoot that she did not like, and she asked him to come around to her house and give her some much-needed assurance.

By now, everyone had come to the conclusion that Papa was dead. Even the Tsarina, who had held to a slender thread of hope, grudgingly agreed with the consensus, and she turned a tear-stained face to her lady in waiting.

"Anyushka, what will we do without him? What will

Aleksei do without him? What will happen if my son is taken ill again?"

"Remember, Vyelichyestvo, Otyets Grigori told you that the tsarevich would have no further illness." But, of course, that was no answer to their growing grief and fears, and they wept together as women have always done for those who are dear to them.

Yussupov's overwhelming compulsion was to flee from the gathering unpleasantness. He did not think the crime could be laid at his door unless he did something to give himself away and, therefore, wanted to avoid additional questioning by the police and by his victim's friends at the palace. He decided that the best place in which he could escape the gathering storm was his estate in the Crimea. But he had sufficient presence of mind to realize that a simple flight would set tongues wagging, and so he first paid a visit to the Minister of Justice to learn what the reaction would be to his planned journey. The Minister assured him that there was no reason why he should not go, but then, the Minister had knowledge that caused him to give that assurance. For several hours, the police had been intercepting telephone calls and telegrams from people in the highest places, including some members of the imperial family, all of which assumed that Feliks had been the ringleader in an as yet unproved murder, and all made it plain that he had their support. And the Minister realized that his caller was too big a fish for his net, and that it would be best for all concerned if he were to be treated with the utmost respect.

Late that afternoon, a police inspector called at our flat, accompanied by Episkop Isidor, who had been a friend of Papa's. The inspector showed us a bloodstained overshoe which we immediately recognized as our father's. He told us that it had been found on the ice near the Petrovski Most.* He also told us that divers had been lowered through the ice, but that no trace of the body had been found.

Varya and I were already convinced that our father was dead, but now that we had seen the overshoe, we were certain that he had been murdered; no other explanation seemed possible. We sent a wire to Mama, saying only that Papa was ill, and that we thought she should come to Petrograd.

*Petrovski Bridge

241

And then recalling the letter that he had shown me on the previous evening, I took it out of the drawer in which he had placed it, and sat down to read it aloud to Varya and Katya.

> *My Darlings,*
>
> *A disaster threatens us. Great misfortune is approaching. The face of Our Lady has become dark and the spirit is troubled in the calm of the night. This calm will not last. Terrible will be the anger. And where shall we flee?*
>
> *It is written: Beware as you know neither the day nor the hour. The day has come for our country. There will be tears and blood. In the shadows of the suffering I can distinguish nothing. My hour will toll soon. I am not afraid but I know the break will be bitter. God knows the path your suffering will take. Innumerable men will perish. Numerous will be the martyrs. The earth will tremble. Famine and disease will strike men down. Some signs will appear to them. Pray for your salvation. By the grace of Our Lord and the grace of those who intercede for us, you will be consoled.*
>
> *Grigori*

As I finished reading the prophetic letter, so correct in its prediction of the cataclysm that was about to befall our native land, I found it impossible to believe that he would not soon come walking into the room and bend over to kiss me. I could actually feel that scratchy beard against my cheek. He had been the central point in my life. He had stood like a giant monolith, in the shadow of which one might play without concern, yet all the while knowing that he was there, protecting me with his love and kindness. And, as I looked up through my tears, I saw that Varya and Katya were weeping, too, their own memories and griefs isolating them in their own private and unreachable worlds.

But they were not alone in their sorrow. All over the

242

city there were those who had been members of his court, and others who had reason to be grateful to him for healings and favors, and they prayed fervently for a miracle that would restore him to their midst. And foremost in her mourning was the Tsarina, but in her heart, mourning was combined with anger, an anger focused upon Yussupov and Dmitri Pavlovich, convinced as she was that they were the ringleaders in the homicide. But when she summoned Protopopov to the Aleksandr Dvoryets and demanded that the criminals be shot without delay, he told her that proof of their complicity in the crime would be needed, and in fact, it was yet to be established that a crime had been committed.

"Well," she said, "the Tsar has been notified, and he will arrive back from the front tomorrow. And then we shall see."

"Vyelichyestvo, it is good that His Majesty will be here. I can only advise you to await his return."

But not all of those who had known my father were consumed with grief. In fact, some of the aristocrats felt that a heavy burden had been lifted from their backs, freeing them to pursue their privileges and perquisites without restraint. They gave, and attended, parties in celebration of the event, drinking toasts to their hero, that most unheroic of men, Prince Feliks Feliksovich Yussupov. But that stalwart was even then packing in preparation for his flight to the Crimea, only to have the police descend upon him and the grand duke and place them under house arrest in Dmitri's palace, where, it seems quite natural, they were both staying. The Tsarina might not be able to order their execution, but that much she could do.

On the following morning, the Tsar and tsarevich returned from the front, and Nikolas immediately ordered that the investigation be carried out with dispatch. And Aleksei tearfully demanded that the murderers be caught and punished. The tsarevich had loved the starets almost as a second father, not only because his friend had saved his life on several occasions, but because of the quality that drew most people to him, an aura of love that seemed to surround him at all times. Aleksei recalled how he had run to leap upon Papa whenever he came to the palace, wrapping his arms and legs about him in sheer youthful exuberance at his friend's appear-

243

ance. And he also remembered with a sad smile how, on the last occasion, when he was thirteen, the leap had toppled his target and they had both fallen to the floor, there to wrestle playfully, while Papa took every care not to hurt him. That was what Aleksei would miss the most; not the healings, for he was not afraid of death, but the pleasure of his company.

Later, on that gloomy day, divers found my father's corpse beneath the ice near the Petrovski Most, and they carried it to a wooden hut beside the river. Protopopov telephoned me with the sad confirmation of what we had all been convinced right along: Papa, my dearest Papa was dead. And still holding the receiver to my ear, I buried my face in my free arm and wept anew. Until that moment, it had all been a little unreal; there had been a hope, however fragile, that he might be still alive. But now, even the small hope was gone; it was true, so horribly, brutally true; Papa was dead.

I had forgotten all about Protopopov, who had been waiting patiently on the line for my first paroxysms to subside. But now his voice came over the wire again.

"Maria, I do not like asking you this, but a close relative is needed to make a formal identification. And since you are the closest relative now in Petrograd, I was wondering if you might feel strong enough to do it."

I could not answer at once, but somehow pulled myself back into the world of reality, or at least enough so that I could recognize what must be done.

"Yes, Ministr Protopopov, I will do it."

"I must warn you, Maria, that he has been badly— how shall I say it?—badly injured, and the sight is not a pleasant one."

But now, my grief had been at least partly replaced by rage, a rage at learning that the killers had not only murdered my father, but had apparently mutilated him. And so I said, with some asperity: "I will come."

When the car that Protopopov had sent arrived to pick me up, I found a determined Varya, who would not be left behind. And Katya, too, insisted on accompanying us, for, until Mama arrived, we were in her charge. Arriving at the Petrovski Most, we found the street blocked by a cordon of

244

police, with a full company of soldiers standing by. Only cars on official business were permitted to pass through. As we pulled up along the riverbank, several police officials stepped forward to conduct us through the deep snow to the hut. And once inside, there was nothing to distract the eye from its central feature: the mortal remains of Grigori Efimovich Rasputin. For it was undeniably he, his face smashed in at the temple, clots of dried blood matting his beard and hair. Most horrible of the visible portions of that still form—for the worst of the mutilations were hidden by a rough blanket—was one of his eyes, dangling against his cheek, held there by a slender thread of flesh. There were deep, raw marks on his wrists, showing the struggle he had undergone to free himself when he was revived by the cold water beneath the ice. And his right hand lay upon his breast, its middle finger bent so that, in combination with the index finger, it formed the classical symbol of the cross seen in many ikoni.

Time had withdrawn into the abyss of eternity. My brain refused to function, and I stood as one in a trance, mesmerized by that horrifying spectacle. I know that I opened my mouth to scream, but no sound issued forth. It seemed to me as though I had been transfixed in a tableau of infinite duration, but of course it was not infinite, and thoughts began pounding in my head. Was it not enough to satisfy them? Could they not be content with killing him? Did they also have to mangle him almost past all recognition? What kinds of people were they? No, not people; what kind of savage beasts could they have been? I knew that in my impotent rage I would be violently ill if I remained in that hut one moment longer, so I nodded to the waiting officials to signify that it was my father, and ran out the door, where I stood panting as though I had run for many miles, trying to settle the queasy feeling in my stomach. Varya and Katya appeared beside me and the three of us looked at each other in outraged silence, until Protopopov came up to us.

"Is the deceased a person known to you?"

I looked at him for a moment, unable to comprehend his words. Then I recalled the reason for my being there. Protopopov knew it was my father's corpse, and he knew that

245

I also had recognized it, but the formalities had to be observed, and I forced myself to answer him.

"Yes. He is—he was my father, Grigori Efimovich Rasputin."

It seemed that there was no strength left in me, and I would have fallen had Katya not thrown an arm hastily about me. Holding Varya with the other arm, Katya led us back to the waiting car. We were quickly driven back to the flat, where we found that Protopopov had given one more evidence of his kindness, for there was a heavy guard around the building as protection against any possible attack upon the dead man's family. And so we climbed the stairs, with nothing ahead but a bleak future, a future devoid of any meaning or purpose.

Ж

The little contingent from Pokrovskoye, Mama, Dmitri and Dunia, arrived at the Petrograd Station five days later. Varya and I met them, and Mama's question was answered even before she could ask it, when she saw that we were wearing black dresses, dresses given us by the Tsarina. When she knew that her worst fears had been realized, Mama, who had always maintained an iron control over her emotions, was shattered. The dam of her restraint broke and a terrible scream burst from her lips, and she began sobbing wildly as we hurried her toward the rented car that was to take us back to the flat. Pressed for details, I poured out the story, leaving out the more horrible aspects, and told them of the funeral on the grounds at Tsarskoye Syelo, in a plot donated by Anna Aleksandrovna. I told them of how his body had been prepared for burial by Sister Akulina, the former nun whom Papa had exorcised; but again, I did not tell them of what she had discovered: the terrible mutilation of his groin and abdomen. On top of what I had seen with my own eyes, Akulina's account had been almost too much for me to bear, and I knew how it would have affected Mama. But when Dmitri asked about the funeral itself, I could not tell him, for the imperial couple had forbidden us to attend, fearing a possible untoward incident if it had become known, as it might have if we had been recognized, that Rasputin was being buried.

The next day, a car was sent by the Tsarina, and Mama, Dmitri, Varya, and I were driven out to Tsarskoye Syelo, where we were lovingly greeted by the royal family, the tsarevich and the grand duchesses, and Anna Aleksandrovna. While the adults did their best to comfort Mama, the royal children took us into their arms and hearts, showing their love and sympathy. But Aleksei stood to one side, struggling manfully to keep from weeping, while the tears ran down his cheeks.

The Tsar, like so many kindly men, always submerged any outward sign of benevolence beneath a gruff exterior, and he did so now, as he tried to reassure Mama about our futures.

"Gospozha Rasputina, I shall be a second father to your lovely daughters. Aliks and I have always loved them as if they were our own. Let them continue their schooling here in Petrograd and I will see to it that they are not in want."

"Vyelichyestvo, you are too kind. I don't know . . ."

"Please do not thank me." And he turned away from her to stop her expressions of gratitude.

Ж

But the Tsar, although he was a man of his word, could not keep his promise for long. There were only a few months remaining for the House of Romanov, and after him were to come the Communists, who were not the ones to keep his, or even their own, commitments.

And there was need of the Tsar's assistance, for when I went to look for the money that Papa had shown me, and then so carelessly thrown into a bureau drawer, it was not there. One of the numerous visitors who had come to the flat after the murder had become known had stolen the three thousand rubles he had left for me. And there was another sum, the amount of which I did not know, that Papa had said was in the safekeeping of the banker Dmitri Rubinstein, but that, too, was missing.

During the month that followed, Mama gradually emerged from the depths of inconsolable misery into which she had been plunged, having spent herself in outbursts of tears and lamentations. Her grief was dulled, rather than diminished, and she began to think of the realities of the situation. The family's livelihood depended on how well the farm prospered, and so she began making plans to return so that she might again oversee its operation. And a few days later, Varya and I accompanied her back to the station, where she, Dmitri, and Katya boarded the train to begin their homeward journey.

And now there were just the three of us in the flat, and I had the leisure to face the situation. Most difficult to accept was the realization of the almost universal hatred for my father. I had seen the celebrations of the mobs in the streets after his murder had been confirmed; I had noticed that few of his former supporters were coming to visit; and, strangest of all, Yussupov and Dmitri Pavlovich were now being hailed as heroes and openly admitting their part in the homicide. As far as I could learn, neither of them had been punished, and the investigations seemed to be fading away, so that it became clear they would not be punished. The only action that was taken against them was that Feliks was sent to his estate at Rakitnoye, from where he later went on to the Crimea, and Dmitri Pavlovich was transferred to a military outpost in Persia. As it turned out, this was no punishment, but rather a boon, for it simplified Yussupov's escape with at least a good part of his fortune after the revolution.

Having faced the fact, I now sought the answer to the burning question: Why? Papa had been loved, truly loved, by nearly all who had known him, from the villagers of Pokrovskoye to the aristocrats of Petrograd. Why had they turned against him?

I turned to Dunia who, I knew, shared more with and of him than anyone else.

My first impulse, of course, was to blame the relationship between them and was immediately sorry.

"Please forgive me, Dunia," I said, after a sudden outburst, more out of frustration at his death than anything else.

"There, there," she said.

"But I had no right."

"You had every right, dear. There is nothing to forgive."

And so peace was restored, and Dunia, to help my peace of mind, told me about Papa. And by the time she had come to the end, I had begun to realize how much Papa and Dunia had loved each other. And along with understanding came compassion, and I wept with her over our mutual loss.

During that period, I was too engrossed with Dunia's account of my father's life, faithfully recording every morsel in my diary, to take much notice of the world outside. At times, Varya would come home from school with tales of having seen long lines of people waiting for bread that never came, or of groups of slovenly soldiers, lounging about the streets in rumpled uniforms—a certain sign that the army had lost control of its men. But the only times that I saw any of this for myself was on my weekly excursions to Tsarskoye Syelo. On Wednesdays, Varya and I spent the afternoon and evening at the Aleksandr Dvoryets, where we were accepted as daughters by the Tsar and Tsarina. The palace was like a haven of peace in the midst of the turmoil of Petrograd, a shelter against the gathering storm in which everything went on as it always had.

I was puzzled by this indifference to actual events. It was not as though the painful truths could be forever locked out. Anna Aleksandrovna Virubova had received several threatening letters, accusing her of having been in league with my father to bring about the defeat of Russia, and the Tsarina had moved her into the palace, assigning a guard to protect her. The Tsar, as commander in chief, must have known of the multitude of desertions from the army; even from far-off Pokrovskoye, Mama had written to tell us of the many farmers who were now leaving their ranks to return home, openly and without shame. The whole national structure was crumbling around him, and yet the Tsar maintained the pretense that all was well.

At the end of February, three months after the

murder, Dunia was called home to take care of her aging father, and once more, I went to the Petrograd Station to bid farewell to someone I loved. We embraced like mother and daughter, and again I stood alone on the platform to wave at the receding train, left alone in that tumultuous city except for Varya and the imperial family. I wept on the way back to the flat, but once inside, I washed away the tears, for a task still remained to be accomplished: Varya had to be looked after while she completed her education.

And now it was very lonely in the flat at 64 Gorokhovaya Ulitsa while Varya was away at school. The concierge came to clean the apartment daily, and cooked lunch, but for the remainder of the day I was alone, and I sat, mourning my father and praying for the well-being of his soul. And then my thoughts would turn homeward, and I longed to be with Mama again, living in the peace of the Siberian farmland.

One day, feeling particularly lonesome, I picked up the telephone to call Anna Aleksandrovna, but I found that the line was dead. I went out into the street to see if I could discover the cause of the trouble, but saw, instead, a large mob marching down the Latinya Prospekt, chanting, "Down with the Germanskaya," smashing shop windows and holding aloft their clenched fists. The service was restored that evening, and I called Gospozha Virubova, who told me that some of the soldiers had mutineed and had murdered their officers. Throughout the next few days, there was more rioting; barricades were thrown up in the streets, and Petrograd began to resemble the Paris of 1871. I kept Varya home from school, and the two of us huddled in the cold flat, aware of the continued rioting from the shouting and other noises outside. Finally, the streets grew quiet, and when, after several days, there were no further signs of tumult, Varya went back to school. But, when I tried to call the palace, I could not get through. Varya had brought home conflicting rumors that she had heard in her classroom: The Tsar had abdicated, would soon abdicate, had been forcibly dethroned, had fled to England, to Germany, to Sweden, to any place the creator of the rumor might imagine, and I feared for his and his family's safety.

I had to know what was happening, and so I hired a

car for the trip to Tsarskoye Syelo. I had no difficulty in gaining admission to the palace, for I was known to the guards who were still loyally maintaining their watch at the gates. A footman went to tell the Tsarina that I had arrived, and Her Majesty came quickly to the anteroom where I was waiting. She embraced me, but said that I must not stay, because the whole family, including Anyushka, was in bed with the measles. She ignored the danger which was more threatening than a case of measles, for at any moment there was the possibility of a take-over by the revolutionaries, and there was no purpose in permitting me to become involved with the other residents of the palace.

The Tsarina led me to the door, and with tears in her eyes, kissed me as a mother would, promising to call me as soon as the situation had calmed sufficiently to permit me to visit again. In the foyer there was a large jar filled with little butterscotch balls, and she took handfuls of them to stuff into my pockets before sending me away. And once I was back in the car, I burst into tears, feeling certain that I had just bidden farewell to my dearest friend for the last time. Now, all were gone; in all of Petrograd, only Varya remained.

And only a few days later, on March 14, the Tsarina's foreboding was justified when the Duma proclaimed the formation of a provisional government, and the Tsar was forced to abdicate. The imperial family was placed under house arrest, and the guards who now stood at the gates were there to keep the last of the Romanovs in, rather than unwelcome visitors out. And a drunken lot these new guards were, shouting filth and exposing themselves whenever one the grand duchesses appeared at a window.

On the night following the Duma's take-over, an unruly mob of intoxicated soldiers broke open my father's grave and dragged his body unceremoniously into the woods. To that ghoulish deed they added a ghoulish sport, tossing the corpse from bayonet to bayonet, until tiring of it, they built a fire and placed the body in its midst. But it was not their purpose to conduct a proper cremation; rather, they danced wildly in a ring around the pyre, and with some women from the nearby village joining in, the celebration ended in an orgy of sex.

251

Hearing of this grisly ritual, Rodzianko, although now out of power, but retaining all his malice toward my father, growled, "A fitting memorial service for a fiend."

As the word of this final degradation spread through the city, it at last reached me, and I telephoned Marusa Sasanova to learn what she knew of the story. A man who answered the telephone said Marusa was there and wanted to see Varya and me at once, adding that it was urgent that we come immediately. Hurrying to the Sasanov house, we found the family and some twenty people who had been friends of our father gathered under armed guards in the drawing room. Startled, we became even more frightened when they told us that we, too, were under arrest.

After determining that no more fish were going to swim into their net, the soldiers herded us out to a line of automobiles, and ordered us to get in. We were driven to a building in which we found a large number of other prisoners, many of whom I recognized as members of the aristocracy. There followed a period of waiting that seemed interminable, although it lasted only about two hours, during which we were permitted to visit the toilet only under the gaze of the undisciplined soldiers. I was finally called up for questioning, and, terrified, I embraced Varya, believing I was to be separated from my only companion in Petrograd.

An unshaven, foul-mouthed private shouted commands in my ear as he half guided, half pushed me down a long corridor into a small bare room. There were two men lounging behind a plain wooden table, and one of them ordered me in a harsh tone of voice to be seated. He then proceeded, without once looking at me, to consult a bulky file before him. This continued for some minutes, the only sound being the turning over of the pages of the various documents in the file, until I began to pray that the questioning would commence; anything was better than this dead silence.

Finally, he looked up, staring at me with an accusing frown: "Your name?"

"Maria Grigoryevna Rasputina."

"You are the daughter of Grigori Efimovich Rasputin?"

"I am."

And now there was a hint of a smile, which was also a leer, about his lips. "How many times did Aleksandra Feodorovna Romanova, lately the Tsarina," and here he almost spat out the title, "sleep in your flat, which was located at . . ." And he riffled through the papers in the file for a full minute. "Ah, yes, the flat at Number 64 Gorokhovaya Ulitsa?"

"She never spent the night. She never even came there."

"Be careful of how you lie to me. She was seen entering there many times."

"It is not true."

"Do you think these reports lie?"

I was furious; the stupid man had heated my rage to the boiling point. "If those silly reports of yours say that, they are worthless."

The other man, who had been silent up to that point, now took up the interrogation. "Did you ever see your father kiss that woman?"

"If you mean Her Majesty, the Tsarina, he kissed her in greeting, just as he did with everybody."

"We have a report that she spent the night with your father, in his bed, and that when you found them there in the morning, this so-called Tsarina bribed you to keep quiet by giving you a bracelet."

This was too much. My nerves had been wound as taut as a piano string, and I began to laugh hysterically. The vision of that narrow cot, hardly wide enough to hold Papa's gaunt frame, acting as a nest for two lovers was more than I could bear, and try as I would, I could not stop laughing long enough to answer the question.

Actually, my uncontrollable mirth answered the inquisitors quite well, for they were embarrassed at being thought ridiculous, and dismissed me, and sent for Varya. Although we passed each other in the hall, we were forbidden to speak, and I could only smile in encouragement, unable to warn her of the two commissars' line of questioning.

But they succeeded no better with Varya than they had done with me, and soon we were both free and told that we could go. Surprisingly enough, a car was provided to take us home. And we huddled together, worrying about the situation of our dear friends at the Aleksandr Dvoryets.

The next morning, the principal of Varya's school sent for her, and although she had been an exemplary pupil and was first in her class, the usually friendly woman glared at her as though she had committed some heinous offense. In a cold and angry tone, she told Varya that she could no longer attend the school, refusing to give any explanation for her decision. Shocked, my sister, who had just turned sixteen, caught the tram back to Gorokhovaya Ulitsa, and ran to tell me, sobbing out her story while I attempted to comfort her.

There was no reason for our remaining in Petrograd. No one who cared about us was left in the city, so when I said that we would go home to Pokrovskoye, Varya agreed, her face brightening for the first time since her expulsion. We packed only what we could carry, leaving most of our possessions in the care of the concierge. We did not know, nor care, if we would ever see them again. But I did take my most prized possession, the school copybook in which I had recorded Dunia's account of my father's life.

As we were driven to the station, I looked out at the crowds thronging the streets, many of them ill-kempt soldiers, dragging their rifles behind them by the shoulder straps. Gone was their pride of service, even, apparently their pride of manhood. These were the same men who cared so little for their own dignity that they would, in just six short months, submit placidly to the Communists and their tyranny. Petrograd was not the same city as the one to which Papa had brought me. Then it had been busy, filled with excitement and bustling people; now there remained but a hollow shell, filled, or so it seemed to me, with the dead. I was glad to be leaving.

And in our compartment on the train, I leafed through my diary, seeking the key to the complex man who had been my father. But I did not seek for long; I was tired, too tired to think of those tragic times. Someday, I would put the whole story together, and when I did, it might become comprehensible. But that was a task for the future. Right now, I just wanted to rest. And I leaned against the back of my seat, lulled by the clacking of iron wheels against iron rails. And I slept.

AFTERWORD

by Patte Barham

In the spring of 1968, while researching this book, I flew to London to interview some White Russian émigrés whose names had been given me by Maria Rasputin. The people I met were quite friendly toward Maria, but most of them were hostile insofar as Rasputin himself was concerned, believing him to have been an evil influence in the affairs of the Romanovs. They did, however, give me the names of some people to contact in Paris, where I was due to go for a meeting with Maria at the home of her daughter Tatiana, who lived with her family outside the city.

After checking into my hotel on the Rue St.-Honoré, I lay down to rest before driving out to Tatiana's house. After a few minutes, the telephone rang and a man's voice asked for a "Mr. Barham."

I replied that there was only a Miss Barham registered in this room. There was a sharp intake of breath, and then the phone went dead. I assumed there had been some mistake, and gave it no further thought until the next morning, when the telephone rang again. The man, whose voice I recognized from the previous day, apologized for ringing off and asked me to meet him for a drink. When I inquired as to his reason for the invitation, he mentioned the name of one of the White Russians I had met in London, saying he had some information that might interest me. Within the hour, I took a cab to the café he had specified on the Champs Elysées, mildly intrigued by his air of mystery. I imagined that he might be one of that legion of émigrés who had managed to eke out a living in France after the Bolshevik Revolution. Perhaps he would offer to tell me some hitherto untold stories about the Russian court in return for a fee. I had been caught in that trap before, and resolved to pay nothing until I heard what he had to tell me. To my surprise, there were two waiting for me, one about sixty, white-haired and shrunken in appearance, and the other around thirty, with close-cut dark hair, and enormous, rather startling brown eyes. He was the one who had called me. They introduced themselves as Gleb and Georges, no surnames.

Georges, whose English was perfect, said, "I am sorry I rang off yesterday. We had expected a man."

"Does it matter?"

They looked at each other in seeming embarrassment, without replying. Georges finally spoke. "You are writing a book about Rasputin?"

"Yes, I am."

"There is someone who wants to meet you."

I looked around. "Where?"

"Not now; tonight."

I was puzzled and somewhat amused by their furtive manner. We set a time, and they promised to pick me up at my hotel. Prompt to the minute, Georges drew up in a black Citroën.

"Do you know Paris?" he asked, as I climbed in.

"Hardly at all," I replied.

He nodded, and fell silent. We drove for almost an hour in what I began to realize was a deliberately circuitous route, so that I would not be able to find my way to wherever we were going again. But by now, I had had enough of mystery.

"What's this all about?" I asked.

"I am taking you to see my grandmother."

"What has she to do with Rasputin?"

"She is one who once loved him."

This seemed to be promising, the most hopeful contact I had made in Europe so far. But Georges had gone moodily silent again and refused to be drawn out. Eventually, we turned off the main street onto some side roads that ran by a small river. I had seen this area, St.-Denis, written up earlier, but there was no other means of identifying my exact location. The car turned into a narrow driveway behind a tall hedge. I saw a dark, gloomy house, surrounded by trees that most certainly obscured the light in the daytime.

Georges showed me into a living room and then excused himself. It was like a faded Tsarist museum. A large painting of Nikolas and Aleksandra hung over the fireplace. A huge silver samovar stood on a table, and there were many other signs of Russian influence. I noticed that there was no number on the telephone, as if it had been deliberately removed. A few moments later, Georges returned.

"She will see you now," he said, holding open the door.

Instead of going upstairs, as I had expected, he led me down the corridor toward the back of the house. Reaching a heavy wooden door, he tapped lightly, and then pushed it open, beckoning for me to follow. It was apparent that the room, probably at one time a pantry, had been turned into a bedroom. An old woman lay in the bed, her wrinkled face framed with sparse white hair, through which I could see the pink of her scalp. But what caught my attention was a greatly enlarged photograph of Rasputin hanging on the wall. Below it were two candles, burning as if at a shrine. Georges was by the bed, speaking in Russian to the old lady.

He turned to me, saying, "She knows French, but she has forgotten it."

"Please ask her what she has to tell me."

He spoke to her and she replied. After another exchange, he translated: "She wants you to know that Father Grigori was a great man, a reincarnation of the Christ." His tone was level, as though he were avoiding personal commentary, even by an inflection of his voice.

"I have not come all this distance just to hear that. How well did she know him?"

As Georges translated, an extraordinary story began to emerge. The old woman had been a maid at the Hotel Europe in St. Petersburg. She had served Rasputin many times at dinner parties he had given in the hotel's private dining room. Frequently, he came to the hotel and booked a room for the night. I gathered that she had had an affair with him, but in considering that withered, mummylike body, sex seemed so obscene that I did not press for details. Georges, too, seemed embarrassed by this part of the story, but his grandmother showed no signs of being ill at ease. There was little about Rasputin's activities I had not already heard before, but I had become deeply interested in the old woman herself. The only White Russians I had met had all been grand dukes, princesses, and ex-millionaires; she was my first self-confessed plebian. When the recital came to its end, I asked, "Why did she leave Russia if she wasn't an aristocrat?"

His answer startled me. "She was in fear for her life," said Georges. "She was a known disciple of Rasputin's. She escaped with some holy relics of his."

My ears went up like a lobster's antennae. "What relics?" I almost shouted.

Georges walked across to the bureau and took up a polished wooden box that lay there beneath Rasputin's picture. It was about eighteen inches long, and six wide, with an inlaid silver crest on the top. He showed it to his grandmother, who nodded weakly, and then brought it to me. Impassively, he raised the lid, and I saw what looked like a blackened, overripe banana, about a foot long, and resting on velvet cloth.

"What is it?"

"My grandmother says it is the Holy Father's sexual organ," he said without a smile.

Seeing my astonishment, he turned away, closing the

box and replacing it on the bureau. I noticed that the old woman made the sign of the cross as he did so.

Recovering my breath, I asked, "How did she get it?"

"One of the servants in Yussupov's house was married to her sister. He retrieved it after they mutilated Father Grigori, and then murdered him."

She was the first person I had met who spoke authoritatively of mutilation. Excited, I pressed questions upon her. Through Georges, she told me what had actually happened on that night in Yussupov's palace on the Moika Kanal. It was as if an eyewitness were describing the Crucifixion. By this time, I had gone deeply enough into Rasputin's life with Maria, as well as through my own research, to realize that he was in no way the monster that Iliodor and others had drawn him. But here I was, face to face with a woman, nearly at the point of death, who regarded him as the Christ. It was an extraordinary moment.

After a few more questions, the old woman's eyes closed, and when I tried to thank her directly, I saw that she had fallen asleep. Georges led me out, and back to the car. I expected him to say something, but he drove as silently as before. I sat for a long time, turning what I had heard over in my mind. Then I looked at Georges, whose face was inscrutable.

"Do you believe it?" I asked.

"Believe what?"

"That Rasputin was Christ?"

"For a start, yes. Do you?"

"Of course not."

There was silence for a moment, and then I asked, "What about that thing in the box?"

He looked at me for a moment. "Is it Rasputin's, you mean? I am sure of it."

"How do you know?"

"I was born in France; the only Russian thing about me is my name. But my grandfather was a very down-to-earth man. He'd been a worker on the railroad. He believed. So did all the others."

"What others?"

He glanced at me with a smile. "The followers," he said. "They used to meet at our house every Wednesday. A sort of prayer circle in his memory."

"How many were there?"

"A hard core of about a dozen. Sometimes many more."

They were, he told me, a group formed by people who had actually met and known the starets. Several, like his grandmother, who had taken part in sexual activities with Rasputin to purge their sins, not only admitted it, but gloried in it. Some of the others had received his blessings or benefits in other ways, without sex. They all shared one common denominator: an adoration of the Holy Man.

"Do me a favor," he said. "Don't try to find out who we are."

"Why not?"

"The man you met this morning is my father. We love my grandmother very much." He shrugged. "We would not like her exposed to ridicule."

"Then why contact me in the first place?"

"Because she insisted. She will die soon, and she wanted someone to print the truth about him."

"What do you think is the truth?" I asked.

He frowned and looked intently at the street. "I think he was a simple man to whom God had given great powers. So long as he remained a peasant, concerned only with God, everything went well for him. When he started meddling in man's affairs, he was out of his depth. He lost his footing and was drowned. It was a great tragedy for him—and for us."

"Us?"

"The Russians."

It seemed a fitting epitaph.

GLOSSARY OF RUSSIAN TERMS

AKKORDEON/*accordion*
AKUSHYERKA/*midwife*
ARISTOKRAT/*aristocrat*
BABUSHKA/*grandmother; term of endearment for an old
woman*
BALOVYEN/*darling; pet*
BITKI/*small meatball*
BLUZA/*shirt; blouse*
BOLSHYEVIKI/*members of the Communist Party*
BRODYAGA/*vagabond; tramp; wanderer*
DA KHRANIT VAS BOG/*God preserve you*
DOROGOI/*dear*
DUMA/*parliament (Lit.: council)*
DVORYETS/*palace*
DYAVOL/*devil-or DIAVOL*
EI BOGU/*by God; an expletive*
EKATERINA VYELIKAYA/*Catherine the Great*

EPISKOP/*bishop*
GERMANSKAYA/*Germany (fem.)*
GOSPOD KHRISTOS/*the Lord Christ*
GOSPODIN/*Mr.*
GOSPOZHA/*madame; Mrs.*
GOSTINITSA EVROPA/*Hotel Europe*
GRUBIYAN/*clodhopper; yokel; rude fellow*
IKONA/*icon*
INOSTRANKA/*foreigner (fem.)*
ISBA/*home of a peasant*
KABACHOK/*inn; small tavern*
KATEKHISIS/*catechism*
KHIZHINA/*hut; cottage*
KHRISTIANIN/*Christian*
KOLKHOZ/*collective farms (pl., kolkhozi)*
KOLYASKA/*carriage*
KOMNATA/*one room*
KOSINKA/*kerchief*
LYUBOVNIK/*lover*
MAKLER/*broker*
MALODUSHNI/*coward or pussilanimous*
MALYUTKA/*my child; little one*
MEDVED/*bear*
MILOCHKA/*my dear*
MINISTR/*minister*
MODISTKA/*modiste*
MONAKH/*monk*
MOST/*bridge*
MOY MALENKI/*my little one*
MUKHA V MAZHYE/*fly in the ointment*
MUZHIK/*peasant*
MYENSHYEVIKI/*members of the minority in Russian Revolutionary Party*
OKHRANA/*secret police (lit.: guard)*
OSTROV/*island*
OTYETS/*father*
PANTALONI/*trousers; underwear*
PIVO/*beer*
POLKOVNIK/*colonel*

POSLUSHNAYA/*manageable (fem.)*
PROSTITUTKA/*prostitute*
PRYEKRASNAYA/*beautiful (fem.)*
PRYEVOSKHODITYELSTVO/*Excellency*
PROSHCHAITYE/*farewell*
PYOTR VELIKIE/*Peter the Great*
RABOTNIKI/*workers; laborers*
RADI BOG/*for God's sake*
SHYELK/*silk*
SLIVOVITS/*plum brandy*
SOSISKA/*sausage*
SOVYET/*council*
SPLYENITZA/*gossip; one who gossips (fem.)*
STARETS/*a lay holy man; old wise man*
STRANNIK/*pilgrim; wanderer*
SUDBINA/*fate (fem.) (old-fashioned slang)*
SVINYA/*pig*
SVYASHCHENNIK/*priest*
TAK I BIT/*so be it*
TEPER/*now*
TISHYE/*silence; quiet*
TOVARISHCH/*friend; comrade*
TROIKA/*three-horse carriage*
ULITSA/*street*
UNIZHENIYE/*humiliation*
VYELICHYESTVO/*Majesty*
VERST/*3,500 feet, about two thirds of a mile*
VOZHD/*leader*
ZAKUSKI/*snacks; hors d'oeuvres*
ZYERNO/*corn*

INDEX

264

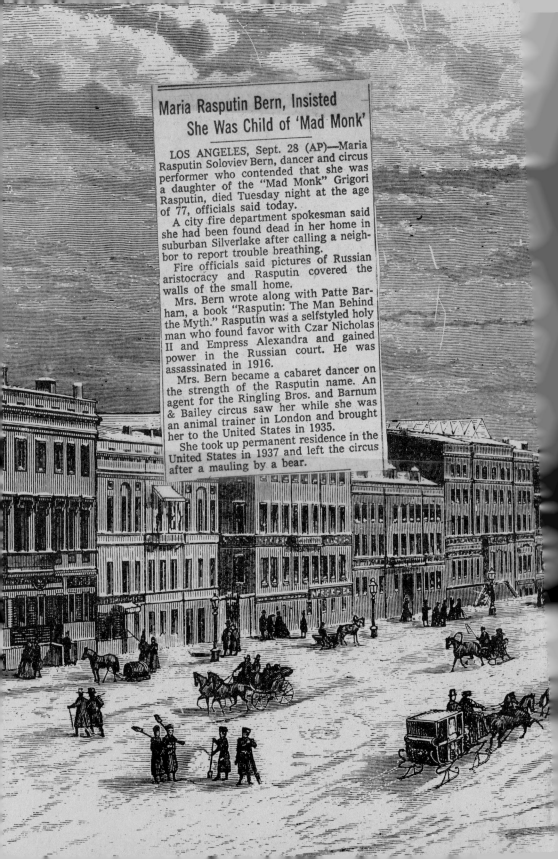

Maria Rasputin Bern, Insisted She Was Child of 'Mad Monk'

LOS ANGELES, Sept. 28 (AP)—Maria Rasputin Soloviev Bern, dancer and circus performer who contended that she was a daughter of the "Mad Monk" Grigori Rasputin, died Tuesday night at the age of 77, officials said today.

A city fire department spokesman said she had been found dead in her home in suburban Silverlake after calling a neighbor to report trouble breathing.

Fire officials said pictures of Russian aristocracy and Rasputin covered the walls of the small home.

Mrs. Bern wrote along with Patte Barham, a book "Rasputin: The Man Behind the Myth." Rasputin was a selfstyled holy man who found favor with Czar Nicholas II and Empress Alexandra and gained power in the Russian court. He was assassinated in 1916.

Mrs. Bern became a cabaret dancer on the strength of the Rasputin name. An agent for the Ringling Bros. and Barnum & Bailey circus saw her while she was an animal trainer in London and brought her to the United States in 1935.

She took up permanent residence in the United States in 1937 and left the circus after a mauling by a bear.